Dear,

Do it with your whole heart.
Here's to happy endings!
Namaste'

Kat

Bringing the Inside Out

Peeling away the emotional layers to self acceptance

Cece Gardenia

BALBOA.
PRESS
A DIVISION OF HAY HOUSE

Balboa Press books may be ordered through booksellers or by contacting:

Balboa Press
A Division of Hay House
1663 Liberty Drive
Bloomington, IN 47403
www.balboapress.com
1 (877) 407-4847

Print information available on the last page.

ISBN: 978-1-5043-5729-6 (sc)
ISBN: 978-1-5043-5731-9 (hc)
ISBN: 978-1-5043-5730-2 (e)

Library of Congress Control Number: 2016908720

Balboa Press rev. date: 07/05/2016

Table of Contents

School Days

Adulthood

Mother and Father Revisited

Healing

Prologue

Screams and wails echo through the hall from the small child, hanging over the cold metal crib, with her arms outstretched. Her mother and father walk quickly toward the exit door, after their weekly Sunday visit. A nun in a grey habit silently appears and waves goodbye to the parents before drying the child's tear-stained, reddened cheeks. Long days pass until the next visit; weeks turn into months, and the girl, confined to a polio ward along with many others, grows resolute in the face of fear, pain, and loneliness.

****

I stand for long moments in the shower, gazing through the steamy clear glass of my isolated haven, as the scene floats through my mind—a wisp of memory, a quiver of distress. I can hear the cries; my throat feels tight. I hold the nozzle close beneath my chin, lost in the past of the physical and mental crippling, while warm water blankets and soothes me. The old neediness for solace, for love, rises up through me.

My baby book tells the story on soft pastel pages. Sentences lovingly written in my mother's hand, documents my hospital stays, including birthdays and holidays, and her longing for my return. I am moved in that isolated moment by the tender sentiments she expressed. And yet they feel foreign to me, as if a stranger had written them.

Seeing through the Pane Now

At twenty-two months, I was ready to see the world on my feet instead of my hands and knees. It was a surprise and a concern to all when I suddenly began to falter. My falls became more frequent, and I developed a fever that persisted for an undue length of time. The stark truth for my parents followed: their baby had contracted polio and would have to be hospitalized immediately. Through the next few years, black and white pictures, secured by photo corners, reflected images of me as a child, wearing the ever-present leg brace and crutches.

I had contracted spinal polio, the most common form of poliomyelitis, primarily affecting my lower right limb, causing weakness and partial paralysis. In actuality, I was fortunate to have this type of polio, considering how much worse other forms could have been. Some who had contracted the infection were completely paralyzed or died when their chest muscles weakened. In 1952, when the polio epidemic was at its highest point in the United States, there were close to 60,000 cases, with over 3,000 deaths and 21,000 people with varying degrees of paralysis. Most who died were children younger than five.

To simplify it, the virus most commonly entered the central nervous system through the blood stream and then infected and destroyed motor neurons. Consequently, the muscles were not receiving signals from the brain or spinal cord, and without this nerve stimulation, they withered and weakened. Those infected would experience a variety of symptoms: fever, sore throat, a mild headache, muscle pain, and a stiff neck. Depending on the severity of the infection, within two to four days, complete paralysis could occur.

Was it from the summer days spent swimming at the beach, as many had thought, or just a chance exposure to a passing wind? A question with no answer to this day.

I was admitted to St. Francis Hospital in September 1950 and entered the infants' ward for a year, along with many other children. The year before I arrived, the hospital was admitting up to thirty patients a day and attending to, in total, almost 400 patients. After my initial admission, I continued to be admitted and discharged for corrective surgeries until I was eleven, with varying lengths of stays.

****

The young girls' ward mirrored something out of the pages of the children's story, *Madeline*—three rows of drab, painted iron beds with matching metal nightstands were meticulously placed throughout the ward, like keys of a piano. Along with my favorite stuffed animal, Mimi, all my belongings fit in a drawer at the top of my nightstand. Below was a washbasin with my personal toiletries.

Through wall-to-wall, double hung windows, I could look out onto the sparkling waters of a harbor from our high perch. Abandoned structures were scattered along the coastline, as the port had once been a busy shipbuilding hub. Of course, at my young age, I was not aware of the history outside my enclave. My primary consideration was to manage my own small world within the confines of the hospital

Awakened abruptly before dawn by the flick of a switch, an explosion of overhead fluorescent lights brashly ignited the room. With little hesitation, I'd quickly make my way by wheelchair to the public bathroom, adjacent to the ward. With toothbrush, paste, comb, and washcloth balanced on my lap, I began my day.

Before we could even think of having breakfast, mass was celebrated in the small chapel beside the hospital. Despite the chapel's stately gothic architecture and the faint early rays of light filtering through its heavy stained glass windows, the setting was a dismal one for me at best. The stagnant air was filled with incense and a familiar candle scent. During this time of abundant illness, candles were kept lit by ever-vigilant churchgoers. A statue of the Virgin Mary on the far left end of the chapel was perched, larger than life, on a marble pedestal. Although I found some comfort in her solemn gaze above me, my wheelchair would bring me at eye level with the snake that entwined her bare feet, as she stood upon a pale blue and golden globe of the world. Always dreading passing the reptile each morning, I wondered why anyone would couple a sinister image at the feet of this seemingly tender and loving woman. But then again, everything about the chapel was dark, cold, and somber.

When finally ready for our first meal of the day, young women circulated our ward and placed meal

3

trays on our individual rolling bed tables. They never engaged in any conversation. I once heard from a reliable source that they were orphaned, mentally compromised children, who were transferred to the hospital in the years prior to the polio epidemic. Not having a place to call their own, they worked at the hospital in exchange for room and board at a nearby residence.

Despite involuntary regurgitations, the nuns insisted that everything on our plates was to be eaten. Before that moment of truth, I often found myself swirling the food around on my plate and wondering why something that was supposed to be good for me could taste so bad. Early on I learned that hospital food left a lot to be desired. One day, however, a server came to take away my tray and showed mercy on me. Noticing I had not finished my gray and lifeless string beans, she pointed to the bottom of my plate, urging me to conceal the remainder of the food. I gladly obeyed. Without a word ever spoken between us, the same young woman came to save me daily. We had a pact of sorts and were never discovered.

The religious order presiding at the hospital were trained as educators or nurses and always ran a tight ship. They were as rigid as the starched white, cotton caps they wore and as stoic as the life-size statues that appeared in every nook and cranny in the halls of the hospital. Everything about St. Francis was sterile, lifeless, and regimented. The Sisters were robotic and distant, but rarely cross. Fun just didn't seem like it had its place; everything was a serious matter.

"Wake up a-little Suzy, wake up. We've both been sound asleep. Wake up a-little Suzy and weep. The movie is over. It's four o'clock and we're in trouble deep," was the popular Everly Brothers tune back then.

The girls delighted in gathering around the small, red-and-white record player while it spun the latest 45-rpm records. Not surprisingly, before we could even absorb the lyrics, the record was banned from the girls' ward.

Rolling through the corridors of the hospital in my wheelchair was one of my favorite pastimes. I never knew what I might discover "cruising" the halls and finding my way through the maze of rooms. During one of my exploratory adventures, I slowed the wheels of my chair as I passed a doorway; I'd heard a strange sound coming from within. It reminded me of windshield wipers whooshing back and forth. Slowly and quietly, I wheeled my chair backwards just to the brink of the doorway and leaned over the arm of my chair to peek in. To my surprise, the room was sizable and filled with what appeared to be rows of metal drums. They weren't ordinary drums. Glass windows, dials, gauges, and tubes were melded on the surface of the cylindrical container. They were iron lungs—or negative pressure ventilators, as I later learned. I had heard about them but never saw one for myself. It was a sight I would not soon forget, if ever. At the narrow end of each drum was a hole that was lined with thick rubber. The rubber was supple so it would fit snugly around a patient's neck, as well as creating a seal for the remainder of the machine. A pillow rested on top of the rubber lining to accommodate their heads. Gazing at the children in those iron lungs stirred up many questions for me. It seemed as if they were trapped and were being swallowed by a living, breathing machine! But they were quiet. Could they be asleep? What could something so awful-looking be doing for them? As a child, I became preoccupied with the haunting image and felt panic for those inside. How did they eat since their hands were unable to reach their mouths on the outside? Did someone feed them? How did they take a shower and go to the bathroom? What if they had an itch on their nose? Could they play? So many questions I was too afraid to know the answers to.

****

Part of my day at St. Francis was spent in grueling, regimented therapies or treatments in the large, rotunda-shaped portion of the hospital. During the early 1950s, hydrotherapy and electrotherapy were used widely to treat the virus. As for me, after the polio ran its course and did its dirty deed, I was left with nerve cell damage and a deformity.

Hydrotherapy became a familiar term during those times due in part to President Franklin Roosevelt's belief in its benefits for his own polio affliction.

Whirlpool immersion tanks were used in the hospital with the expectation that circulating water could change blood flow and reduce pain. In addition, this therapy was used for physical rehabilitation and exercise. I was placed in the vast tub of water with the assistance of a swing, to help me perform resistance exercises, which they hoped would build muscle strength and create less strain on the bones and joints. It was a pleasant enough to be in the water and exercise, but it was questionable whether progress was being made.

Electrotherapy was another story altogether—and not a happy one. The goal was to encourage muscle contractions by using direct currents applied to the skin, otherwise known as the "warming affect." Since the voltage was so powerful it would often cause the skin to blister.

As a young child, I received electrotherapy rehabilitation often. Nothing could prepare me for the treatment of repetitive and punishing electric shocks. Each time I entered the sterile, white room, I was transferred from my wheelchair to a stretcher that was tightly wrapped in an icy white sheet. It felt like sandpaper against my exposed limbs. As soon as I saw the electric probes positioned near me, I would begin to shiver. I knew what to expect, but it didn't make it any easier. I told myself that if I squeezed my leg muscle as hard as I could, maybe I wouldn't get stung. A Sister would give me the order as she applied the connections. "Tighten your leg now." Bizzzz! It never worked. Over and over, the shocks would come.

Why did Sister have to hurt me? I kept thinking. I tried hard not to cry. Over and over again, the treatment went on until I could feel tears welling up in my eyes.

Perhaps far worse than my treatments were the surgeries I faced during my adolescence. Over the course of time I had undergone numerous surgeries in an attempt to correct my gait and improve mobility. Nerve grafting, tendon lengthening, bone and tendon transplants; limb lengthening and bone fusions were used.

During my youth, I became very familiar with what to expect on the pre-op and surgery days. In preparation for one of my first surgeries, a Sister instructed me to wheel my chair to a designated room just down the hall from where I slept. The doors were mullioned with opaque squares of glass so you couldn't see through. I wasn't given any information, but as I waited outside the doors, I suspected that it wasn't going to be a good experience. After waiting for several nerve-racking minutes, the French doors opened and one of the doctors inside asked me to stand up and walk into the room. In front of me were two long rectangular tables placed several feet apart to make an aisle like a fashion runway. Several male physicians were seated at both tables, facing the makeshift aisle. One of the doctors then asked me to walk through the path and back. As I timidly made my way, they would discuss their thoughts amongst themselves and make notes on their pads in front of them. I was sure that they were talking about my hospital gown. It had two small ties below the back of my neck, but the remainder was open. I could feel the coolness of the air in the room and was terribly worried my bottom was the topic of conversation. I was unaware that this was a gait evaluation prior to one of my many corrective surgeries.

On the day of a surgery, I would be wheeled on a gurney into the operating room. There was a light above me that was blinding and the room felt very cold. Within minutes, a nun would approach me.

"Do you know how to count down from 100?" I'd nod yes and tremble. "Okay, now we are going to give you something to help you sleep," she explained in a soft tone.

Oh God, how long could I hold my breath, was all I could think of. *If only I could run away!* Thoughts of feeling alone and vulnerable began to swirl in my head. *Where are my mommy and daddy? Could someone please hold my hand? I am so scared.*

I tried with all my might not to breathe as the ominous, black domed mask began to envelope my tiny mouth. One breath, *No, take it off!* Two breaths, *Oh no, I can't let it in!* Three breaths…There was no way out, I was trapped and desperate to escape, but I couldn't. The sweet, sickening smells entered my nostrils and consumed me. But the assault wasn't over. After the surgery, I could hear faint voices around me in the recuperating room. "Check her; see if you can wake her up."

"Dear, wake up now; can you hear me?" I could hear them but didn't have the strength to answer. Suddenly, I was overcome with violent nausea. There wasn't time to let anyone know, but they were ready. Ether had an insidious way of making your system revolt to its horrid and pungent gas. And revolt, it did, for what seemed like an eternity.

The rigid braces and casts worn for months after the surgeries led to muscle atrophy, due to the limited use of my leg. All in all, most of the treatments provided little therapeutic value. It was a guessing game of sorts, and even a considerable mistake was made after my last surgery at St. Francis. I was turning in on my ankle as I walked, and as a result, walking on the outer most side of my foot. After my surgery, my foot began to turn inward even more; my ankle would cave from the stress of my weight, and I developed a thick callous that was trying to make up for the continuous pressure on the soft, pliable skin. I often found myself losing balance and would end up on the floor. There was no fault or lawsuits considered at that time. I believe there were only dedicated doctors trying to fix what they didn't always or readily understand.

****

Despite the vicissitudes during my stays, I sought to make the best of my situation when I could. There were times when we were allowed to venture outside and visit the playground site that overlooked the harbor. If the weather didn't cooperate, we raced our wheelchairs down the sloped linoleum-lined corridors of the hospital wings, providing a nun didn't catch us. In the basement of the hospital was a playroom filled with donations of toys, dollhouse, board games, stuffed animals, and the like.

Even on the best of days however, bedtime was the hardest for us all. I often wondered what caused the reoccurring nightly phenomenon. One girl would begin to audibly weep and it would spread to any number of girls who would be awakened by the crying. Perhaps it was triggered by a nightmare, or the overwhelming grief of being separated from our families. Within no time, the cries would spread throughout the girls' ward.

One Sister was assigned to a bedroom next to our ward and would come out to investigate the commotion. With the harsh beam of her flashlight, she would point it down at each child's face till she found the ones in distress. She would talk to them for a moment and tell them to go back to sleep. I remember crying myself at times, but also recall nights when I would just lie still in my bed and wonder what my family was doing. Were they sleeping in their beds? Were they talking about me? Did they miss me? I survived with those thoughts as best I could. Despite the fact that we rarely exchanged words, I would think about the other young girls who flanked my bed and held on to the idea that I was not alone during those long dark nights. I longed to be in my home and my own bed.

Much later in my life, I had the opportunity to have one of my questions answered when I met one of the Sisters who was there during my stay. She was much older and frailer but still wore her habit, unlike many others who had replaced the heavy, itchy, woolen garb for more comfortable attire. Her face was still recognizable. I introduced myself and we reminisced for a short time. Among other memories, I reminded her about the frequent emotional chain reaction that occurred back then in our ward.

"There wasn't much we could do to calm the girls," she explained.

"Really, why was that?" I asked.

"Because if we hugged or kissed one child, we would have to hug and kiss them all."

Stunned by her rationale, I walked away thinking that my years as a patient there were as grim as I remembered.

Still, there was one significant ray of light during my stay. From a young age, I was aware of the head therapist and her legendary achievements. Besides the obvious distinction that she was the only one not wearing a gray flannel habit, she was a wonderful and caring individual. According to my parents and by all accounts, she was untiring, dedicated and knowledgeable. In my years of hospitalization as a young girl, I couldn't remember a time when she was not there, relentlessly working and trying to make a difference.

Age was difficult to judge as a child; every adult was old to me at that time in my life. Although I was unaware of her age, her striking good looks were very apparent. Slender and graceful, she carried herself with an air of dignity. She kept her soft, brown, curled hair off her face, secured with bobby pins on her crown and behind her ears. Her face was unadorned with makeup, and her features were as refined and slender as her frame. She had gentleness in her approach and was a vision of poise and strength for me.

When I left the hospital for the last time at the age of eleven, I was not consciously aware that I probably would not see this woman again, but I never forgot her.

Twenty years ago, when I was active and volunteering at my church, I would often spend time with Sr. Marguerite during our fundraising events. While we worked on the charity plans, I would retell my experiences as a child living in the hospital. I mentioned the therapist I grew to be so fond of. She suddenly placed her hand on my arm and stopped me. "Do you know that she attends mass here during her summers?"

"What? Are you sure?" I replied in disbelief.

"Yes, she comes with her friend, who drives her."

I was dumbstruck! The thought of actually seeing her again after so many years was astonishing.

That very summer, a few months later, I was at mass. Sitting on the left side of the altar, facing the pews on the opposite side, I glanced over and noticed an elderly woman sitting almost directly opposite me. It didn't take more than a few seconds for me to realize who she was. My heart was beating faster, and I could hardly wait till mass was over. After the last hymn I hurried out of the church, down the staircase, crossing the grounds to the other side of the building to see if I could catch her as she exited.

As she approached me, I stood nervously in front of her. "Are you Miss McCready?"

"Yes, how do you know?"

I told her I had been a patient of hers. Then I teasingly added, "Your white blouse was a dead giveaway; you were always in uniform."

We renewed our relationship from that day on and became close friends. Although she was away a good part of the year, we visited with each other during her summers in her bungalow by the sea. I learned even more about her compassionate nature. We talked about her life back then, with conversations like: "Paid overtime was unheard of; you just did it." The endless evenings spent soliciting door-to-door to raise funds to fight the epidemic was, "Just necessary." She was innovative. She told me she took photographs of the children and the interior scenes of the hospital during those epidemic times to encourage the generosity of potential donors. Today, numerous black-and-white and sepia-colored framed photos remain throughout the hospital hallways and offices.

She remained single, without regret. Although she denied it, I couldn't help thinking her uncompromising dedication left little room for personal relationships. I came to know her not only as the caring and warm person I remembered, but also as a woman who continued to be highly regarded and respected in her field for her lifelong commitment. She became a legend in the wards and to the staff. I was happy to be a part of the functions that honored her, including using her namesake on their new therapy wing. She was always embarrassed and humble about the recognition. I, however, knew first hand, what an impact this remarkable woman had made on my life and many others.

****

The best of all my memories at St. Francis were Sundays and Wednesdays, family visiting day. My father always remembered to bring a cup of ice cream from the popular ice cream shop in town on Wednesday afternoons. On Sundays, I was able to leave the hospital for the day and make the lengthy trip with my father to my home. Halfway there, he always took me to a diner where I could order anything I wanted on the menu. He would always introduce me to the waitresses and explain our plans for my visit. "This is my beautiful daughter, Colette," he would proudly announce.

Sunday was the day I got to be part of my family and spend time playing with my younger brother.

Although my gait was very compromised, I remembered hobbling, stumbling and giggling my way through the grassy lawn with my brother and feeling free. But the days always ended too soon, and I found myself in the car once again after dinner, knowing I was going to be away for another week. Sitting in the back of car, mile after mile, telephone pole after telephone pole, I dreaded my return.

"How many more weeks do I have to stay?" I would ask.

Most times, the answer was the same. "When you are better."

Some hospital stays were months long, others were shorter, but no matter the length, it always seemed like the doctors would come up with another reason for me to go back. Keeping my thoughts to myself, I looked out into the blackened night and darkened roadway, feeling sad and wondering when it would all end.

After my last surgery, my parents began to look for medical alternatives. Later on, there was speculation that these treatments had little value and might have in fact destroyed healthier parts of the neurological area. Unexplored medical territory encouraged experimentation with the best of intentions. However, as a child, nothing made sense, and the pain I was put through was frightening and dreadful.

We went from one recommended physician to another, including a chiropractor. My parents finally decided upon a highly esteemed orthopedic surgeon. Dr. Richgood evaluated and performed additional surgeries to correct and make significant improvements to my leg and gait. He was my hero.

Papa

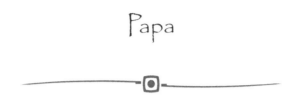

One of the saving graces of my childhood were the family visits to France to see my grandfather, Papa, and grandmother, Henriette, on long summer vacations from school. When I was six, we travelled on the SS Queen Mary. Aside from the adventures of traveling the Atlantic on a cruise ship for seven days, spending time with Papa still remains one of my sweetest memories.

Papa served in WWI in France, then married and settled with his wife in a small village; the same village as the builder of New York's Statue of Liberty. Little did Papa know that WWII would take his eldest daughter from him, to live in the very same state where this famous statue stands.

Papa had a very round face with cheeks and nose to match, and was balding, with the exception of some sparse strands of hair fighting to stay on either side of his head. Everything about Papa was full and compelling. His chubby stature likened the image of a cuddly teddy bear and his ever-present, broad smile would light up a room. His voice was soft-spoken and soothing, despite the fact that I barely understood a word. No better idiom than "actions speak louder than words" could suit the kind of relationship we nurtured. I always felt cherished when I was with him. Though limited by distance, I would find his acts of love comforting during our times together.

On one of my first visits to France, I learned that Papa was a diesel mechanic by trade. His residence accommodated an attached gas station on one side of the structure. Their house included a door that conveniently led to an open sided, attached roof area supported by pillars that housed two gas pumps. The garage was immaculate, no neon signs, no oil laden floors. Potted planters containing multi-colored flowers were strategically positioned to embellish the open-air stop. Customers parked to buy fuel for their autos and chat with the cheerful, engaging middle-aged owner.

Entering their home from the front, you couldn't miss the charming feel of it. Large wood shutters opened to hand-cranked, mullioned windows, overlooking the park in the center of town. And like many homes in France, you could sit upon the screen-less, extra wide sills, and watch the world go by.

I learned a little French by the end of my stay with Papa, but it wasn't until my next visit that I connected on a deeper level with him, although there were still very few words between us.

Papa and Henriette moved to a second story apartment after my first visit. The kitchen had three wide steps leading to a double casement window, and three equally wide steps outside, which descended onto the one story raised concrete patio. But in Papa's mind's eye, this patio needed a more protective barrier for his young grandchildren. Giving it some thought, he came up with an idea. He would create an atmosphere of illusion to please us, as well as provide a safe environment. With several long sheets of gray corrugated metal, a good imagination, and creative talent, he transformed the dull, lifeless courtyard walls into a fantasy town. All hand-drawn and painted in brightly colored hues, he created a mural that included people on bicycles, dogs running after cats through the streets, children flying kites, and ladies going to shops. We spent many hours happily playing there under the canopy of trees in this gentle man's vision of a daydream.

I looked forward to our walks, hand in hand, through the forest in search of the much-desired mirabelle plums or raspberries for that night's tart. Papa's collection of twigs and flowers on the way were transformed into my new crown for the day. He didn't forget my brother. A wide and shallow stone fountain set in the middle of town was perfect for the launching of small hand whittled boats with white cotton fabric sails.

Papa was a wonderful cook. My favorite was the leftover, seasoned roasts and raw onions that he ran through the manual meat grinder attached to side of the kitchen table. Cored-out raw potatoes would house the ground meat mixture and slowly simmer in a big Dutch oven while the room filled with mouth-watering scents. He also ground coffee every morning by placing the beans in the top of a wooden box, then turning the metal arm in circular motions, round and round. When the beans disappeared into the box, he would have me pull the small drawer out from the bottom. There appeared, to my delight, the wonderfully aromatic beans magically transformed into fine morsels. It seemed that everything Papa did was captivating.

****

Noelle, a girlhood friend of my mother and aunt, must have also enjoyed being in Papa's home, as she often paid us a visit. I enjoyed her visits and was mesmerized by her looks. Noelle sang Frank Sinatra tunes, as we sat sidesaddle, face-to-face, on my grandparents' kitchen windowsill, while the glow of the sun warmed our shoulders. Papa often hummed along with us,

""*Fairy tales can come true, they can happen to you, if you're young at heart......*" While I learned her signature song, I couldn't help staring at her face. She was a beautiful woman, but I decided that Noelle either had the most peculiar upper lip or she was attempting to start a new trend in the world of beauty. Instead of following the natural line of her upper lip, with two symmetrical curves from the center, she ran the lipstick straight across. Not that it mattered to me: this was a woman with such a gay spirit and presence that it began to seem normal to see her lips colored in that manner.

Love and War

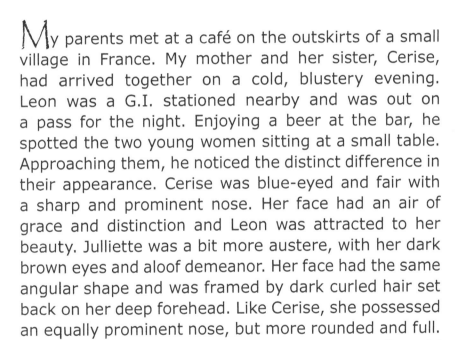

My parents met at a café on the outskirts of a small village in France. My mother and her sister, Cerise, had arrived together on a cold, blustery evening. Leon was a G.I. stationed nearby and was out on a pass for the night. Enjoying a beer at the bar, he spotted the two young women sitting at a small table. Approaching them, he noticed the distinct difference in their appearance. Cerise was blue-eyed and fair with a sharp and prominent nose. Her face had an air of grace and distinction and Leon was attracted to her beauty. Julliette was a bit more austere, with her dark brown eyes and aloof demeanor. Her face had the same angular shape and was framed by dark curled hair set back on her deep forehead. Like Cerise, she possessed an equally prominent nose, but more rounded and full.

Cerise seemed more approachable to Leon. "Would you care to dance?"

She was a bit reluctant, but accepted the soldier's request. He was tall and thin, with striking almond-shaped, blue eyes and a sensual presence about him neither woman could ignore. His face was oval and his mouth was thin but his upper lip was noticeably heart-shaped. He possessed warm, straight, thick, brown hair that he wore parted on the side.

"Where do you come from?" Cerise asked as they danced to a slow, big band tune.

"New York," Leon proudly answered. "I've been here for a year now and have been assigned to grave yard duty."

Cerise's eyes dropped and looked away. "What a terrible time to live in. So many lives have been taken and destroyed."

"Yes, but a necessary evil at this point if we're ever going to get rid of that mad man," Leon replied.

To lift their spirits, Leon invited Cerise and her sister for a ride in his army jeep. It was a cool autumn night and getting out of the smoked filled café for a while seemed inviting.

"And what is your name?" Leon asked in his broken French.

"Julliette."

"Well Julliette, I hope you like open air vehicles since there's quite a nip tonight."

Cerise sat in the front with Leon. Climbing into in the back, Julliette made herself as comfortable as one could in the cramped space, buttoning up her coat to her neck. They drove along the river that ran through their small village and toward the mountain route. Leon loved the countryside of this part of France. There were farms dotted along the valley and majestic trees blanketing the mountainside foothills of the Black Forest. Conversation was difficult as they competed with the roar of the jeep's engine, so they headed back to town after their drive. When they returned, Leon introduced his passengers to some fellow G.I.s. Cerise drifted off to engage in a conversation with one of the men and Julliette stood alone. Hearing another big band tune drifting through the windows, Leon turned to her and invited her back into the café to dance.

"Are the stars out tonight, I don't know if it's cloudy or bright, cause I only have eyes for you ….dear."" They danced to the "30s song by the Ben Selvin and didn't seem to notice when it was over. Standing on the floor, they just clung to the sense that there was someone in this maddening world to hold on to. They sat together for the remainder of that brief evening, sharing stories about their families and what they were going to do when the war was over. This song would become their song when they said their marriage vows shortly after the war, but could those sentiments sustain them?

What Happens at Grandma's, Stays at Grandma's

It was a traumatic time for my mother, at the tender age of twenty-one, to leave her homeland as a war bride and move to a foreign country. She often shared stories with me about her difficult life adjustments. Living with my father's parents initially, and barely speaking English, was one of her more repeated vexations.

"Your grandmother thought I married your father just so I could come and live in this country," she would explain with her French accented English. "She really wanted your father to marry an American girl she knew in town."

"But Mom, after a while she must have realized that was not true?" I would ask. Julliette never really believed that and never had a good relationship with her mother-in-law, Esther.

Most times I took it all in, but there were times I would turn off her tirades and thought of my times spent with my grandmother. Grandma Esther had fiery, strawberry-blond hair, cropped short, which framed her very freckled face, as well as the rest of her boxy and overweight figure.

She lived over a railroad station for many years after her husband died. "Pop Pop" Dunne worked for the railroad as a conductor. When she became his widow, she was offered the much- desired apartment. It was comparable in size to the expansive station below and offered more than ample sized rooms, including two large attics that sat like bookends on either side.

It was unlike anyone's home that I knew. The kitchen table sat under two large double hung windows with a chair flanked on either side of the table. We had a bird's eye view of train arrivals, with passengers disembarking and boarding without anyone knowing we were there. That is, except for the conductors who knew that my grandmother and my aunt Gaye lived there. Aunt Gaye made up train schedules for many of the conductors. It was a way for her to earn money, since she was a sickly woman from early childhood with whooping cough and subsequent epilepsy. Her uncontrolled grand mal seizures did not allow her to keep a job, but she was phenomenally quick with numbers. She breezed through to their tedious timetables, and they were grateful for it. She even made the newspapers once for having the ability to play twenty Bingo cards without chips! She logged her winnings and took her mother to Florida one year on the savings she accumulated from her Bingo games. Likened to a savant, she experienced the severity of one part of her brain malfunctioning, while another part would over compensate.

On those lazy Saturday mornings at Grandma Esther's, I sat at the screened window, eating my favorite breakfast: an English muffin with butter oozing all over it and a glass of tomato juice. Grandma never forgot my favorites and often made sure she prepared a batch of homemade baked lima beans for her only granddaughter. However, since her cooking repertoire was not very extensive, she often would take me to the local eateries, which was something our family rarely did back then. Some afternoons we would stop at Grints, the department store where she was employed. We always visited the pet department to see the many cute animals waiting for a home. Grandma had bought her dog, Sandy, and her parakeet, Tweety Bird, at Grints.

After we checked out all the pets in their cages, we were off to the toy department! Grandma would begin to talk to one of her fellow employees, which gave me a chance to wander up and down the aisles of toys and deciding, if I had a million dollars, which ones would I buy! I never left the store empty-handed, either. Grandma would let me select something small and reasonably priced to bring home. Mom would not approve because she felt it was indulgent on my grandmother's part, but despite her chagrin, I always received a plaything.

On our way home, Grandma Esther and I would sing one of my favorite songs by Patti Page.

"How much is that doggie in the window (arf, arf) the one with the waggley tail, how much is that doggie in the window (arf, arf) I do hope that doggie's for sale...."

There were always songs to sing as we traveled in her car. We often sang Lucille Ball's hit from the '60s musical.

"Hey look me over, lend me an ear, fresh out of clover, mortgaged up to here. Don't pass the plate folks, don't pass the cup. I figure whenever you're down and out, the only way is up....!"

Singing with Grandma Esther was a happy time for me.

Our next stop would often be Howard Johnson's for dinner. Yum, my mouth would water on the way, just thinking about the wonderful grilled hot dogs sitting in their specially toasted split rolls, with lots green relish and mustard smothered all over. Being a connoisseur of HJ's menu, I would also order a side of their baked beans, served in a little, brown, glazed pot to make it a balanced meal, along with a wonderful thick shake float to top the sumptuous repast perfectly! What a treat that was!

There were days spent at her home when I would look forward to adorning myself with the clusters of flashy costume jewelry, kept in shoeboxes in grandma's bedroom. I was quite a sight to behold with my equally heavily-applied makeup and a hairbrush microphone in hand in front of her bedroom dresser mirror, singing my songs "on stage." Grandma would often be in another room, singing along or talking to the TV. Arthur Godfrey would be on the air with his Talent Scout show. She said he was her boyfriend. Aside from the fact that they rather looked alike, I wondered about her choice in men! There he would be, in all his glory, "talking" to grandma. If he was not on the air, there was always the torn magazine page with his image taped to her wall for her to swoon over.

Staying at grandma's for a sleepover was something I would not have traded for the world. My brother and I would compete for the chance to be selected. Actually, it was more like a contest of who begged, pleaded, and whined the most when she paid us a visit. I was really good at it.

After the sofa bed was made up for me in the living room, I would kiss my grandmother goodnight. This would be just the beginning of another adventure for me. I would lie in bed under the covers waiting. Finally, after some time, it would begin. I could barely make out the sound at first. Like the far-off rumbling of a thunderstorm, it would slowly draw near. I could feel the faint vibrations increasing through the room. The bed quivered, and anything hanging loose, like the chain on a lamp, would start to jingle. The whistle would begin to call in the night, and the apartment accelerated to a tremble. Within a few short minutes, the noise was deafening and the apartment would be like an uncontrolled jackhammer on concrete. As the train rushed below, the tracks brashly clicked to a frenzied rhythm. Grandma slept through it all, it appeared. I guessed you could get used to anything if you were tired enough. The vibrations and sound continued and slowly became a subtler tune. I would lie back in bed with the cover to my chin and smile, feeling thrilled and satisfied.

My mother, however, found fault with grandma's lifestyle. "For God's sake, she works for Grints and has had a pension since your Dad passed away, but she can't save a dime?" My mother cursed grandma's Daughters of America conventions that took her to different states for long weekends a few times a year because she thought it was a frivolous expense. Having a running car was grandma's priority and a prominent irritant to my mother. She did not relate to grandma's urgency for her car to be on the road, perhaps because she never learned to drive. My father would give in to his mother and help her out when she needed extra funds for those trips. When I would tell him later on in life that I had fond memories of his mother, he would say that grandma gave my mother a hard time. He defended my mother despite the fact that she would have plenty to say about the disappointment he was to her throughout the years.

The Center of Attention

---●---

When I was perhaps five or six, my parents rented a large, two-story pre-war home. Entering the front door, a stairwell led to the second floor where my brother, Buster, and I shared an L shaped bedroom. The longer part of the L—Buster's space—was wallpapered in blue and red cowboys on brown horses, while the shorter part of the L was my space, the surrounding walls covered with pink ballerinas. My dolls were lined up on the floor along the inner wall and ran parallel to my brown metal bed. To my delight, the solid, massive headboard was decorated with decaled, pastel colored, smiling teddy bears. My brother and I shared the double hung window on the outside wall of the room. I spent many nights, my elbows on the sill, and hands cupped under my chin, looking out upon the vista below. We lived on a side street off of a "main drag" and behind a one-story tire shop, that sat across the street from a Carvel ice cream stand. The larger-than-life ice cream cone, which glowed brightly above the stand, always fascinated me. It lit up the sky like a torch of a lighthouse that showed the way in the night. I felt special thinking I had the only view of this much-enamored symbol.

Sometimes when my imagination ran wild, I conjured up an image of myself lying on a magic carpet, tummy down, and gliding across and around the cone, having a bird's eye view of it, and the customers standing in line below.

One night when we were on the verge of sleep, without forewarning, my father burst into our room. I have no memory of what prompted him, but within seconds I was the object of several punishing blows. Pulled out of bed by the shoulder of my pajama top, I was thrown to the floor near the top of the hall stairwell. In my struggle to recover without my leg brace, I began to stumble and tumbled down the stairs. I was lucky. The staircase had a landing about five steps down, which broke my momentum. To this day, I couldn't even tell you why it happened; I was too young and most likely traumatized by the event. Looking back, I often wondered what would have happened if I did fall down the second, longer set of stairs that night. Would I have survived or perhaps broken my neck? My brother had witnessed the scene, but we never spoke about it, ever. Did my mother come to my rescue? A limited terrorizing memory frozen in time.

****

Being home from the hospital for intermittent periods of time meant I was also attending my elementary school. I was easily singled out because of my polio affliction. "She wears baby shoes, she wears baby shoes," was the sing-song chant that came from my schoolmates in the '50s. A thick leather waistband with buckles secured the brace around my waist. The heavy gauged metal posts attached to the waistband, ran down both sides of my leg and were bolted to the dark brown, high-laced shoes that went above my ankle. The brace was clumsy and heavy, but a necessary evil.

Much to my chagrin, they were right. I was quite a unique image with my cumbersome appendage and a pair of wooden crutches. No one looked like me in grade school. At least I didn't feel ostracized when I was living at the hospital.

Despite the fact that I attended classes during my long hospital stays, it was never equal to the public school education program. I missed a great deal in my childhood during the lengthy hospitalizations. Somehow I managed to catch up on all my subjects, except for math. Looking back on those days, I would jokingly explain my plight by saying, "God must have been taking a coffee break when He was about to give me math skills, and forgot to finish the job when He got back."

Early on, I was stumped with my math homework, and my first choice for help was my mother. She explained to me, however, that her French math was not at all like American, so she could not help. I pitifully struggled so much with my adding and subtracting that she might as well have explained it to me in French. I just didn't get it. That left me with no choice but to go to my father.

Often, I would find him sitting at the faded, red, floral tablecloth that covered our dining room table, writing out bills or reading the paper. With great trepidation, I would meekly ask if he would help with my math problems, taking a seat near him when he agreed. At first he would explain them to me in a calm manner. Again and again, I would give him a look of confusion. When he asked me for an answer to a problem, in desperation, I would nervously throw out an answer, hoping it would be a lucky guess. His stature would become rigid and again, after a briefer explanation, he would ask me the same question. Pretending I was pondering about the answer, and for fear of saying the wrong thing, I would hesitate. After a short pause his voice would rise, "I said, what is the answer?"

"I don't think I know, Daddy," I replied, in a whisper.

The volume of his voice would increase. He pounded his fist on the table. The glass vase of garden flowers in the center began to shimmy as if it were in fear as well. After another stern explanation, he would ask, "**Now what...is...the...damn...answer, Colette**?"

On the verge of tears, my eyes cast downward, with my voice quivering and hardly audible, I replied again, "I really don't know, Daddy."

My math book took flight, deflecting off a near wall to the floor, spine and pages bent and crumbled now. While I absorbed what had just happened to my schoolbook, out of the corner of my eye I caught a glimpse of my father's other hand descending. Careening towards the side of my head the impact hurled me off my chair, tumbling to the floor. Breathing deeply, my father sat back, trying to collect himself after the blow. That was the end of my lesson for the night. My mother then ushered my trembling, recoiled body to my bedroom. I spoke not a word in fear that it would provoke his anger again. As I climbed into bed, I hugged my mother's neck and told her I was sorry. "Just go to sleep now Colette," was her only reply.

To this day, I struggle when it comes to math. If I have to do the simplest math, on a restaurant tab or a checklist of numbers on a receipt, I am stymied. Something in my head just shuts down. To my embarrassment, I still can't add in my head, failed algebra in high school, and barely made it through

business math. Would I have ever been a math wiz?
Unlikely.

When I was about eight and my brother was six, we
moved again, but unlike previous homes, my parents
purchased this house. I liked our new home and street.
There were a number of kids on the block who went to
school with us. Buster and I still shared a bedroom, but
now we slept on bunk beds when I wasn't hospitalized.
I loved the bunks. Because of my physical limitations,
Buster got to climb the ladder and sleep on the top and
I on the bottom. I felt secure within my cubbyhole. The
head of my bed was bounded by the side our dresser
and the spring and mattress that was suspended above
me. Buster and I were entranced for hours in our beds
with our "best" stuffed animals. He had a pale blue
rabbit and I had my black and white kitten. Or at least I
thought it was a kitten. A family member gave it to me
as a gift when I was an infant. I called it Mimi. I wasn't
even sure if it was a kitten. Over the years, it was so
worn it could have passed for a panda. It had long ago
lost its eyes, which were replaced with white buttons.
The nose was squished in, due to a shift in stuffing. To
compensate, the nose and mouth were replaced with
a few strands of red thread. Mimi lost just about all
"his" fur, too (what did I know about gender and the
relationship to names back then!). His cotton "skin"
showed through everywhere except his tail. It had been
permanently pushed sideways, but if you lifted it up,
you could see the soft and shiny coat surviving under
the fold.

Buster would push his rabbit between his upper
bunk and the wall that ran along our beds to pay Mimi
a visit. Mimi would invariably greet his rabbit with a kiss
or hello. Many happy adventures played out through
that narrow passageway. Today, Mimi is still alive and

well in my steamer trunk that houses all my favorite memorabilia.

I was happy in our new bedroom. I had a record player, a small metal desk that I spent hours drawing on, and not one, but two, double-hung windows in the corner of our room, looking out our backyard and the neighbor's. During the summer, I would grow marigolds from the seeds I collected from last year's flowers, and watermelon from the collected seeds of our summer desserts. I had a good view of my "garden" under my window, and delighted in seeing their growth, despite the fact that I never reaped fruit off the vines.

My play days weren't always tranquil. Tranquility did not last long in our household. It didn't take much to sense an air of mayhem brewing within the confines of our home. As a youngster I was very sensitive to the chastising and criticisms by my mother.

Within a few minutes of my father's arrival, I could hear my mother speaking to him down the hall from my room. She knew. She knew if she complained about me, he would follow through.

Suddenly, I was numb with fear again. Down the short hallway of our Cape Cod house, pounding footsteps would draw near, keeping time with my head and heartbeats. The door of our bedroom was open, so there was no need for a dramatic entrance. Without uttering a word, he lunged at me in a rage. His thick, powerful hand slapped and catapulted me to the carpeting. The strikes kept coming as I cowered on the floor. Moments later, my mother entered. As my father silently left the room with my mother in tow, I made my way to my bed, crying from the badly bruised areas. Within a few minutes, my mother returned. She had fetched washcloths soaked in cold water to put on my welts and reddened body.

No more than a ten minutes later, my father returned. Still whimpering, he approached and sat himself on the edge of my bed. In a calmer voice he spoke, "If you were a better kid, I wouldn't have to do this." Strangely, I was somehow comforted by his words. I felt gratified that he was so remorseful, and I began to feel some sense of well-being again.

I did not tell anyone about the beatings, not my grandmother, not even my friend who lived a few blocks from me. Brea and I spent a lot of time together during grammar school and junior high. Most times we hung out at her home during those adolescent years. Her mom worked during the day, and we had the whole house to ourselves. We were rarely at my house. One day, however, we decided to spend time in my parents' basement.

Half of the basement was finished with wood paneling, vinyl flooring and furnishings, on the order of a recreation room: a good place for two girls to sit, play music, and talk about boys and school. The other half of the basement was unfinished and housed the washer, dryer, and assorted storage, along with a makeshift office for my father. Near his desk was a wooden bookshelf with variety of books stuffed on all five levels. It was kind of an oddity, as I had never recalled ever seeing him reading. As we scanned through the collection on this particular day, we noticed a sizable book with the bust of a woman on the spine. She was a blonde, the Mae West type, with lots of jewels and makeup, and she was wearing a shiny pink top that showed an ample amount of her voluptuous bosom. We began to giggle as we started to pull it off the shelf. My friend suggested we take it upstairs and outside so we could take a look at the rest of the pages. I knew if I got caught, I would be in trouble, but I was willing to take the chance with my friend's repeated urges. We left my house safely and began to walk down my street. Halfway down the block, we found a spot alongside of the road with several trees and shrubs. We agreed that we were far enough away from my house now. Sitting ourselves down on the curb, we began to explore this forbidden volume. Much to our surprise, it was filled with more photos of of semi-nude women. It was pretty tame by comparison to today's material, but no less intriguing for us. The storyline was about burlesque and in bold print on the front cover was the name, *Little Me*. Before we leafed through no more than a few pages, I heard a car approaching. We didn't look up at first, since we were ogling over the many photos, but as I raised my head to see the passing car, there was my father! He was on his way home from work and slowed down as we feebly attempted to hide the book. I knew he saw it by the frosty look on his face. Rolling down his car window, he ordered me home and told my friend, if he ever saw her on the block again he would kick her butt. (He actually said worse.) Without a word of goodbye to Brea, I quickly headed to my house and entered the back kitchen door. I set out toward my room when my father entered from the front door. His strapping hand grabbed me by the arm. With his firm and forceful grip, I was thrown across the kitchen floor. I slid over the vinyl surface to the other end of the kitchen and hit the corner of our rectangular garbage can with my leg. It broke my careening motion, but the sharp, copper edge left a thick, half-inch gouge on the inside of my knee.

My friend could surely hear my father as she hurried home. Many a day, his thunderous voice roared like a jet engine and spilled out into the streets of our block. All the neighbors knew about my father's rages, especially since our windows were screened in those days.

I never got stitches for my laceration that day, but some fifty years later my scar is still clearly visible. The recollection of pain is long gone, but the emotional scar from his brutality remains.

When I reached my early teens, during the blur of my father's assaults, I often thought of sharing my secret. Who could I turn to and how could they even help me?

At our church, we were introduced to a new priest who had joined our congregation. He was much younger than our residing priests and had a different personality than what we were accustomed to. He was cheerful and funny, and played hymns on his guitar during Mass. I found him refreshing and not at all like the other austere and solemn priests. Our parish embraced him, and he became very popular with the younger parishioners. He could relate to us, and we gravitated to him. He was engaging and easy to talk to, and I often wondered if I would dare ask to speak to him. With all the courage I could muster, I finally decided to try. It was late in the afternoon and I was leaving my after school religion class. Before I headed home, I decided to stop by the rectory.

The secretary greeted me, "Can I help you?"

With a bit of hesitation, I meekly asked, "Is it possible to make an appointment with Father Collins?"

She was pleasant enough and did not hesitate to look at the oversized, black, covered calendar she kept for the several priests who lived at the rectory. "Okay, how about next week?" She pointed to a day the following week, which seemed like an eternity, but I accepted. Now that I had the nerve, I wanted that day to be right now. It was hard living with my parents, knowing I was about to do something they knew nothing about. How would they feel if they knew? To say I was nervous would be an understatement.

The day finally arrived. I was at the rectory not a minute too soon or too late. I was committed and didn't want anything to go wrong. The secretary directed me down a long narrow hall to the office, where I was to meet the youthful and approachable priest. He was seated behind his large wooden desk. He looked up, smiled, and asked me to sit in the chair opposite him. "What's going on, Colette?"

"Well Father," I stammered.

"I wanted to know if you could speak to my parents."

"What about?"

This was my cue. I began to explain the recurrent beatings the best way I could. He listened, but did not make any comments as I spoke. When I was done, he asked in a soft tone, "Would you like me to talk to your father?"

"I think so, but I am afraid."

"I understand, let me see what I can do. I have your phone number; I will make a call."

He never told me when or where he would ultimately speak to my father, but I thought maybe it would be at my house. I waited. One week went by, and then another, but nothing appeared to be happening. My parents never approached me, nor did I hear from the priest. Thoughts kept swirling in my mind. *If he did call my father, wouldn't my father tell me? Would he give me a beating for it? Would the priest contact me to tell me what happened? Should I run away if I sensed that I would endure the worse beating imaginable?* But nothing did happen, and nothing changed. If I couldn't trust a priest to help me, then whom could I trust?

****

In my freshman year of high school, I met a boy through my friends, who lived across the street from me. Darin was in his last year of high school, and would soon be on his way to college. Darin and I dated for about two years, when I decided to break up with him. I was becoming disenchanted with his possessiveness and jealousy. Besides, there was Kip. Kip was in my English class and sat in front of me. After a few flirtatious comments before class began, he passed me a note one day. "If you weren't dating 'Joe College,' I would have liked to ask you to the prom."

I wrote a message back saying, "I'll go with you!" Darin was not happy about my decision, and went to extremes to try and change my mind. At the time, he was attending a State College several hours away. I phoned him at his dorm to explain that I wanted to end our relationship. That very night, in a frenzied state, he climbed on his motorcycle and drove over two hundred miles in the dark and pouring rain to see me. It was too late; I had made up my mind.

Darin was a rebel, and very liberated in his thinking on just about any topic. Unlike my father, who was controlling and dictatorial, his parents allowed him to be a free thinker in all regards. I enjoyed Darin's open views on issues, but he also had some radical behavior that made me eventually long for someone more conventional, like Kip.

Darin was undaunted and pleaded with me to meet him the next morning. Sneaking out to see Darin, in order to clarify my reasons for breaking up, would be crossing the lines of what my father would tolerate. Being a teenager with poor judgment, however, I told my parents I was going to walk to the end of the block to meet a "friend." Not an outright lie mind you! As I approached the end of the street, I saw Darin sitting in a parked car. He rolled down the window and asked me to get into the passenger's side. I did. After he gave me a kiss on the cheek, we sat for a few minutes and talked about the prospects of our getting back together. In the midst of our discussion, I heard a car, and turned my head toward the back driver's side window. My father approached Darin's car and demanded that I leave and come home with him. I was terrified. As I opened the door to climb out, I began to shake uncontrollably. Darin urged me to stay, "Keep your ground and stay with me."

"No Darin, enough damage is done. I have to go!" I knew that would only escalate my father's temper. After entering the passenger side of our car, my father, now crazed, spun our car around and raced back to our house. He made a sharp right turn into the driveway and slammed on the brakes so hard I had to stop myself from hitting the dashboard with my hands. Without any time for an explanation, he slapped me across the face. The impact was so severe that my nose began to bleed profusely and my face swelled up on one side. Before I could get myself out of the car, without any tissues at hand, the blood streamed down my face and onto my white tee shirt and shorts.

My two friends who lived across the street noticed our car and were making their way to greet me. Seeing my bloody exit, they turned around and walked back without a word spoken. I wasn't shocked at their reaction—they knew my father's wrath and knew enough not to stick around. I was grounded for the entire summer that year. On some level, because of the humiliation I endured, I was grateful not to see anyone. But it was torturous, spending my entire summer vacation in my room, day after day. My only salvation was being allowed to speak to Kip once a day on my Princess extension phone. I thanked God for small miracles.

There was an end to the beatings, eventually. It occurred during my early twenties. I was working for a large company and still living at home. I decided to join the company bowling team that met after work on Thursday nights. After the members of our teams finished up their games, we would spend the last hour or two of the night in the adjoining bar area. It was a time to unwind and get to know each other outside of work. Of course, the bar was not exclusive to us; there were others who enjoyed having a drink or two before going home. I met one of those people one night. He was the owner of a gas station near the bowling alley. He was considerably older than I but we began dating and I quickly became smitten with him. He spoiled me, and I was swept off my feet. At some point during the relationship I asked, "Could we hang out at your house tonight?" That's when he broke the news. He was married. But because I felt addicted to his positive attention, I didn't want to walk away from him. Within several days however, this man's wife called my home. When I returned from work that day, my mother confronted me. I explained that I knew he was married, but that in my heart I couldn't stop seeing him. It felt like I was falling in love.

Later that day, in my bedroom, I heard our car pull in the driveway. This was never good. I was in a cold sweat again, frozen in place, heart muscle tightening. I had my own bedroom on the second floor now. *Oh, dear God, I know what's coming,* I thought. *Will he give me a chance to explain?* I knew the answer to that as I began to hear those heavy footsteps climbing the staircase leading to my room. When my father entered my door, not a word was spoken between us; we both knew it would not impede his intent. Only this time it would play out differently. I was standing in front my bed, bracing the bedpost when he faced me. Within seconds I lifted my free arm in front of my face. The first massive blow knocked me to the floor, parallel to my bed. It was searing and painful, but I didn't cry. Unlike all the other beatings, I began to speak. I turned my head to him and said, "Go ahead, do it again. Keep going, if that's what you want." He complied with more blows to different parts of my body. I continued my remarks, "That's right, do it again." He obliged. What was going on in my head? Total abandonment and a lack of feeling. "Does that make you feel good?" I asked him. My remarks incensed him, and he hit me again.

As always, Juliette soon appeared, "Leon stop!" So fruitless were her remarks, I had begun to mentally refer to her as "Nurse Juliette." Despite her attempts to play the role of a caretaker after each beating, it did not erase her responsibility and insincere concern for my welfare.

"I don't care," I said to her. By this time he was kicking my side, and I began to inch under my bed from the repeated impact of his shoe.

"Enough," she said. "Stop!"

I guess she was right; the job was done. I lay under my bed for a long time, wondering why I verbally fought back. I knew full well it would only incite his rage more intensely, but I felt defiant in that moment. For a long time after they were gone, I laid there, aching so, I could only allow myself shallow pants of breath. Tears finally began to stream down my face, and my nose filled with mucus. I was in relentless and commanding pain, but I believed the tears were for much more than I could explain at the time.

Waking up the following morning, I quickly discovered that I could barely move. Sharp pains radiated from my side; my rib cage full of deep crimson and blue contusions. I didn't think I could get out of bed much less go to work. What now?

My father drove me to the emergency room that morning. This trip to the hospital proved to be quite serious. I had torn ligaments and a bruised rib cage.

"What happened?" asked the nurse.

I gave a carefully rehearsed response prompted by my father: "I fell down the stairs."

Fear

*"Now I lay me down to sleep, I pray
the Lord my soul to keep,
if I should die before I wake, I pray
the Lord my soul to take."*

~Joseph Addison

My mother often encouraged me to pray for our safety. Before my prayers however, she would discuss, in great detail, the memories of her life during WWII as a young girl in France, and the dangerous and frightful scenarios she witnessed. There were myriads of haunting bedtime stories, some about German Gestapo soldiers, captured and kept in caves near her house. She and the townspeople were forced into the shelters with them during air raids. The captive Germans would make overtures to the young girls, and she admitted that they were often handsome. She always added, in earnest alarm however, "They were not to be trusted; they were the most evil of all the German soldiers."

One very impressionable story that she reenacted for me was the day she and her girlfriend attended a movie in town. During the show, they began to hear the air raid sounding. She explained that this alarm happened often and since they were under the protection of the solid and stable movie theater, they stayed put and waited for the all-clear signal. They were out of harm's way and felt confident they could now make their way home. Heading toward her friend's home on foot, they made a harrowing discovery. A bomb had destroyed her friend's house, and her entire family had perished. "Can you imagine something like that happening?" she asked, her gaze intently holding mine. In shock by the horrid outcome of the story, I slowly nodded my head no. I took the tragedy to bed with me that night and felt sorry for my mother. I would often be drawn back to her recollections and wondered how people could be so evil. Dwelling on the dreadful events that consumed me at night, I would resort to easing myself into her bed to feel safe when I could not find solace on my own.

I was fourteen in 1962, during the Cuban Missile Crisis. The country, as a whole, was engrossed with the foreboding situation at hand. While Soviet ballistic missiles were deployed in Cuba, my mother focused on her own emergency preparations. When I asked what was her intention, she had me follow her to the basement so she could present her pantry. She had organized a set of shelving to store canned foods, bottled water from our tap, and a manual can opener. I felt a sense of panic looking at her meager supplies. I wondered what would happen if the supplies only lasted a few weeks. Then what?

"This is where we will go and huddle, so we will have the most protection from the atom bomb fallout," she said, pointing to the designated corner of our unfinished basement that had no windows.

I had learned a lot about the atom bomb from my mother during my early teenage years. The way your skin would be eaten, the way your insides would decay. What could you do? The solution for her was to have nourishment to sustain us, to appoint a designated shelter that wouldn't protect us at all, and to pray. I had a great deal of trepidation about her illogical efforts, even though they seemed to satisfy some of her own fear.

Praying was a nightly ritual. My First Communion rosary beads hung from my bedpost, and if that wasn't enough of a reminder, every night my mother would enter my bedroom and ask, "Did you say your rosary?"

"Yes, Mom, I did." I did so without fail. I was so terrified of dying, that this religious mantra set precedence in my survival. I was constantly preoccupied with the prospect that the world could be annihilated in the blink of an eye. At night, alone in my own room, the darkness always enveloped me in a shroud of despair that I had no control over. I was grateful for the dim beam from the streetlight that peeked through my bedroom blinds. Sometimes when my spirits were very low, I would turn my nightstand light on so I could fall asleep. It was necessary to wake up and turn it off before dawn, however. Should my mother find my light on, I would be reprimanded for wasting electricity and fined a quarter. That was monumental for me. Since I was fined any time I forgot to shut a light off, my $1.00 allowance for performing household duties would often be severely threatened.

****

I was young, but I struggled to be fearless. I longed to enjoy the endless possibilities that life had in store for me. Anything I might consider an adventure, was in my mother's view, a hazardous or dangerous situation. Despite her anxiety, at the end of my teen years, I would jump on the back of my boyfriend's Harley or drive my car hundreds of miles to visit a friend or fly on my own to Europe to visit my aunt and uncle. I suspect that my father had something to do with my growing freedom, since he had none of her fears. Looking back however, I remained largely powerless. It was a hard-fought battle for me to remain separate from her fears.

Thunderstorms were another unnerving experience for my mother. In the summertime, during the early '60s, no one in our community had air conditioning. You found yourself sleeping on top of your sheets, spread-eagled, with your screened windows wide open, in hopes of catching a hot night breeze. If there were a fan perched nearby, it would offer no more than intermittent hot streams of air. Along with those long, sweltering summer nights came the occasional earth-shattering thunderstorm. In my house, it would be an event! My mother was convinced that the lightning could aim its electrical bolt at us in various ways. Throwing on her robe, her hair tousled and her expression anxious, she would call us from our beds and assemble us in what she considered the most sheltered area of the house: the hallway.

"Why do we have to sit in the hallway, Mom?"

"You could be hit by lightening lying in bed because the draft can carry it in." So convinced it was dangerous, my mother would rush from door to door to close each one. She explained that we would be sheltered from the draft and it would keep the noise of the thunder and bolts of light out. The three of us huddled in the hallway for the storm to pass, while Dad slept in his bed. Years later, when I was older, she warned me that sleeping with metal hair rollers (how did we sleep on them anyway?), would make you an even greater target for a strike.

There were countless disclosures for alarm. According to my mother, we could fall into harm's way by driving over bridges. Perhaps today, when you see or read the news, you might actually consider that a risk. Back then, the idea of accidentally driving off a bridge or having it suddenly crumble before your eyes, was highly unlikely.

Flying was also a terrifying option. My mother made it impossible to even visit her own parents living in France. In lieu of boarding a plane, she believed the better choice was to cross the ocean on a cruise liner for seven days. Many times, the ship would rock and roll in the great, turbulent ocean, and we in turn would be green for days. The intercom orders from the ship would often command that we put on our orange life jackets, as we witnessed the staff attempting to secure furniture while they slid from one side of the room to the other. My mother was frightened beyond reason, but it seemed, perhaps to her, there was greater possibility of surviving a sinking ship than a careening airplane.

Because she was chronically afraid, she never learned to drive a car and depended on my father for all her needs outside of their home. There was always something to worry about, and worry, she did.

"Be careful eating tuna or salmon from a can. There might be a bone that could rip open your stomach."

"Don't light candles because they can start a fire."

Don't, don't, don't. There were so many possibilities of doom and gloom and they slowly seeped into the crevices of my mind. How did I survive it all? Well, maybe I didn't.

By the time I was in high school, I kept most of my fearful thoughts to myself. Once in a while, they would manifest themselves suddenly.

In October of 1965, I planned to attend the World's Fair in Queens, NY for the last time, with my boyfriend, Kip. The exposition was a wondrous place for me and I enjoyed every visit I made. But this visit was quite different as the fair was about to close. After a fun-filled day, Kip and I decided to ride the cable car one last time before returning home. As we slowly glided above the grounds, I watched the scenes below me. There were handfuls of people walking around the garden areas, helping themselves to flowering plants, leaving gaping holes in the ground. Various attractions were already being disassembled. The fair was taking on a different complexion and fading away before my very eyes. My thoughts began to drift to my own personal demise. I contemplated on how much longer I had in my life. Would I be around long enough to experience the many remarkable events and sights that the world had to offer? Droplets began to surface in my eyes and blurred my vision. Kip, who was seated next to me with his arm around my shoulder, looked down and asked, "Babe, what's wrong?"

"I don't know, but I feel very sad," I responded.

"Is there anything I can do? I hate to see you this way."

"I'm sorry. I just feel a little depressed."

"Come on babe, be happy. We are together."

"You're right, I'll try to shake it."

He held me close as we continued our flight across the park's exhibits. Before the ride was over, I experienced a sudden transformation in my thoughts. *Girl, if you continue to worry and wonder when your life will be over, you will be wasting the time you do have to enjoy it.* It made complete sense to me. And it was so simple: how could I waste a minute of time? Live for the day! Or, as the Latin expression goes, *Carpe Diem.*

I came to discover in the years to come however, that it was easier for me to say than do.

Never Good Enough

I spent most of my years, through adulthood, trying to please my mother. It's a daunting task to take on when the receiver cannot be pleased. Some of my many attempts have become a blur now, but others created such heightened emotion for me, I could not erase them if I tried.

The one that perhaps stands out the most was when I was a young teenager and working part-time after school to earn an income of my own. Mother's Day was approaching, and I was excited to have my own earnings to buy a present. My mother had mentioned that she needed a new purse and I knew all about her requirements. It had to be a certain size, color, lots of interior pockets and dividers, a particular outside closure, and a lengthy shoulder strap. I searched one store after another in pursuit of the perfect handbag. I knew all too well how unwavering my mother was about her needs. Yet, as I took on this endeavor, my excitement began to build. I thought, *She will be shocked when she sees it. She will wonder how the heck I managed to find the right one!*

After many days of handbag hunting, there it was, sitting on the shelf in Macy's department store. I left the store that afternoon thinking five days is a long time to wait to give it to her. But wait, I did. I carefully wrapped the box with paper and matching ribbon, and slipped it in my closet behind my clothes rack. This was going to be the best surprise ever!

Mother's Day finally arrived, and we had company. My Aunt Cerise and uncle were visiting from Spain for a few weeks. After dinner, we were all seated at the kitchen table having dessert. The time was right and I was beyond excited. I left the kitchen and went to my bedroom. Finally, I would be able to offer my gift. I handed the box over to my mother, who was still sitting in her chair. I bent down to give her a kiss on the cheek and wished her a Happy Mother's Day. Holding my breath, I watched as she carefully unwrapped the box. She always saved wrapping paper for another event, carefully folding it and putting it aside. I was about to bust! As she opened the lid and exposed the purse, she said not a word. Pulling out the purse she began to inspect it. Color, check, size, check, pockets and dividers, check, strap, check.

"I don't think it has enough dividers. I like a zipper on at least one of the dividers," were the first words she uttered. To say I was destroyed would be an understatement, not just for this isolated incident, but for all the others times before it. I had no will to listen anymore and I left the kitchen through the back screened door. When I reached the driveway, tears were pouring down my face and hitting the concrete. Before long, my aunt and uncle came out of the house. I was inconsolable. My aunt wrapped her arms around me while my uncle spoke softly to me and held my hand. I don't remember what either of them said, but I can tell you I needed that tenderness so desperately. I was very grateful to them.

My aunt visited our family many years later and told me she remembered that Mother's Day very vividly. She offered only the excuse that it was my mother's personality. She could attest that her sister was the same when they were young.

I never received an apology that day from my mother. Not then, not ever.

And I never learned from my experiences, because I continued to set myself up for disappointment time after time, wanting to earn her approval and thinking maybe this time it would be different. They call that unrequited love.

Even later in my life, I was still trying to earn my mother's approval. You'd think by my thirties, I would have figured out that it was not meant to be. I was still not ready to face the reality.

When my mother and father decided to visit my mother's parents in France for four weeks, it took her a month just to mentally prepare for the visit. She attended intense therapy geared especially for the fear of flying for weeks, and now she was as committed as she would ever be.

My grandparents were elderly and were struggling with some serious illnesses. My aunt lived out of the country in Spain, but often flew back and forth to France for weeks at a time to care for their needs. Cerise often urged my mother to visit while she could and before it was too late.

Besides her anxiety about the trip, there was a long list of things she needed to do before she would leave. My father would say that those things could wait, but she could not rest until every detail was accomplished. The one thing she had no control over was the watering of their lawn. They did not have an automatic sprinkler system to water their front and backyards. My father, attempting to resolve her concern said, "Yeah, it will die, but it'll come back."

"But then people will know we are not home and might try to break into the house," she exclaimed with conviction. She always had another obstacle to replace the last.

Without saying a word to them, I decided I would be the one to give them a big homecoming surprise. Despite the fact that I lived about ten minutes away, I spent every day of those four weeks going back and forth to their house. I would set up the manual sprinkler for a half hour, return home or run an errand, and return to adjust the sprinkler again until all the areas were tended to, often taking up the better part of the day. The joy and eagerness for me would be the look in their eyes when they drove up their driveway to see their lawn lush and green.

After a month in France, they returned home. No phone call initially from them. Shortly thereafter, they called to say they were going to stop by for a short visit. We sat and had some coffee after they arrived and began to share the many photos my father took during their visit. When the last of the photos was gleaned over and the doughnuts were finished, it was time for them to go. Not a word was mentioned about the lawn. *Perhaps it just slipped their mind with all the excitement of sharing their trip with us,* I thought. As they were about to leave, I finally caved. "Mom, didn't you notice the condition of your lawn?"

"Oh, yeah, I did," she replied.

And then they were gone. Though a small incident, it began part of a greater collection of incidences of careless regard. I was powerless to establish healthy boundaries. In time, I learned why I needed to modify my behavior—and how hard it would be to adhere to!

Square Peg

My father's nickname for me during elementary and junior high school was "Crisco in a Can." Not very flattering, but apparently humorous to him. Admittedly, I had filled out some during those awkward years. Having perhaps what you might consider a well-upholstered bottom and ample thighs, but I wasn't considered fat. Had I clamored for a few more of those banana splits he made regularly for the family, I would have surely been on my way.

I was my father's daughter: I had the same bright, steel blue, almond-shaped eyes and sandy brown hair, which I usually wore long and often in a pony tail. My face was oval shaped and my nose donned a sprinkling of freckles that I had inherited from my Grandma Esther. My face was my best attribute, I modestly admit. Considering my perceived physical liability, it was the one asset I felt good about. You could say my face was my saving grace. If I became discouraged or self-conscious about my awkward gait, I could feel better by looking in the mirror and seeing my face staring back at me.

I had a few friends and enjoyed our relationships and times together, especially when I was invited to their homes for dinner or, even better, to stay overnight. I loved the gaiety and the relaxed feeling of their homes and the sense of peace I felt. I knew that they liked me and were happy to see me. I was always polite and very appreciative of anything they did or said. Best of all, in their homes I could forget about my disability. My friends and their families embraced me for who I was and no one said a word about my differences. They made me feel equal, and it was a priceless validation.

Faith, one of my friends from grade school, and I have managed to continue our relationship throughout these many years, even though we have long lived far apart. I always tease and remind her of how well-liked she was in school. She laughs and is embarrassed to accept the compliment, but I remind her of the days when a mutual classmate and I used to fight over who would get to walk to the candy store with her. The rule at school during recess was that only two students at a time were allowed to leave the premises during recess. I suspect the faculty's fear was that more kids would be off to the candy store than on the field getting exercise. I "won" Faith's friendship in the end, however, because we are the two who remained friends throughout our lives.

I was also close with the twins who lived across the street from me. We spent endless time together after school and during the summer months. They rarely spent any time at my house, however. Even if my mother was the type to invite a friend to dinner, they were too painfully shy to have accepted. My times with Bonnie and Jeanne were primarily spent upstairs in their attic bedroom that expanded from one end of their brick Cape Cod house to the other. With two double hung windows on either side for light and air, I recall the room being sparse and dark: bare floors, brown ceiling-to-floor paneling, twin beds flanking the one window and a built in bookcase and closet. It was a sanctuary for me and I loved being there. When I was with them in that room, I felt free. Bonnie was crazy about horses and would pour through magazines, then scotch tape horse pictures onto their walls. An act like that was unacceptable in my room at home.

When we weren't hanging out in their bedroom, we would take walks to the nearby hamburger stand or go for ice cream a little way's down the street. Some early evenings were spent on one of our front stoops listening to DJ Murray the K on my transistor radio. Some nights when their cousin and brother were around, we played badminton in the middle of our street under the glow of the streetlight. I ate and slept over at their house as much as I could during the summer, even when their bedroom would be unbearably hot and beastly. It didn't matter; I was content to be there.

Bonnie and Jeanne's mother worked outside the home. Their dad ran his own gas and repair station in town. When he returned home in the evenings, I remember well his smirking expression, seeing me in his home like I was part of the woodwork. I imagined he was thinking, *I guess I have an adopted daughter too.*

I ate kosher salami and drank egg creams made from the seltzer water delivered to their house in glass bottles. There were few parallels between our households, and I happily acclimated to their family, including their pesky older brother who found it delightful to relentlessly tease his sisters.

Having a polio affliction as a young girl caused lingering issues for me—a distinction I never quite got over. Moreover, it caused serious insecurities for me when I was in school, attempting to fit in with my classmates. Junior high is a tough time for any kid; you could be the object of ridicule for just about anything. I was a square peg. I'd go to school in my oxfords that looked like the ugly version of saddle shoes, while girls my age were deciding which dainty pastel-colored flat would go well with their outfits. Most days, I would run to my locker from the bus and change into my gym sneakers. It didn't offer a lot of support to my weak right ankle, but at least I could tighten the laces and walk pretty steadily. They were something that everyone else wore; what a relief knowing my footwear didn't once again define me.

In gym class, most coaches would have a "runner" for me when we played baseball and various other sports; all I had to do was swing the bat on my turn, or shoot a basketball at the hoop. I actually believed I could have run those baseball bases back then, but I think the coaches felt my ability to run was slow at best, and that would not be fair to my teammates. Besides, as I got older, my mother would always remind me not to run. Apparently, I looked less than graceful when I tried. She would say, "Don't run Colette, you don't want to bring that kind of attention to yourself." The biggest lesson I learned was if she was embarrassed, then I too would be embarrassed.

Occasionally, there would be a snide remark that I would be privy to. In high school, it occurred in the cafeteria during a study hall period. As I set my books down on one of the long tables and took a seat, I heard one of three boys a few rows behind me say, "She's okay, but she has crazy legs." How I managed to sit there the whole hour without bursting into tears is still a mystery to me since that comment was now etched into my brain. *You can't get up now Colette, it will only draw more attention and that's the last thing you want to do right now*, I thought. Pretending to be studying, the statement swirled in my head like a spinning top. The bell finally rang for our next class. I hesitated for a moment, pretending my books needed straightening out, just to make sure those boys were gone and I wouldn't have to face them or walk past them.

Some of my classes were a challenge. I hated to walk into the class, knowing that the "cool" kids would all be seated in the back of the room, and I would have to take a seat just in front of them. Generally, they were what we considered collegiate kids. They were the boys who strutted around the halls in the letter jackets or cardigan sweaters, with their one arm hugging their books to their hips and the other around their latest girlfriend. The collegiate girls were donned in perfectly matched A-line skirts and soft cardigans, and had their hair styled into what we called "the flip" back then. I attempted to emulate them in every visual way I could. I wanted so badly to overcome the stigma I carried with me like a ball and chain.

I pretended not to hear their taunting remarks, but it sunk in deep. And just when I thought it couldn't get any worse, it did. I was always punctual leaving the classroom after the bell, since I needed to physically have the time to get to my next class that would sometimes be on the other side of the building. Or worse yet, having to climb a set of stairs, which had always been my hardest task. The last thing I wanted to do was walk in after the others. With my arms tightly hugging my stack of books, I would be off. My plan didn't always work out, however. Walking too quickly, my weakened leg couldn't keep up the pace, and I would suddenly find myself falling. Desperately attempting to retrieve myself, as well as my dignity, my legs would flail out and ultimately my bottom broke my fall. I often found myself in awkward positions where my skirt would expose, at best, my slip, or at worst, more than my own brother would ever see! My books followed to the floor and laid scattered around me. Pages of my opened notebook continued to glide across the polished hall like thin chards of broken ice. There wasn't much more I could do to mortify myself when all I wanted was to blend in.

But I was the type of girl who didn't want to give up. I wanted the opportunity to have a more fulfilling life, especially when I saw a chance to go to a dance. The Sadie Hawkins dance came around, and I was ecstatic. No waiting for someone in my 8th grade class to ask me. Instead, I strategized how and when I would ask a boy in my history class whom I had a crush on. He really didn't take much notice of me, outside of a passing grin or a question about our homework. He had a small frame, very curly brown hair, a sharp jaw, and a chipped front tooth that I thought made him look cute. His shirts were always neatly tucked into his pants and his stomach was very flat. He always rolled his long-sleeved shirts up to his elbows to expose his firm looking arms and hands. He was funny and cute, or at least I thought so then. Looking back at his photo in my yearbook now, I wonder if I had similar taste in men as my grandma Esther!

After the classroom bell rang, I scooted around the desks and caught up with him, but then lost my nerve. The next day, I promised myself I wouldn't let the opportunity go by again. What's the next best thing to do when you can't speak? Pass a note. He answered with his own note, "Yeah sure." Eureka! I had a date!

I rushed home that day to prepare for the dance that would be held the next day, after school. I had to make sure everything would be perfect. I took my best outfit from my closet and scheduled in extra time to get up early to style my hair. The school day dragged by so painfully slow but finally, it was over. I saw my soon-to-be date in history and hoped he would look over my way. I was only one row behind and over his right shoulder, but he did not. Off to the gym I went with a bit of the jitters. All I could think about was dancing with him, maybe even a slow dance. When I asked him where we should meet, he had said he would be at the doors to the gym on the right side.

As you might have guessed, he didn't arrive. I was certain he didn't show that day because he was embarrassed to be seen with me. So I made my way home on the late bus after spending most of the dance in the girls' locker room, crying on one of the benches. I had given him ample time to arrive, but couldn't bear to have anyone witness me standing by myself for any longer. I couldn't stay in the locker room forever, either. I didn't want any of the other girls to detect what had happened, so I went to the row of sinks, wiped my eyes with a paper towel and left for the gym. Perhaps for one last survey of the room, in hopes that he was just late. While I scoured the gym for the face I so longed to see, a boy suddenly appeared in front of me and asked if I would dance with him. I danced with a boy who had the worst case of pimples and the runniest yellow nose that I had ever seen in my life. Yes, two school misfits dancing as if we were actually having a good time under the harsh gym lights.

When my mother asked if I had a good time, I explained to her that the boy never showed. "We all have crosses to bear Colette, and this is yours." Geez...I felt doomed!

Reunion Revelations

—————————————●—————————————

Years later, I was on the fence about whether I wanted to go to my 40th high school reunion.

My friend, Faith, said that she didn't really need to go. "I keep in touch with the friends I made in school. I don't need to see the rest."

I supposed she had a point, but I kept thinking, what did I have to lose? Besides, I had gone to the last few and wasn't sorry I attended. I was a different person at that point—or was I? There were weeks and days before the reunion in which I wavered about the prospects of going. Why was it such a big decision, anyway? What did I expect or not expect from attending the reunion? Was the affirmation of my former classmates so important to me? After all, I'd only see them again in another ten years.

Despite my deep insecurities, I did have my first two significant relationships during high school. Later, out of school, I began dating quite a lot, but I vacillated about my self worth. My friend, Kathy, and I would keep track of our dates on a piece of lined paper, as if it were a race or a goal. And in the next breath, I would be questioning why a boy would be interested in me. With a measure of self-imposed preparedness, I would make sure my date knew about my limp and my surgery scars, in case they hadn't noticed. Early on I might have even said something like, "Did you notice my limp?" or, "I have one leg that's shorter than the other from polio." The opening statement would often be awkward, I knew, but I felt compelled to beat them to the punch, as it were. Nice way to start a first date! I wasn't good at rejection and it saved me from any deep emotional investment. In turn, most times they would shrug their shoulders, or act surprised and change the subject quickly. I couldn't bear the possibility that they would be embarrassed to be with me, or even turned off by my awkward gait. One of my most vivid memories of a first date was when a consultant at my job asked me to a gala that his firm was holding for all the computer programmers and systems analysts. I was flattered that he asked me, but all the while very nervous. He had only worked at our facility for a few days when he invited me. After he picked me up at my home, and we entered the glamorous catering hall, we were directed to the ballroom. Before long, after introducing me to his friends at our table, he asked if I wanted to dance. I readily accepted as I enjoyed dancing. Out on the dance floor I began to dance with leather soled, dainty shoes, something I had no business wearing. The flooring was made of what looked like stone or marble. Half a minute into the song, I took a serious fall. Trying to gather myself up in front of hundreds of people, including my date, was completely demoralizing. Perhaps I could have survived that moment, but when I fell twice after that incident in the same night, the only thing I wanted to do was crawl into a hole and die. The ride home was still. I offered no excuses and he offered no comfort. I blamed myself.

Wearing shoes that may have been appropriate for the occasion was not prudent for someone whose physical capacity required more caution. To answer any lingering question, no I never saw him again.

When I dated my first husband, Mario, I remembered he once told me his best friend questioned him. "Mario, why are you dating that girl?" When Mario questioned in turn, what he meant, his friend's answer was, "You sure you want to date someone with a disability?" I have to give my ex-husband a lot of credit, because he really never gave that notion any thought, and felt his friend was totally off base. Here was a guy who loved me for who and what I was. What more could I ask for?

Well, maybe wearing high heels instead of less attractive shoes my whole life would have been nice. Or maybe not feeling embarrassed about wearing revealing attire, like a bathing suit. It was beyond my comfort level to expose the surgery scars and residual effects of the disease. Stitch marks along my thick surgery scars lined the sides of my right leg and were scattered over my right foot and ankle. My leg, from my knee down, was shapeless; my calf was missing due to atrophy. My knee had a distorted bulge. Years ago this was referred to as a "handicapped knee." My right leg was shorter by approximately an inch, and the same foot, two shoe sizes smaller.

It also would have been nice to pass a store front and see a reflection of a young woman walking without limping and throwing her hip out in her gait.

Looking back, I may have made a bigger deal over it than I should have, because after my divorce, I again had my fair share of boyfriends. I was hired, during my divorced years, to tend bar at watering holes that served businessmen's lunches. I did very well in tips and had no shortage of interested men. Make no mistake about it however; I continued my masquerade because I couldn't shake my ever-mindful personal embarrassment. I deliberately avoided walking back and forth in front of them while they had their hamburger and tap beer, calculated my moves by waiting until they looked up at the news or sports feature on the TV, or sauntered slowly, making stops on the way, to a customer in need. Not an easy task but where there is a will, there is a way.

****

My present husband and I fell in love after our dating period, but I do remember a time when he was a bit dubious about what would happen if I became more disabled. He was afraid of the monetary implications. Fortunately, his love for me was stronger than his financial concerns, so that hurdle dissipated over the years.

Even though I was celebrating twenty-five years of marriage to this man, whom I couldn't be happier with, I was still facing my demons. I wanted to walk into that school reunion and feel confident that I was no longer one of those "rejects" or unpopular students that I once felt I was. I am sure many of us have felt this way over one issue or another.

Despite the assurances people gave me about my worth as a person, I never embraced my success. I was able to attain positions in the work force by my persistence and untiring energy to do well, learning that my winning smile and positive attitude could go a long way. At the time, I didn't see it as self worth but simply luck and perseverance.

I even got to experience my fifteen minutes of fame. I earned the title of Freshman Class Sweetheart at Kip's college, and was a runner-up for Miss National Bank of North America while I was employed there. Being selected for two beauty pageants, shouldn't that be enough? I couldn't shrug off my need to be perfect in every way.

I had the unique experience to meet with the comedian, Joey Bishop (member of the famous Rat Pack), at a resort where he was performing. He was very charming as we spoke side by side in the lounge; he invited me to his suite in the hotel, along with his bodyguard and my two friends. I knew he was smitten with me as he gave me two free tickets to see his show that Friday night and signed a paper napkin that said, *You're beautiful, Colette. Joey Bishop.* All this may not seem like a lot, but for me, it was the affirmation I continued to crave. Having said this, it never made up for what I considered my physical disfigurement but was more a mere temporary Band-Aid. And yes, I still have that napkin tucked alongside Mimi in my trunk!

It wasn't easy for me to attend the reunion on my own since my husband had attended the last reunion and vowed he would not go again. He wasn't interested in hearing the old stories he knew nothing about or talking to people he didn't know, shouting over loud music. I couldn't blame him.

A conversation with a former neighbor made it even harder. He was the older brother of the sisters who had lived across the street years ago. Burt was dropping off his daughter in my neighborhood one Saturday morning. On his way home, he noticed that I was outside doing some gardening and pulled his car up to the curb. We had discovered a few years prior that we lived only a few blocks from each other and renewed our long-time friendship.

I walked down to his car from my lawn, as he opened his passenger side window. During the course of our chat, I asked him if his sisters planned to go to the reunion and that I looked forward to seeing them again. He replied that in all likelihood they wouldn't. He went on to say that they had their own school friends they kept in touch with and had no interest in seeing classmates they essentially had no relationship with. I understood.

"I get it, Burt. I always felt like a square peg in school. I am hoping that time has changed people and most of them have grown up and matured."

He agreed, and then added, "Yeah, that's right, you were left out because you were the gimp." OUCH! The harsh reality of how I was defined was a crushing blow. Burt's brutal remark took the all the wind out of my lungs at that moment. He affirmed all the judgments I carried of my history in one short sentence.

To add insult to literal injury, I took a fall the week before the two-night reunion. After spending a few hours in the emergency room of the local hospital, I was relieved to find I had only a bad sprain and hadn't broken my ankle, as I had assumed. The injury left me with my ankle wrapped in an ace bandage and on crutches. As the week went by, I kept hoping that I would be able to ditch the crutches and walk in on my own accord that first night. Getting ready for the first gathering, I decided I would try to go sans bandages and put on my stretchy supportive sandals. I managed to walk into the darkened and crowded bar without anyone noticing my wincing. Everyone was shuffling slowly around each other, so I felt at ease. The evening went by and I enjoyed myself, being among my former classmates. By the time the evening was over, however,

I could barely get myself outside and to the car without collapsing on the sidewalk from the pain.

I knew this wasn't going to work for the dinner dance the following evening. But what could I do? Could I grab the DJ's mike and say to everyone, "Listen, you all remember me limping my way through school, but if I am walking even worse tonight, it's not because I am more crippled. I sprained my ankle seven days ago!" God, why did I even feel compelled to give any explanation?

I was bound and determined to go, however, because I got a taste of what the night would hold. At the bar, I was approached by many of my former classmates, including some popular guys who couldn't get over how great I looked and how I hadn't aged much. And as for the men who said they had a crush on me back in school, what the heck had they been waiting for?

The next night of the dinner dance, my foot was surprisingly better. I wore my sandals with my ace bandage and a long skirt to cover the "damage." I ran into a guy that night that had been out of my reach so many years ago. As I recalled, Ken was actually nice to me in school, always had a smile and a hello, like a big brother. His smile was totally infectious; he had the looks of Kevin Costner and his personality equaled his good looks. Now, we were face-to-face, complimenting each other and thinking about missed opportunities in the past. At the time that brief flirtation was an ego booster, but I knew I had the real deal at home and didn't need another hero.

Driving home that night, I wished I hadn't put so much emphasis and effort on concealing what I considered my physical deficit. I had come across confident and relaxed that night, but inside I still had the need to conceal the part of me that I was sure they would still spurn, if exposed. My healing journey was not over. As long as I continued to believe in the ingrained notion of not being good enough, I would not be able to rise above and feel whole, or even my true self. The only thing I was sure of was reaching the safety of my home and being with the love of my life.

Great Expectations

---•---

In 1970, when I was in my early twenties, I worked for a large firm that employed 900 employees. Initially, I worked in the secretarial customer relations pool. My primary responsibility was typing replies, dictated by department supervisors, addressing customer complaints or inquiries. After my first year, I received a sterling review and was plucked out of the pool for a promotion in the personnel department. Working in personnel, I had the added perk to meet eligible men looking for employment with our company.

Mario, who was two years older than I, had completed his tour of duty in the Air Force during the Vietnam War, and was looking for work. The day Mario arrived for an interview, I noticed him walking through the glass entry doors. My position was at the front desk of the long and narrow office, so I could clearly see the comings and goings. Not wanting to stare as he approached, I arched over my desk, looked down, and pretended to be madly working. As he entered the office, I looked up. He gave me a smile and stated his purpose for being there. Looking at him more closely this time, I noticed how tall, broad-shouldered, and very fit he was. He had that wonderfully thick, dark, brown hair most Italian men are blessed with. He wore it parted on the side and brushed across his forehead. He was easy on the eyes: a handsome and strong nose, dark brown eyes, a prominent chin, and soft, full lips.

I was taken with him, but repressed smiling back. After his interview with my boss, I thought I would catch a glimpse of Mario leaving, and perhaps wish him good luck. Out of the office on an errand, I lost my opportunity.

For some time, I only knew Mario as the manager of the printed matter department. I did make it my business however, to get to know him better. Our department was often in need of supplies, paper, pencils, paper clips, and the like. I scanned our inventory and volunteered to fetch these items as often as I could, making frequent trips to the other end of the building where his department was located.

We began to notice each other in the company lunchroom. It was a sizable room with a large variety of tables, floor-to-ceiling windows hosting a beautiful view of the lush grounds, and a more than ample patio outside when the weather cooperated. It was a convivial meeting place and very conducive to sitting and chatting away your free time. Mario often sat with his employees at one of the long, rectangular tables. It was apparent that he developed a good relationship with them all. Most days I would purposefully pass their table, giving a general hello to them all. In no time, I was invited to sit with them. Mario and I became friends and enjoyed more intimate lunches and coffee breaks thereafter. My unnecessary visits to his department became more frequent. Eventually, we became part of a small group of friends who worked for the company, attending many events together: house parties, picnics, the beach, and bowling.

One night, at one of our house parties, Mario introduced me to his good friend, Skeeter. Skeeter was invited despite the fact that he did not work for the company like the rest of us. After a brief conversation, he asked me out that night and we subsequently began dating. Why Mario and I hadn't dated yet was a mystery. Perhaps Skeeter was not as shy as Mario. And since one good turn deserved another, I introduced Mario to my friend, Sarah. Still, my friendship with Mario grew and soon we found ourselves calling every day on our inter-office phones. We were cognizant that our daily conversations were becoming lengthy and could hamper our positions, so we decided calling each other on our home phones was the only solution. Mario finally made the first move and asked me out and I gladly accepted. During that first date we decided that we were a much better match than with Skeeter or Sarah. They took it well, and Mario and I became inseparable.

> *"Love can be right or wrong,*
> *And if I chose the one*
> *I'd like to help me through,*
> *I'd like to make it with you."*

During our first year, we often listened to the song by Bread, "Make It With You." It played on all the major radio stations that year, and wherever we were, we would pause to take in the lyrics. It mirrored our feelings to a T. I was such a hopeless romantic; I bought the single and ran the risk of grinding down the grooves from playing it so often! As much as we felt we were in love, we did not know each other well, but we did want to "make it." That would have to wait a bit, however. I had a previous commitment. I had planned to visit my aunt and uncle in Spain for part of that summer. My tickets had been bought and they were anxious for me to arrive. As much as I felt torn, I thought this might prove to be a good test for our budding relationship.

Mario took the hour's car ride to the airport, with my parents, to say goodbye. We sat in the waiting room before it was time to board, holding hands and regretting the plans I was about to fulfill. With my parents nearby, we managed to give each other a goodbye kiss. Oh, how hard it felt to leave him. Tearfully, I managed to turn away, squeezing his hand one last time. Handing my ticket to the stewardess, I stepped through the doorway onto the ramp that led me to my plane.

> "...*Have a good time but remember there*
> *is danger in the summer moon above.*
> *Will I see you in September or lose you to a*
> *summer love (counting the days 'til I'll be with*
> *you, counting the hours and the minutes, too)*"

I suspect, much to the chagrin of my aunt and uncle, playing their 45-rpm record of the 1960's tune "See You in September" by the Happenings, reflected where my heart was.

However, I was thoroughly enjoying my visit with them. I had the opportunity to see amazing sights, landmarks, and pastoral vistas of the countryside where my uncle was born and most proud of. My aunt and uncle utterly spoiled me. They took me out to the best restaurants and bought me lavish gifts. They had a son several years younger than I. Despite the fact that they obviously were crazy about him, I would never forget when my uncle shared his feelings with me: "You are the daughter I always wanted." My heart melted as we embraced. I knew my connection with him was indelible from that point on.

I was happy I made the trip, but I continued to get lost in my lagging thoughts of what I would be facing when I returned home. Could I lose him to a summer love? Worrying about the possibility of being "out of sight, out of mind," I wrote often. I shared all my wonderful experiences, but most of all, I expressed my longing to see him again, hoping my words could insure my place. Mario hadn't written at all, which made me all the more anxious about our fate. What was he doing while I was gone that prevented him from writing a few words? He was an affable, good-looking guy. What girl might be lurking around him at work, attempting to steal him away?

Despite the distance and time apart, it looked like we were destined to be together. I was so relieved to see Mario standing at the airport, along with my parents, when I returned. *You are a sight for sore eyes, Mr. Olivieri,* I thought, as I turned the corridor to the waiting room. We flew into each others arms basking in that glorious moment. Within a few days, he asked me to marry him. I was beyond excited. It didn't take long before the news was out to all our family and friends.

There was yet another hurdle to face after I returned home. I was at a crossroads and was about to embark on a very exciting career endeavor. I had been selected, and was being trained, to convert all of the firm's manual personnel files onto computer files. The company was a well-known international business and the possibilities for me were endless. I had already made several trips to their main office at Rockefeller Center for the administration files, and soon I would be on my way to converting the regional auditing files around the nation. I was learning more about computers than I probably could have if I had attended school. With one-on-one training at my job, it was a chance of a lifetime for me. I was thrilled at the opportunity and had never felt so engaged and excited about my future. Now the question was, would Mario be able to handle the many out-of-state or even international trips ahead of me?

****

At that time, the 1970s feminist movement had made its mark, and women began making their way in the work force and playing a new role in society. At the forefront of this movement was the desire to achieve more than the standard role of overseeing household responsibilities, and women were fast realizing the winds of change and their new opportunities. I wanted to be part of these changes and longed for the chance to pursue a career.

My mother, on the other hand, reflected another generation's point of view and had no desire or ambition to be more than a housewife. Being completely dependent on my mother's opinions, I asked for hers—big mistake. "What do you think I should do, Mom?" She answered without hesitation, "Mario wants to marry you. Who is going to keep you warm at night if you don't accept his proposal? Besides, he is willing to accept your disability. What if you don't find anyone else who will?"

Still under the grip of my mother's controlling spell, and taking her opinion for face value, I reluctantly squelched my aspirations, foolishly believing that she had made a valid point. Who else would accept me? Nothing I had done in my life until now was ever revered, and the cost of being wrong in her eyes was more than I could bear. Looking back now, I think if I had been forthcoming with Mario, he would have been honest and supportive of me. He was a reasonable person, and not as rigid as my mother in his thinking. After all, his mom worked. He was not raised to think a wife should only take on the role of housewife. But I was too timid and unworldly about these issues at the time; I would learn soon enough that independence was another hard-won battle.

With some reservation about my decision, I began to concentrate on our upcoming wedding instead. It was a wonderful time. What woman in love didn't enjoy the preparations of an engagement party, being surprised by showers, and making plans for her wedding day with the man she looked forward to spending the rest of her life with?

We were off on the right foot, having had the means to buy our own new house and watch it develop together before our very eyes. From the foundation up, we would make trips on weekends to see how far along the builders had come. We were still within a reasonable distance from our families' homes, but far enough away to feel on our own. The high ranch with its natural wood siding, red door and shutters, on a quarter acre, was more than we thought was possible. Mario gave up his dream to buy a Corvette. Pooling our combined savings, we were on our way to becoming homeowners. There we stood, hand-in-hand, on the sandy, uneven construction site, witnessing the results of our decisions. I surely didn't want to throw this all away. Aside from feeling that Mario was the one, meeting and getting to know his family made my decision all the sweeter.

More to Love

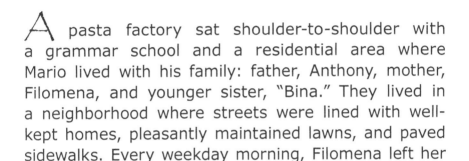

A pasta factory sat shoulder-to-shoulder with a grammar school and a residential area where Mario lived with his family: father, Anthony, mother, Filomena, and younger sister, "Bina." They lived in a neighborhood where streets were lined with well-kept homes, pleasantly maintained lawns, and paved sidewalks. Every weekday morning, Filomena left her home, cut through a six-foot chain link fence entryway of the schoolyard, and crossed through to the factory where she worked on the assembly line.

She had a remarkable zest and balance to her life. She enjoyed her work, her family, and home life, none ever being overlooked. What would perhaps appear to be a seemingly ordinary existence to others was the life of an extraordinary woman to me.

The first time I met Filomena, she greeted me with twinkling eyes and a wide, welcoming, contagious smile, instantly making me feel comfortable and relaxed. Her frame was average and shapely, her hair mid-length, black, and wavy. She possessed the same rounded and prominent nose as her father and son. Perhaps one of the most notable distinctions about her, however, was her husky voice. If you closed your eyes and listened, you would swear you were hearing Louise Jefferson, the raspy-voiced wife from the sitcom, *The Jeffersons.*

She had a genuine and engaging way about her. Always speaking with a lilt in her voice, listening intently, and laughing hardily. She was the personification of a loving mother. Even though her title a year later would have "in-law" after it, I couldn't wait to call her mom.

Over those months of my engagement to Mario, I spent as much time as I could at their home. At the end of the workday, Mario and I would leave in our respective cars and be joined again at his house to have dinner with his family. Before long, the dinner visits mushroomed into overnight stays. Even when my migration there increased, it was never an issue for either of our families. I was in love with Mario, but I was also enamored with Filomena.

Sundays were special days at Mario's home. I would wake up in his twin bed, facing his favorite iconic poster of King Kong on the Empire State Building, while he slept in a spare bedroom. My senses were quickly aroused by the first wave of garlic being sautéed downstairs in the kitchen. I scrambled from bed to help Filomena prepare for the weekly feast for family and friends. She was in charge of the sauce, but I was ready to be her sous chef. She definitely had things under control and would often shoo me away, but I would stay near to watch her magic. The least I could do was chop onions or wash lettuce. Red Italian sauce with pasta of different variations was always the first course, accompanied by sausage, meatballs, stew meat, and one hardboiled egg. I never did ask her if the egg lent itself to the taste, or perhaps was a token of good luck. A roast would follow with quartered, roasted potatoes and several side vegetables, maybe even a bitter green (that was the only thing I would opt out of). Just when you thought you'd bust from another mouthful of pasta, the second course arrived. One whiff of these dishes would arouse and provoke you to carry on and partake of it all. The food was simply divine, and I learned early on to pace myself, taking smaller helpings to get through the meal. I often think about Filomena serving her signature dishes; she taught me how to cook a number of her recipes that I still use to this day.

I tried to help her in the preparation and cleanup, as it was a daunting task for one person. Yet she never appeared to be stressed. It was so unlike my own home, where no one was ever invited to dinner as making a meal was always overwhelming to my mother. For Filomena, cooking the Sunday meal was a celebration of life.

There was always enough room for another person at the table as well. "Just pull up a chair. There's plenty of food," was how unexpected guests were greeted. Sunday dinners were an all day ritual. After a multi-course meal, the nuts and fruit and nutcrackers would always appear in a large crystal bowl in the center of the beautifully set dining room table. Playing cards would then be pulled out of the breakfront drawer, for the entertainment. I was never interested in card games myself, but enjoyed the banter and conversation that lasted for hours.

Filomena treated me like her second daughter and I thought of her as my second mother. She was such a loving person and always made me feel welcomed in her home. I learned to embrace the art of gathering a community around me, and today, I owe it to Filomena that my own home is a place for family and friends to come together.

Mario and I did spend a good deal of time in his bedroom, with the door closed, lying side by side on his bed and watching TV. Filomena would never say we couldn't, but we knew her comfort level, as a concerned mom, was being tested. Every once in a while she would knock at the door and burst into the room with what essentially seemed like a lame question, comment, or better yet, to bring a snack that we did not ask for. We smiled at each other as she left us, with the door this time a tiny bit ajar. On one occasion, an incident involving Mario's mom actually made us giggle for years to come. Early one evening, Mario opened the bedroom door and found his mom just outside, on her hands and knees. It was a sight you could only imagine seeing in a comedy movie. "What's going on, Mom?" he asked. She shooed him away and pretended there was something that needed to be addressed on the carpet she was scrutinizing. You had to love her; she was only doing what most caring moms have an inclination to do. Mario and I had often reminisced about that encounter.

I loved spending alone time with Filomena, too. We would go shopping or run an errand for my upcoming wedding. Many times, we would just sit in her modestly small kitchen, talking. Mario would often be in the den on the first level of their split ranch, watching a sports game with his dad. I would be content to linger in what was now my "assigned" seat against the wall, facing hers at the kitchen table. When the dishes were done and the kitchen cleaned, Filomena and I chatted about everything over a cup of tea and cookies. Our bond would last a lifetime.

A Dream Shattered

"We've only just begun to live,
White lace and promises
A kiss for luck and we're on our way.
We've just begun..."

Our wedding song encapsulated my longings and expectations. We danced to Karen Carpenter's dreamy words of bliss, and for a short while, we even lived them. After a number of months passed however, life was not falling into place as I had expected. I was lonely.

Shortly before our wedding date, Mario began working for the railroad. My father, having worked countless years for the same line, was able to help secure a good job for Mario, but it came with a price. Without seniority, Mario had the dregs of entitlements. The position required 24-hour on call availability. Mario was assigned hours between 11pm to 7am. His long commute meant that he left our home two hours earlier and didn't return until late the following morning.

In addition to working nights more times than not, he was also on call on his scheduled days off. Living an hour away from my job, I decided to leave, and took a receptionist position near our new home. With the change, I would at least be able to see my husband on my lunch hour. Unfortunately, most times, I would find Mario fast asleep. As my lunch hour ended, my only connection with him would be a kiss on the cheek before I left.

After dinner, Mario would take his shower and get ready for work. Before we knew it, he would be leaving. Most nights, I passed the time watching TV and reading in our den. We bought a dog for companionship, but it was no replacement for my husband. By the time I was ready for bed and in a deep sleep, Mario would return from work. With an unnatural schedule, falling asleep for him was difficult. In order to wind down, he would conduct his nightly practice. While watching TV in our bed and propping his pillow against the headboard, he would place a bowl of fresh made popcorn on his lap. After the last kernel was eaten and the early hours of the morning arrived, he would finally fall asleep. There was no blame in this atypical living arrangement, but it did put a strain on our relationship, especially since I loathed being alone at night. I had an unhealthy fear and my own nightly practice reflected my extreme and unrealistic concerns. After numerous acts of securing my home: check and double-check the locks on my doors before it became dark, keeping lamps lit in all the rooms and outside lights of my house on all night, pulling all the drapes tightly shut, I urged my dog to follow. If he suddenly barked or showed sign of alarm, my nerves would unravel. More often than not, I would eventually call my father to come and check my home. My level of comfort was never satisfied. Mario knew my concerns, but not to the depth of my fear and subsequent actions. Besides, there was little time for talking and sharing when we were together.

Mario was a sports fanatic. When we dined together, he would invariably turn on the kitchen television and watch a game during our meal. Even if I did feel compelled to talk about my fears, it never seemed like a suitable time. If we managed to have a rare weekend night together and invited friends for dinner, the television was purposefully positioned to face the dining room. He could never let the opportunity pass to glance over and catch a score. He loved every sport with a passion. Did you know you could go from baseball to football to hockey to basketball and never have to watch another thing on the television? I didn't know that until Mario. This might seem like a small issue, but it did contribute to the failure of our marriage.

In my infinite wisdom, as a young twenty-three-year-old wife, I thought that perhaps having a child would bring us closer together; it would be an extraordinary life event that we would share and enjoy as a couple and a family. I longed to engage with him the way he did with his interests.

Within a few months, I was pregnant! When I told Mario, his reaction was what I had hoped for. He was equally thrilled with the news. I'll never forget how he would giggle and rub my belly, while the camera was clicking or the recorder was running. This was it; this was what would fill the void in our relationship and give us the solidarity we needed.

As the months passed, Mario continued to work the night shift and was called in more often than not on his days off. It became so unsettling to hear the phone ring in the middle of the night. It began to happen so often; I placed the phone inside the nightstand drawer, muffled with a pillow, hoping we could somehow avoid the call. Maybe there would be an outside chance they would give up and call the next traffic controller on the list. That never happened; they would relentlessly pursue their goal. The more you didn't want to hear it, the more you did! When the phone would ring for the better part of a half hour or more, Mario would finally cave in and answer.

I was getting more and more disillusioned about my life. Since we rarely had a free weekend, I hoped for perhaps one weekday when we could do something together: go to the beach, have a picnic, like we once enjoyed. But Mario was not on the same page as I was. He was feeling the pressure of his job and studying for a better position. If he had the opportunity, he pursued his own releases: playing softball or a round of golf. That's not a bad thing, mind you, but it did present a problem if you ended up spending next to no time with your wife because of it. For me, there is a difference between passion and obsession.

We had two days coming up, back-to-back, that Mario knew he would have off. I was so pleased and looked forward to planning some time together. It was nearing the end of the long summer-like days, but the temperatures were still moderate enough to go out to the ocean and relax.

Money was tight. We had received a letter from our bank saying our mortgage payment was going to increase every month, a considerable snag for us back then. I was ever so vigilant and cautious about all our expenses—my only occasional frivolous purchase was buying a diminutive plant for my dining room windowsill at the farm stand. We could surely splurge and eat out at a café or diner, if I kept close count on my clicker the following week when I went to the grocery store.

My thoughts and plans became irrelevant. Mario called from the office before his day off, and explained to me that he had just made plans for those upcoming days. Much to my shock, he said that he was going to drive to Connecticut with friends to watch a football game. *No, I can't be hearing this right,* I thought. "What about spending the time with me, Mario?"

"I already made the plans and I really want to go," he answered somewhat defensively.

"No, Mario, I want to spend some time with *you*. It's been too long now."

He, in turn, stood his ground, "I want to go to this game. It's real important to me, Colette."

"But what about what's important to me?" Nothing. The phone was silent.

"If you go to this game, you are not going to find me here when you get home," I proclaimed. He went to the game and I packed and left for my parents' house. I was in disbelief and crushed at the lack of concern he had about my feelings. Of course, he probably figured out where I was and knew I was safe. To add insult to injury, my neighbor called me to report witnessing Mario leaving the following morning with his golf clubs.

I knew it wasn't in my best interest to be upset while carrying my baby, but my anguish was great and I cried myself to sleep for several nights at my parents. After a few days, my mother took things into her own hands and called Mario's parents. It now became a family crisis, much to my chagrin. It wasn't a pretty picture. After a lot of phone calls between our two mothers, eventually Mario picked me up and I returned home.

The nine months of my pregnancy were largely unsettling and turbulent. During one of our many arguments, I was so frustrated, I put my hand through my bedroom window. Reviewing that moment now, I know I was trying desperately to make Mario understand how close to the end of my rope I was; willing to resort to a frantic act for attention, discovering a place inside me I was unaware of.

In the wee hours of the morning of September 29th, I woke suddenly. I hadn't been sleeping well those last few months. Not feeling right, I wondered, could this be the time? I laid in bed in the dark, not knowing exactly what to expect. Within an hour or so I experienced my first feeling of discomfort. It wasn't strong; in fact, it felt fairly dull. But it was definitely there. I waited a bit longer until the next isolated throb and decided I should wake Mario up now. By now, the light from dawn was just peeking through the bedroom draperies. He was relatively calm. In his robe, he headed downstairs to wake my parents. They had been living with us temporarily while their new home was nearing the end of construction. When he returned, he called my obstetrician. "How many minutes between the labor pains, Colette?" It wasn't enough yet. By now I was sitting on the side of the bed, my head facing my feet, feeling strong achy jabs of pain. This was it; our baby was finally coming. Another phone call was made when the pain intervals got closer. It was time. My parents were up and ready and everyone was still calm and collected. No excitement or panic like you often witness in the movies or on TV shows. We were in charge of our mission as we made our way to the car. It was a rainy morning and right about the time children were heading off to school. When we reached Southdown, a town beyond where we lived, we were confronted with commuter traffic making its way through the single lane of Main Street at a snail's pace. As luck would have it, a lady traffic monitor suddenly stepped out off the curb and put her hand up for us to stop in order for the children to cross the street. We were beginning to panic a bit at that moment. Mario was driving and became exasperated. "There's woman in labor in this car. You can't hold us up!" he exclaimed loudly within the confines of our closed car. It was pretty funny looking back now. At that time, it did seem like it took forever for those kids to cross to the other side and before we were able to continue to the hospital. When we finally arrived, my pain was kicking in with more severity and frequency. Mario had me sit in a wheelchair when we arrived at the curb, and away we went. After admission, the nurse began to take the steps necessary for the delivery—monitors and the like. I heard my son's heartbeat; it was so strong and ready. Mario and my parents were outside waiting. Once the sedation set in, I remembered little outside of the staff's muffled voices. Suddenly there was the most incredible pressure happening. It must have been close to 11:22am. Hello, my baby boy!

My next recollection was being in my hospital room. There was an opened, clear plastic box at the foot of my bed. My head was still so foggy; I didn't realize at first that my baby, Dana, was so close. Mario soon came in with a pale yellow gown and cap. He had a big smile on his face that stretched from ear to ear and carried a small, blue football squeeze toy. He bent over and gave me a very appreciative and tender kiss on my forehead. The nurse brought our baby over so I could nurse. I was surprised to see my son's head was a bit misshapen along with the facial marks from forceps. He invariably gave the doctor a good fight! He had tons of dark hair like his daddy and a sweet pudgy little nose. It was love at first sight! After he was full and content, Mario held his son proudly. There we were, the three of us as a family.

My parents arrived at my room shortly there after. I remember little about their visit. My father was proud of the arrival of his first grandson. I wasn't surprised my mother showed little emotion, however. Looking back now, I realize that my mother was always void of excitement and laughter. At best she might have smiled that day—that was just who she was.

Perhaps with her own circumstance, it brought back memories of the birth of her daughter. Growing up, during one of our many talks in her bedroom, she revealed that I was conceived out of wedlock. It was surely a disgraceful time for her; particularly back in the late '40s. She was faced with either a forced marriage to my father or to go on with her life, carrying the humiliation of the times.

****

Dana was not even a year old when I began to have serious back issues. I was able to carry him full term and escaped having a cesarean childbirth, but it took a toll on my back. I would be in the most pain during the night. My back would stiffen. Changing positions, I would scream out loud, always frightening Mario from a sound sleep. I needed to find out what was going on, and quickly.

The orthopedic surgeon from my earlier polio surgeries was still working and conducted an evaluation. My lower spine was so deteriorated from the residual of polio; the nerves were being squeezed together. After reviewing the x-rays, he indicated that I required a spinal fusion. This involved removing a piece of bone from my left hip, the stronger side, and fusing it to the part of the spine that had become so thin. I didn't have a choice. Now I faced necessary major surgery while having an infant to care for.

After two weeks in the hospital for my surgery, I was discharged with a metal slatted back brace, adjustable straps to keep my back in place for healing, and told that I would not be able to lift anything over ten pounds or do any strenuous activity.

By that time, Dana was becoming a rambunctious boy. Mario was able to help, but he couldn't be at home and at work at the same time. I asked my mother if she could help us out. At this time, their home was complete and they lived within walking distance, no more than two blocks away. The plan proposed that Mario or my father could drop her off if the weather was inclement, or if she didn't feel inclined to walk. Her answer was what I expected. I don't remember the reasoning, because my mind had already moved passed the "no." She didn't have a job and I knew it would not interfere with her social life, as she didn't drive and had few friends or activities to attend.

Mario was obliged to turn to his mother. Without hesitation, Filomena said yes. Despite the fact that she had to request a leave from her job that she enjoyed and depended upon, she would help us out. Since a trip from her home to our house was about 50 minutes or more, it made the most sense for Dana to live with his grandmother while I recuperated. I was incredibly grateful to her, although my heart broke thinking that my son would be spending so much time away from me for that six-month period. Mario and I would make the trip to his parents on his days off, but it was a hardship on us all. There was one redeeming side to this event, however. Filomena adored her first grandson. He was the one person she would always defend vehemently and not allow anyone to criticize. Even later, when I would share a minor disappointing aspect or event that involved her grandson, she would markedly defend him with, "Ah, but he's a good boy, Colette." Spending those months together on a daily basis intensified their bonding, surpassing perhaps the common levels of relationship for a grandmother and her grandson. In Filomena's words, "He's the best thing since sliced bread." And Dana always held his grandmother deeply in his heart, because of the undeniably close relationship they had forged. Although some of us are lucky enough to experience generational love and bonds, it would be one that my mother would never know.

Filomena never said a word about my mother's refusal to help, which was the kind of person she was. I would complain to her often about my mother. "She never invites you and you always have them over for dinner; it's just not right," I would state in frustration.

"Colette, don't worry, your mom feels stressed and I don't mind doing it," would be her reply. She was genuinely compassionate and would often nod her head up and down about my feelings, but would always try to find something more positive to say. She never escalated an issue. She was like that with everyone. During conversations at Sunday dinners, when someone would begin to criticize an individual, Filomena would always mention a good trait we failed to consider about that person. We would all smirk and wink at each other, listening to her kind attempt to find a way to soften our comments. Taking notice of her efforts, I began to see the world in a different way: you cannot find peace for yourself, until you can find a way to make peace with others.

Things didn't really change in my relationship with Mario. Yes, we adored our son and enjoyed the times

Bringing the Inside Out

we spent with him, but the constant discord and strife between us never ended. Our values and outlooks were indisputably dissimilar. Our fights became screaming matches, and eventually escalated to violence. Our heightened emotions paved the way for destruction: Mario became physical and I know I pushed him to his limits. I was in a pathetic state of mind. If I couldn't get positive attention, I unconsciously pushed for negative attention. Mario's uncontrolled temper left me once with bruises all over my back. To be physically abusive was not in his nature, but our relationship was out of control. With this certainty, it became the pivotal point in the destruction of our marriage. I am *not* suggesting, and would never suggest, that anyone deserves this kind of treatment, but I knew I was on my own path of destruction as well. Feeling worthless and unloved were emotions I had carried with me for years, and my marriage brought them to the forefront.

Now our relationship felt beyond repair. Two and a half years after our marriage vows, I went to an attorney and asked for a separation. I chose to go to my parents' attorney, not knowing any others, and not wanting to share my intentions with anyone else. It was a big decision to make, but I felt I had no choice. I had to try and make it on my own. I would miss the dreams and relationship I believed I was going to have with Mario. But how could I forget what was done?

Small Voice

The poet Maya Angelou once said, "You did then what you knew how to do, and when you knew better you did better." I have embraced these wise words to get me through events in my life, but no more than this particular time, while living apart from Mario. As my memory unfolds, I find it's the hardest occurrence for me to share. I believe I sank to my lowest and it is a time I am least proud of.

After Mario left, I was finding it difficult to keep up with some of the more physical jobs in my home. My friend recommended a landscaper to maintain the grounds and take care of minor repairs. I didn't really take notice of him, except for the polite chats we had once in a while. When my relationship with Mario remained in limbo, Reese apparently could read it on my face. He would question why I looked so down when he appeared at my door for payment. Starved for attention, I slowly began to purge myself by explaining my situation. He supported the idea of my separation, despite the fact that I vacillated with the pros and cons. I didn't want my toddler son to grow up without his dad, but I didn't want to live feeling depressed and lonely either.

At first I believed Reese was just a friend who listened and became a shoulder to cry on, especially since I knew he was married. He never spoke of his wife or marriage, but I assumed it was a good one.

During the time Mario moved back with his parents, Reese and I became more and more involved. We often sat on my front stoop, after his job was done, and talked about our values, issues, shared musical interests, and life in general. After years of loneliness, Reese brought energy and excitement to my life. He broadened my mental horizons and introduced me to his views on religion and philosophy. Never having the opportunity to go away to college, I was isolated from any progressive thinking. I did not live in the kind of environment that would allow me to explore different outlooks and opinions, since my parents didn't feel I needed to continue my education. I found our talks fascinating and freeing. It was like he was unlocking a door in my mind. Even if I dared to think outside the box before my marriage, I always worried about the repercussions from my narrow-minded parents.

When we had our first kiss, my mind was spinning. He was passionate and tender, but what the heck was I doing? I certainly couldn't have a clear head about my thoughts regarding Mario. Could I salvage our marriage or was it even possible considering our history? Besides Reese was *married*!

Well, as such affairs usually go, he began to explain his unhappiness. "We don't have the same connection as you and I do. You are so different, Colette," he stated with compassion in his voice.

I was different all right; I was such a weak person that I bought into the whole package, hook, line and sinker. And besides, he knew how to push my buttons. He was flattering, engaging, and had those interesting insights on life that I wanted to know more about. He introduced me to a world so foreign I couldn't get enough; I was like a sponge.

But as with every affair, we also had sex. Crazy sex. I lost all my inhibitions and caved to all his suggestions. When I called on his business phone to let him know my son was taking a nap or was down for the night, he would come to see me. Sometimes we even met at the beach. We would talk for long periods in his four-wheel drive and play with Dana until he fell asleep. More sex. I was deeply in love with this man, and I foolishly believed he was with me. He was still living with his wife, and when he told me his wife was pregnant, the red flag should have whipped up and slapped me in the face. How could I not connect the dots? He was still having sex with her! But I was too far-gone to deal with the reality. I was pathetically addicted to this relationship and willing to settle for a part-time friend and lover. When Reese's wife was in the hospital to have the baby, we made love at his house. Oh, how that hurts to say it now. How low does one get before waking up from the nightmare? After many long discussions about leaving his wife, something finally happened.

Reese's wife found a book I made for him. It was about twenty pages long, folded and quartered neatly, carefully written in black calligraphy, and bound together with satin ribbon threaded through the top of the punch hole I had added. With my heart bruised and battered, I filled each page with poems I wrote. My words flooded every page with love and desperate longing and emotion.

She called me. She said that she was angry but wanted to know the woman who wrote this book. As frightened as I was about meeting her, a part of me wanted the torture to end. Besides, didn't I deserve this punishment for the sins I'd committed? At least we could both get the answer we wanted. Was he going to stay with her or leave her for me?

Shaking like a leaf on a stormy day, I arrived at their home carrying nothing but a knot in my stomach. I did not see his car in the driveway but I knew Reese was due home shortly. A few short steps to the front door felt as if I was wearing iron shoes on my feet, or perhaps the weight of those saddle shoes that I resisted wearing long ago. I rang the doorbell lightly, as if I could control the harsh announcement of my arrival. She invited me in to her living room that I unfortunately knew all too well. She asked me to sit on the sofa and seated herself across from me. We began our brief talk. I have no recollection what we spoke about, undoubtedly because of my nerves. I duly noted that she was calm and controlled. She never lashed out at me that afternoon. In fact, I sensed she knew how desperate and piteous I was.

Little did I know the great service she'd bestowed on me that day. I was living in a world of fantasy. It was like I had discarded all the sensibilities that lived deep in my core. I had chosen to immerse myself into the dark and turbulent waters of an eddy. Drowning and grasping for air, her hand was extended and I took it.

Reese walked in and his face was devoid of expression. His one eyebrow was naturally positioned slightly higher than the other that always gave his face a look of surprise. In this case I knew he was not surprised at all. I believe he knew this would eventually happen. He had obviously observed my car in the driveway and knew what was coming. Standing at the threshold of the room, he looked at us both and sunk his head slightly into his shoulders, with one hand in his front jean pocket, but did not utter a word.

"Reese, we are both here for the same reason," she began to say. I said nothing, just stared off at an inanimate object in the room. In a tempered but strong voice, she asked, "How long did you think you could carry on this charade?"

I felt like I was in a nightmare and needed to wake up from it. I wanted to melt into the sofa. It didn't take long for him to make his decision, however. A simple, "I want to stay with you" was all he offered, in a pleading but prideful way. Was I devastated? You bet I was, but at the same time I was relieved. Like a great weight had removed from within me. On some level, I had known it would turn out this way. Was I reluctant to turn my back and walk away without an explanation for myself? Most definitely. My disappointment and shock was almost impossible to grasp at first. I cried myself to sleep many a night thereafter, reliving all the intimate moments, all the words of love, all the romantic gifts, including a "what lies ahead" diamond ring. Those stolen times were now only a mirage. But even in my despair, my thoughts reverted back to his wife.

I ran into Reese a few years later. He was divorced. He had his son with him and couldn't say enough about how great it was to be a dad. I had always felt he didn't really know how much my son meant to me. He would ask me to make concessions—"Get a baby sitter" he'd say. "We don't have to wait 'til he is asleep; let him cry." At least I had the wherewithal not to compromise my son's needs, loving him too much. Yet, I still felt caught in an abyss, the best of myself flowing from a gash deep inside me. What good I thought I had, I gave away in that relationship. Sometimes I look back now on all the strife and hardship my and Mario's divorce brought on, and wonder if I was so brave at all with someone else to lean on, a crutch I was reluctant to discard.

Despite the fact that Reese was no longer a part of my life, Mario would soon be the same. Mario was now involved in a relationship and wanted our three-year separation to come to an end.

Now my life would truly be different. With a naïve and cluttered mind, I didn't have a clue of what to expect. Since Mario and I would be moving on, we made the decision to sell our house at this time; the responsibility of keeping up the house was becoming more than burdensome for me as well.

My father was very handy and decided he was going to finish off half of their basement and convert it into a small apartment. Their intention was to gain an extra income and it was quite ideal. The tenant would be able to enter the apartment from the garage door, then down a hallway to the apartment's front door, without infringing on my parents' basement space.

Since I would be soon be facing the need for a place to live, my parents asked if I wanted to rent it. I accepted the offer. Dana and I would have our own full kitchen, bathroom, living room and his own bedroom. I would sleep on a sofa bed in the living room. The arrangement was fitting and the timing was right. They took their ad out of the classifieds.

Mario accepted his responsibility to pay the alimony and child support, but it still wouldn't be enough income to survive. Somehow, someway, I needed to find work to supplement the expenses. In such a broken state of mind, making sound judgments was hardly possible; I would be flying by the seat of my pants and going with my gut.

The day our divorced was finalized, Mario and I left the courthouse and drove back to our home together. We remained silent through most of the half-hour drive. About five minutes before we arrived home, Mario turned to me. In an even and almost light tone he said, "Well, you got what you wanted, Colette." I nodded some at his comment. Staring straight ahead for the rest of the trip, I asked myself, *Did I really get what I wanted? Not really. It's not how I planned it, but now it was done.*

I doubt that anyone wins in a divorce, most especially the children. That remains one of my biggest regrets. My son had no choice in the matter; through our failed marriage, we had mapped out his life.

After my divorce from Mario, I had no idea how Filomena or the family felt about me. It was heartbreaking not to be a part of their family any longer, but it was the decision we chose in the end. Later, when Mario remarried and was raising his own family, I felt that even if my emotions hadn't changed for the ones I knew and loved, my place in his family was no longer appropriate.

Years later, I learned from my son that Filomena and Anthony had moved to upstate New York to be near their daughter. Bina and her husband, Hank, had bought a house near the college they graduated from. When Filomena and Anthony retired, and began to need more assistance, Bina decided to have a home built on her expansive property to accommodate them.

A number of years after their move, Filomena's husband suddenly died in a terrible car accident. He was driving with one of his grandsons while running an errand one afternoon. When I received the news from my son that his half brother had survived but his grandfather had not, I was in shock. I longed to be with

Filomena. There was nothing I could do to console her, but I just wanted her to know I cared. I never stopped caring. Shortly after the funeral, I sent a card and expressed my true sadness, but that wasn't enough for me. I finally picked up the telephone one Sunday night and called her. It had been some time since her son and I had divorced. I was now remarried, and I worried she would feel uncomfortable hearing from me. To my relief, she was very receptive. Why would I have trepidation for this woman who had always possessed such an open and forgiving heart? She was so grateful for our phone call that they became a practice every Sunday night for twelve years. I would make the call about the same time each week and we would converse for the better part of an hour. We were right back in her kitchen again.

I had little physical contact with Filomena, except for a few occasions. Dana and I took a car trip together to visit her once. After driving an hour to pick up my son, we still had hundreds of miles and approximately seven hours to our destination. Leaving on a Friday afternoon and returning on Sunday was quite an endeavor, but was so worth the trip. When we pulled up, Filomena was at the door, beaming with the smile I remembered so well. All the memories came rushing back to me, and I was thrilled to see her again. It didn't occur to me until that moment, that I had missed the experience of having someone anxiously waiting for my son and I, with the warmth and welcoming manner she gave so freely. It was a gift.

Dana and I slept in the loft above Filomena's charming cottage home. It was more than ample in size for a retired couple and I savored every nook and cranny: lots of wood, an open kitchen with a large country-style table, sofa, TV, and Filomena's chair. Mullioned windows with scattered sun catchers she had collected offered wonderful views of her front porch, where her two cats lounged on the railings, and open pastoral images beyond. Our phone calls became more vivid afterward for me; I could envision her and her surroundings now.

Filomena made the same arduous trip to visit us, while on her way to her brother's one summer afternoon. She took the journey once more to Dana's 30th birthday party, along with Dana's dad, aunt, and family. She had visibly changed this time. Signs of frailty and the result of multiple medical issues were catching up with her, but I knew nothing would keep her from seeing her grandson for his special celebration. I suspected it would be her last long trip. And it was.

She is gone now, and I miss our phone calls. Her absence is a great loss to those of us who knew how exceptional she was. She left a wonderful legacy: always keeping a stiff upper lip in difficult times, finding grace in her heart for others when it was often well hidden, loving from her core and knowing the importance of showing it, being generous without expecting anything in return, and having a happy spirit. I am still bewildered about her resolve to continue loving me, disregarding the pain I must have caused so many years ago. Perhaps she knew me better than I knew myself. She knew I would embrace her life lessons in time. For this, I am forever grateful, because I was lucky enough to experience what a mother's love can be.

Mario and I have had new lives with our respective spouses for more than thirty years. I like to think we both made the best of a very sad situation. We are friends now, and I know we wish each other well.

Keeping My Head Above Water

During my legal separation from Mario, the most sobering thought I had was finding a way to supplement my income. In addition, knowing my mother would not make herself available, I needed to find someone I could trust to care for my young son. At that point, I had been out of the work force for a number of years. Most of the positions I was qualified for offered salaries that scarcely covered babysitting services.

I made friends with a woman who was divorced and had two young children around my son's age. She was looking for work as well. Putting our heads together, we decided that we could cover each other's time by taking care of each other's children. But what kind of work could we do on a part time basis?

I spotted an ad in the paper for waitresses at a new café opening in a local shopping center. We sat face to face at her kitchen table, wondering if we could fake it, since neither one of us had any experience. "It's worth a try and we might be able to make some good tips," I said. "I'm in," Sonia enthusiastically replied. We both managed to get hired and split the workweek. The cook was a slight Greek man with a robust voice and short fuse. Right off the bat, the first issue he had with us was our inability to abbreviate meals outside of a BLT. One of the seasoned waitresses that worked on my weekdays was kind enough to give me a crash course in the most common food abbreviations, and I managed to get by. Of course, I shared my newfound knowledge with Sonia.

Being assigned to the station nearest to the kitchen was an additional obstacle for me. I was required to cover the lengthy wrap around counter, as well as three sizable tables that ran parallel to the counter on the other side of the room. Since I worked lunches, customers generally had less than an hour to get back to work. Given that framework, it was crunch time for all. Along with the demands that came with quick food lunches, there was always a request for extra tomato, more coffee, darker toast, extra butter. Back and forth I went, from counter to tables to the kitchen, working alongside an unhinged Greek screaming expletives that ricocheted off the kitchen walls. I was still young but my legs were screaming, "We need a break!" By the time I was done with my shift, I dragged myself to my car, limping more severely than normal. As soon as I picked up Dana at Sonia's, I would head home and collapse for a few minutes on my sofa. With swollen feet soaking in a small tub of hot water and Epsom salts, I would begin to give some thought to starting dinner and chatting with Dana about his day. Most weeks I made quarts of assorted soups on my day off and divided them into freezer containers. I could pull out the plastic receptacle before I headed for work and in no time we would have a hearty meal. During warmer weather we ate lots of cottage cheese and assorted fruits.

Before pulling out of Sonia's driveway one afternoon, I shared my foremost thought. "I don't know how long I can keep this up, Sonia. I am exhausted and my leg can't handle it." The next thing I knew, she was losing her job. My guess is she never mastered the art of waiting on tables as she continued to be the recipient of much flak from the hotheaded, fiery cook in the kitchen.

So, there we were, facing unemployment again. Back to the classifieds. Scanning through the newspaper, I noticed an ad for a day-time bartender. Looking up from the paper at Sonia, I asked, "You think we could try and fake it again?"

"What have we got to lose? I liked the idea of earning tips," she answered. She was always game.

I called and the night bartender answered. "I am calling about the job in the paper."

"The owner is not here right now, but come down and we can talk about the position, hours and salary."

"I'll be there in fifteen minutes, if you want."

"Sure, I'll be here."

Without hesitation, I dropped Dana at Sonia's and left for the bar with directions in hand.

I found a middle-aged man behind the bar, with half a dozen seated customers, and introduced myself.

"Hi, can I help you?"

"Yes, my name is Colette. I called you a little while ago about the available position?"

"Yes, step on down to the end here so we can talk."

I found him to be a very kind man, who was genuinely willing to help me out.

"I could really use this job but I only have waitressing experience."

"Okay, I'll make a deal with you. Come down during my hours, I will teach you how to mix drinks and give

101

you the heads up on anything else you need to know about." I was hopeful during our chat but I provided the additional hurdle. "That would be great but I need to explain my situation."

"What's that?"

"You would need to hire and teach my friend as we need to help each other care for our kids." He agreed to my surprise. Before long, with his generosity of time, I was actually making martinis and all kinds of mixed drinks by eye.

In addition to offering customers drinks at the bar, the relatively new establishment was also a grill. Sonia and I covered the daytime shift that soon became very busy, once they introduced the businessmen's lunches. Not too many mixed drinks but lots of beers were served, especially for my "regulars." A few mailmen, men in suits, and construction workers came in for lunch, or a drink or two after work. I also had my share of loners, as I called them, who just wanted to be a part of the atmosphere but rarely looked up from their beverage.

With tips, the job paid well—so much better than the lunches I served at the café and a lot less work!

There were times the customers felt inclined to buy me a liquor shot in lieu of a tip. I managed to discourage them by sharing my story about having a son and needing to buy groceries. I wasn't really that desperate, but it worked in dissuading them from buying me a drink.

Thereafter I bounced from bar to bar for a while, always working during the day. Sometimes when things were quiet behind the bar, I would sit on a stool and read. Sometimes I would just sit and listen to the jukebox, pondering on how I got myself into the situation I was in. I did make very good money—on average one hundred dollars a day in tips. That was my main objective, but I wanted I do better than this from a career standpoint. But how?

I continued to search for employment positions in the paper. I couldn't stop the feeling that lingered in my thoughts. I wanted to be independent but also proud of what I succeeded in becoming. One morning, after Dana was off to school, an ad caught my eye. There was an opening at a nursing home for an assistant, five minutes from my parents' house. To my delight, when I called to inquire about the job, I obtained an immediate interview appointment.

The following day I arrived at the nursing facility to fill out an application. The admitting director explained the job and gave me a tour of the building. When we returned to her office, she offered me a seat beside her desk. Our conversation was interrupted when an important call came through. Not wanting to feel like I was invading her privacy, I began to turn my head to study the room. It was quite impressive. It was the kind of office you have when you host the public, a comfortable yet professional appearance for the prospective residents and their families. I began to envision myself in this office. It was cheery: one wall facing the front of the brick building was solely made up of ceiling to floor windows. They offered a wonderful vista of the circle driveway, the columned overhanging entryway, and lush lawn beyond. The admitting assistant's desk sat nearest the office door and perpendicular to the over sized panes of glass. There was a feeling of importance, with its grand draperies and wall-to-wall carpeting, loose-leaf binders and medical texts stacked neatly in a bookcase, with a convenient coffee pot ready for brewing. This was so much more than I expected. I would work in a closet, if need be, to get this job! After my first interview with the director, I knew this would be a defining job for me. I would make enough money, be close to home, and have a career possibility within my grasp.

My second interview was my last chance to convince the director that I should have this position. The day before, I went to the mall and charged a business suit on my credit card for the interview, because my wardrobe was, at best, inappropriate. I could hardly afford this outfit, but I was willing to gamble on the investment to make the best impression I could. I was not going to leave any stone unturned.

When I arrived for the interview, I noticed there was another young woman seated in the lobby that appeared to be waiting to be seen as well. I nervously announced myself to the receptionist and took a seat not far from my competition. What could I do or say to convince this woman I would be the best person for the job? The other woman was called in first. The director noticed me and smiled as she closed the door to her office. I waited for the better part of a half-hour, watching staff and elderly residents passing in wheelchairs and walkers, or taking seats in the spacious lobby. Staring down at a magazine that I had not read a word of, I began to worry. *The longer it takes, the less chance I have, please, God, let me have this job!* I thought.

The young woman finally opened the door and exited the front lobby doors, adjacent to the admitting office. She had no visible expression. There was no way to surmise how it went for her. I was called within a few minutes.

"Yes, I can stay overtime."

"Yes, I only live five minutes away and I am a fast learner."

"Yes, I have a dependable babysitter." On and on went the questions.

The admitting director finally sat back in her chair with a clearly pensive look on her face, "Colette, I think I have made my decision." A moment of silence.

"Okay," was all I could respond with, my arms resting in my lap and fingers clasped so firmly together, my knuckles turned white.

"I have seen approximately twenty candidates for this position but I think you will be an asset here and I would like to offer you the position. Can you to start next week?"

I took in a quick short breath. As I exhaled, I replied, "Oh yes! Thank you so much; what time would you like me to be here?"

"You'll punch in at 9am."

I was so lightheaded by the time I left the building, I felt I was floating on my magic carpet, as I once had imagined as a child from my bedroom window. I couldn't wait to get home to tell my parents the news. As I pulled into the driveway, my mother was on the front lawn pulling weeds from a planter. As I shut my car door I exclaimed, "Mom, guess what?" She pivoted around on her knees, wiping her forearm across her forehead, and replied, "What?"

"I got the job," I excitedly yelled across the lawn.

"Oh, yeah? How come?"

"What do you mean how come?"

"Well, didn't you say there were a lot of women applying for the job?"

"Sure, but the woman thought I was the one," I answered in an exasperated tone.

There was no, "That's wonderful, Colette." No, "Good for you dear." No, "I knew you could do it." Impervious to my news and continuing her job at hand, she finally asked, "When do you start?"

After many inquiries, I managed to arrange for my son to be cared for at the home of a daycare mother. It didn't take long to realize this woman was not acceptable, however. A number of times I picked up Dana in diapers that I later discovered she'd left his bottom red, if not still filled with a bowel movement. That could only mean she was not changing him regularly. At the time of that discovery, Dana told me during one of our drives home, "Mommy that lady gives me peanut butter and jelly sandwiches every day." Being partially reimbursed by the county, a huge jar of peanut butter can go a long way, I decided. After my realizations, I contacted the county office and told them I was very dissatisfied. When I told my mother what had transpired, she offered no alternative suggestion.

Holding my breath, I asked the dreaded question, "Mom, couldn't Dana stay with you? He would be in his own environment and you have a fenced in backyard..." I went on and on, giving examples of why it would be so much better for him.

"Oh, no, Colette, he is too much for me. He is too active. Look at my storm door. I have to clean those marks all the time." It was true; living in my parent's house was like living in a hospital. Nothing was more important to her then making sure the house was immaculate all the time. Not even when the welfare of her grandson was at risk.

I was on my own and feeling stressed. I was beginning to develop headaches during this time. At first, they were random. As time passed, they became chronic and more intrusive. My father experienced chronic headaches too. He took aspirin like most people take daily vitamins, so I decided I had the same gene and tried to shrug them off.

I didn't have time to dwell on my mother's refusal because I had a limited period to find another caretaker. I met with a new daycare mother closer to where I lived. She was already watching three children during the day. Initially I was dubious about how she would manage an additional child. Pam was older than me and had two teenage children living at home—an older daughter and son. Greeting me at her front door with a smile, she invited me in as if I was a guest coming to dinner. She was easy to like. I watched her kind and peaceful interactions with the other children. She had a well-kept, simple house, comprised of many small rooms that quite possibly were additions over the years. The children had a bright room in the center of the home with carpeting and lots of windows that looked out onto her sizable yard, full of trees and greenery and a swing set. There were assorted toys scattered on the floor and a bookshelf filled with children's books. Pam's daughter watched them while I spoke to Pam, all the while thinking to myself, "This is going to work out, thank God." My positive hunch about this woman was realized within the first few weeks.

Not long after Dana's started staying with Pam, he developed a high fever. After work I rushed him to the pediatrician, as the hours would soon be over that day. The doctor gave Dana an exam, wrote a prescription for an antibiotic, and gave instructions for his care. By the time I arrived home, it was after dinnertime. I changed him into his pajamas, tucked him into bed, gave him baby aspirin for his fever, and placed a cool wet washcloth on his searing forehead. Within a few minutes, his hand went limp in mine and he turned to his side. Giving him a kiss on his cheek, I left his room with only a small nightlight to show me the way. I continued my way through our apartment into the unfinished part of the basement and went upstairs to tell my mother what had transpired. She was sitting in her den watching her favorite show, *Little House on the Prairie*. She must have taped every show they ever produced; she literally had a library of them. She turned to me and said, "I love this program, it's what a real family should be like." What irony. This was not at all what my family was like, but she admired these fictional characters and their relationships. Without acknowledging her sentiments, I, in turn, asked if I could leave Dana home in his own bed just for tomorrow, as he was not well. As I expected, she said that she could not as she had an appointment or some such thing to do. There was no more to say. My muscles stiffened, I turned from her and made my way back down to my apartment. I picked up my phone and called Pam to explain my situation, that I would have to miss work. Without hesitation, she replied, "Don't worry Colette, I have a bed in my back room, away from the others so he can sleep and they won't be exposed to him." What a lifesaver.

My job was considered an administrative position at the nursing home. Union employees made up most of the staff: nursing aides, housekeepers and kitchen workers. Since lunches were provided, there was a policy for non-union workers. In the event that there was a strike, we were not allowed to leave the premises at any time. We would ultimately be responsible for the residents if the union workers walked. With this policy in place, I pled my case to the administrator. It was urgent that I drop off the prescription at the drug store for my son during my lunch hour. He was unwavering. Undaunted by his inflexibility, I continued to reason with him. I couldn't take the chance of losing this position, but I was not going neglect my son. After a prolonged exchange, I was allowed to drop off the prescription, providing Pam's daughter would be able to pick it up for me at the drug store. What a relief. I realized after this small success that I was becoming more comfortable advocating for myself, or at least for my son.

****

After working for the nursing facility for several months, my brother, Buster, suddenly lost his wife. She was in her early twenties and became ill on Thanksgiving morning. After a week of evaluations in the hospital, she was gone. Chip, their baby boy, was just six months old. It was all very sad and shocking for our family, especially since the reason for her death was vague and questionable. Legionnaires Disease had surfaced at that time and it was considered a possibility for her demise. The other potential reason was even more curious. Without anyone's knowledge, she had been going to a lab nearby her home. She was volunteering to take certain clinical trial drugs in exchange for a monetary stipend. My brother had no knowledge of the part she played at the lab. He was left with raising his baby boy on his own. At the time, he lived about two hours away from my parents. On my parents' suggestion, Buster and Chip moved into their house almost immediately, and we became a family of six living under the same roof. Dana and Chip enjoyed each other's company and forged a strong bond during that time. My mother took care of Chip daily, and for up to ten hours a day, since my brother's commute to his business continued to be long and arduous. My mother never complained.

****

When I look back on my relationship with my mother, I realize that even though I needed her help, love, and approval, I couldn't dictate or complain about how insufficient I felt her feelings were toward me. And no matter how much I tried, I couldn't convince her I was worthy of her love, pride, and attention. Over the years, history would repeat itself, and I was incapable of stopping the wheel from turning. My expectations of her would continue to be dashed. The setting would change, but the outcome was always the same.

When I decided ten years later to leave my nursing home position as the admitting director, my desire was to go back to school. I enrolled in a trade school for a certificate course in Interior Design and Decorating Applications—something I always wanted to learn more about. After completing the courses, I found I had quite a flair for the field. I submitted an entry for two contests: the *Long Island Monthly* magazine and the Greater New York Apartment and House Show. Not only did I win first place for the "finest living room," a full page spread in their magazine and a $500.00 award, I was also honored at an indoor arena. As for the House Show, I was the first place winner and my prize was a brand new hot tub and media coverage. I was thrilled and excited. My husband, Joe, along with a few family members, were there to support me, but the one person who should have been there was not.

Over the years when I persistently invited my mother to charity events I chaired, she again, was a no show. I had to accept that, like the old saying goes, "You can

lead a horse to water but you can't make them drink."
I knew I needed to find my own worth, be happy and
satisfied with my own achievements, and stand tall.
If others were supportive and happy for me then that
would be the icing on the cake, and I did like icing! But
then again, sometimes what your mind knows to be
true is not what your heart is feeling.

A Journey to Love

―――――――――――――◉―――――――――――――

"The very best way to love someone, is not to change them, but instead, help them reveal the greatest version of themselves." – S. Maraboli

In 1977, in a not particularly romantic way, I met the love of my life. My friend, Sonia, and I had gone to see the hit movie, *Saturday Night Fever*. After the movie, she suggested we head to a popular dance club for a drink. We felt comfortable frequenting the club, as it catered to patrons most often divorced and over twenty-five. The club was crowded for a cold, February, mid-week evening. The DJ was playing tunes at the far end of the room, behind the dimly lit dance floor, with cocktail tables dispersed around it. A sizable, rectangular, free-standing bar filled up the rest of the club. We greeted the bartender and took a seat nearest to the front door. It would have to be an early night, since we both had to get up for work the next day.

During the '70s, there was a significant rise in dance clubs. The disco scene and dance offered a new music genre with driving, repetitive, catchy beats and steps. A unique dance style that was as much fun to watch as it was to learn. Of course, I don't think I would be kidding anyone if I said I was there just to learn to how to dance. The clubs were conducive to meeting eligible singles, perhaps looking for a relationship, or out to have a good time. I experienced both that very night. Joe approached me and asked if I would like to dance. He had been sitting across the bar. Due to the crowd I hadn't noticed him initially. He was a cute, small- framed man with thick black hair parted on the side, and a matching, tidy, dark mustache. As he took a step back for me to leave my stool, I was taken by his soft, brown, grape eyes, which matched the brown turtleneck he wore under his camel wool blazer. As we made our way to the dance floor, I turned to him, "Have you been here before?"

"Yes, I actually came here a few times with my wife to dance years ago, before we separated."

We danced to several disco songs and then decided we needed a break. "What made you decide to come tonight?" I asked.

"I am out with a tennis buddy. We went to dinner after our game and he suggested we stop by for a drink. I don't think it would occur to me to come here, if not for him."

He followed me back to my seat. As I sat back down on the bar stool, Sonia asked me a question. Before I could turn back to introduce my new dance partner, he had disappeared. "Where did that Joe guy go?" I asked Sonia.

"Don't know; he was here one minute and he's gone the next."

His disappearing act happened several times that night. When he returned for another dance, I finally decided to say something. "Joe, why don't you stick around so we can talk?" And so he did. But before long, I realized Sonia and I needed to leave.

"I think I need to say goodnight, we are heading home," I announced with a smile.

"Wait, would you like to go to dinner on Saturday night?" he asked.

"Sure, let me give you my phone number," I replied. Driving home with Sonia, I turned to her and said, "I am not sure why I said yes to that guy. He seems pretty shy and I am not used to that. But he's cute, so what the heck?"

It was a tender and romantic date. He took me to what became our favorite restaurant on the south shore. It had an old world charm: dark woods, soft, low lighting, wall-to-wall carpeting, crisp white tablecloths and waiters dressed in tuxedo-like uniforms. Over drinks, he said that he noticed me across the bar and thought, *That's a beautiful woman.* As I suspected, however, he also admitted he was unsure of himself. He had been married for fifteen years and was a bit rusty with the dating scene.

The more I got to know him that night, the more I realized what a special and authentic person he was. Joe slowly began to open up. He was an architect and shared that, at his wife's request, he'd designed and built a home for his family vacations in the Virgin Islands. They had frequented the island a number of times beforehand, and she became enamored with the whole idea of being there for long periods of time. While he was working back in the States and the house was under construction, his wife prolonged her stay with their youngest son, who was not of school age. Joe managed to finish up his work just before Christmas, and flew down with his two older children to spend the holiday at their new getaway home. On Christmas

Eve, his wife announced her desire to divorce him; she had been having an affair with a native man she had met prior to the construction of the house. To say Joe was in shock was an understatement. Feeling spurned and despondent, Joe left for the States on Christmas day with his daughter and his older son. His youngest son stayed with Joe's wife. Later, after accepting his wife's monetary demands, he received custody of his youngest when their divorce was finalized. I was quite taken by his devotion to his children and his struggles to raise them on his own. This was a good family man, I thought. The kind of guy you know has his heart in the right place.

Prior to the finalization of their divorce, on our second date, he invited me to his home to meet his older children. He announced during our phone call that he was going to prepare dinner. I accepted the invitation. With a bit of trepidation, Dana and I arrived. As we walked along the brick-paved sidewalk, we reached a long set of mullioned French doors. Opening the entryway door, we entered into a passive solar room that I later learned was designed and built by Joe. As I rang the doorbell, I took a glance back at this seemingly peaceful setting. On the far end of the room, the western sun shone zealously through to the sizable, lush plants clustered on the brick flooring. I decided the simple rattan, cushioned, loveseat centered and positioned facing the French doors was an ideal place to relax or even perhaps read a book. As I turned back, Joe opened the front door and greeted us with a big smile. "Come in! Glad you found the house!" Giving each other a peak on the lips I answered, "Yes, it was easy, we are happy to be here, aren't we Dana?" He nodded yes.

As we stepped further inside, the remainder of the home was decorated with a mixture of furnishings that offered a tasteful, eclectic style. I could see touches of Joe's architectural and construction refinement everywhere I looked.

Now approaching the kitchen, the appealing aroma from the prime rib dinner Joe was preparing stimulated my senses. I thought to myself, no one starves in this house! He later admitted to me that when he realized he was on his own to prepare meals for his family, he would have to learn some basics. He signed up for adult education classes in French and Chinese cooking to help him be more creative, outside of hamburgers and pork chops. He was so refreshing, unlike many of the men I had previously dated. I knew this was the kind of man I longed for in my life.

Keira and Chase were sitting at the round, white mica table in the kitchen as Joe introduced us to his two children. Dana and I sat down. While I attempted to connect with his children, Joe put the finishing touches on dinner. Keira, his oldest, and Chase, his middle son, were somewhat reserved. Joe became the intermediary, as we sat together sharing bits of the meal and ourselves; no one had a clue where this first meal together would take us.

Dana was about five-years-old and took to Joe early on. We began to plan family outings when Percy, Joe's youngest, moved back: movies, water skiing, and fishing on their boat; even going on trips together to Hershey, Pennsylvania and Orlando, Florida. In light of our group events, Joe and I had made a pact early on to keep Saturday evenings as our date night. In addition, we would often meet for a quick breakfast before work, and Dana and I continued to be invited to their home for pasta dinners on Sunday afternoons.

As time passed, Saturday nights turned into Sunday mornings at Joe's and before we knew it, Dana and I began to stay for longer and longer periods of time. His divorce was slated for the spring now. We were starting our lives together, but things weren't as blissful as we had wished. Integrating our families proved to be much more difficult than foreseen. We found ourselves attending family counseling to try and mend all the broken hearts. Joe's daughter was most visibly affected by her parents' breakup. I look back now and realize how hurt and broken she felt. Lashing out at me was her only outlet. She disapproved of me being in their home, and she expressed her resentment in hurtful ways. I believe anyone would have received the same treatment; I represented a change in her life she didn't want to believe would happen. I made a gallant effort to become her friend, but she was not ready. Unfortunately, I was not emotionally equipped to understand her pain at the time, and it caused tremendous discord for us. We were both dealing with our own pain and needs, and neither of us had the capacity to put ourselves in each other's place. Keira and I often found ourselves vying for a position of importance with Joe. Positioned between us, Joe added to the conflict. If we planned a date, Joe would invite Keira. If he bought a small gift for me, Keira would receive the same. Caught in between our triangular relationship, Joe exacerbated the strife and hostility between Keira and I. I wanted him to show his support for me, and she wanted things to be the way they were, without me. I was shocked and crushed in the aftermath of Keira's recurring acts of hostility toward me as well as Joe's defense, "You are the adult and you should overlook it." However, at that time, I could not overlook or accept the attempts to sabotage our relationship. There were times when

117

I became out of control much the same as I was with my first husband. I wanted to be loved and I needed support and attention desperately. I felt like I was pleading my case, but the jury wasn't listening.

My relationship with Chase was less eventful. I am sure he had his apprehensions about me, but I was not the focus of his life and I was grateful for that. He, at times, became my confidant, someone I could share my disappointment with. Joe's youngest son, Percy, who was the center of attention before Dana's arrival, had accepted me more readily than he did my son.

At one point, I decided that there was too much drama and turmoil within this family for me to deal with. As much as I believed Joe and I were meant to be together, the variables being played out were more than either one of us could control. Our timing was simply wrong. I left with my son and went back to my parents' basement apartment with a sick heart. Dana was not happy with this idea at all. He would not unpack his backpack and threatened to go back to Joe's without me. What had I done? He was losing another male figure in his life, and I was totally responsible for it.

About six weeks after our separation, Dana and I were at a movie. After the show, we were following the crowd up the aisle toward the exit door. Dana called out, "Mom, there's Joe!" I looked across the center seats to the parallel aisle and there he was with his three children. My heart yearned to meet them, but despite my son's urging, we left without saying hello.

During those separated weeks, I tried to analyze the situation. I saw so many attributes in Joe that I admired. Aside from his dedication to his children, I most especially loved how he interacted with Dana. He was very fair to my son when it came to his treatment of all the children. All four kids had been assigned chores. Many of the chores involved assisting Joe. It was a time where he got to bond with them. If the task was to help him plant some new shrubs, Dana received the same alone time with Joe, and the opportunity to have one-on-one chats as the others did. If they were rewarded, Dana received equal gifts of appreciation. If he granted permission to one, all were granted the same permission. There was never a time that "equal" wasn't played out among them. Joe helped them all with the same enthusiasm and caring attitude.

I was his biggest fan and knew that I was falling deeply in love. Joe excelled in anything that interested him. He was a talented artist. He had a green thumb and was well-versed on gardening and the specimen trees he cultivated. He had a keen sense of finances, reflected in his architectural and building career, as well as his business endeavors. He was grounded, loyal, funny, and unselfish. He was the embodiment of a gentleman.

He had told me that he loved me, but he was conflicted and confused. He had the responsibility of his children, his career, and a heart that was trying to make sense of it all. But it was overwhelming. He wanted me in his life but after his wife had betrayed him, was he even prepared to commit to anyone else so quickly? Perhaps I was the impatient one, I began to think. I loved Joe. And I knew if he needed me to, I would wait for him.

I made the first overture. I called his office and he answered. I asked him if he was interested in meeting for a drink at our favorite restaurant. He agreed. We met at the beautifully appointed restaurant within minutes of our homes. The setting was romantic, and many a night we had danced the night away there. On this night, we met and embraced so deeply, we knew we couldn't let each other go again. Sitting at one of the cocktail tables, we began to catch up on each other's lives. How were his children doing? How was my son? The DJ was playing soft music, as we sat facing each other and the candlelit votive centered on the table. It was as if we'd never parted, and the sparks between us smoldered. When the song "Reunited" by Peaches and Herb began to play, without a word, we stood up and went to the dance floor.

"I was a fool to ever leave your side
Me minus you is such a lonely ride
The breakup we had has made me lonesome and sad
I realize I love you
'Cause I want you bad......"

Dancing so close in that moment, time stood still. We both knew we were ready to face whatever life had in store for us, good or bad.

Shortly after our reunion, things started to slowly fall into place. Nothing was perfect, but with therapy and persistence, we had the determination to make it work. I was still working fulltime for the nursing facility, making dinner for the family when I returned from work, and trying to make a home for us all. Joe pitched in whenever he could. It was a sizable challenge, and often stressful, but we had a goal we did not want to give up on.

We all settled into a relatively normal lifestyle, until one night several months later. After falling asleep for a few hours, I suddenly woke up. I was experiencing the most unexpected and unmerciful headache imaginable. This was nothing like my steady stream of headaches I chronically dealt with. This time I could barely speak.

Nudging Joe, I tried to explain how I felt. "Please help me, Joe," was all I could manage to whisper.

"Do you want to go to the hospital?" he asked. I nodded yes. Even the movement of my head ached. Driving to the hospital, I was in absolute and relentless agony. "I want to cut my head off," I kept muttering as I held my head against the car's headrest. "God, make it stop. Joe, help me."

"We are almost there, babe, hang on," he answered with urgency in his voice. When we arrived at the emergency room, I was placed on a stretcher from the car and brought into the triage area. Joe began to explain my symptoms, and within seconds I found myself being wheeled into a storage closet. *What is going on?* I thought, in a panic, too overcome with pain to ask. After the initial paperwork was finished, Joe came to my side. He wore a mask that covered his mouth and began to explain, "They are calling a neurologist. They think you have meningitis. They put you in here because it might be highly contagious, depending on which kind you have." The room was dark, with the exception of the florescent lighting in the hall. I struggled to speak, "What does that mean?"

"They said they needed to determine whether you have bacterial, viral, or fungal meningitis first. They can treat you for viral or fungal, but bacterial can be fatal."

"Oh my God, Joe," was all I could utter as tears rolled down my cheeks. Joe offered tender words and tried to reassure me that I would survive.

He was right; I did not have bacterial meningitis. I was transferred to a hospital by ambulance, where they were equipped to provide me with a private, isolated room for what became my home for a little over a week. A lumbar puncture (spinal tap) was required to take a sample of the cerebrospinal fluid, so they could determine the diagnosis of meningitis. I was asked to lay on my side in a C shape, drawing my knees and chin to my chest. Local anesthesia was injected into my spine that was supposed to suppress and relieve some of the pain. For me, it did not. As the fluid was administered between two vertebrae, I released a deafening and ear splitting cry, fiercely clutching the sheet crumbled around me. My headache immediately increased, if that was even possible. I wept and wanted to die.

The pain from meningitis is exacerbated by light. Drapes were drawn in my room during the day, and only the hallway fluorescents through the window of my door gave light to the room at night. I was alone, in the dark, for the duration, but with their findings, I was out of fatal danger. Slowly, my headache began to lessen, and the fever decreased. I hoped this would be the last hospitalization I would ever have to experience. Little did I know how many more I would endure.

Joe was not at the hospital as often as I would have liked. Between his business responsibilities and the children's needs, he didn't have a lot of extra time to visit. I would get teary-eyed when he would announce he had to leave. "Don't you care about me? I need you to be here for me." I wouldn't listen to reason back then; I just didn't want to be alone, especially in a hospital setting that I was all too familiar with.

My parents came to visit me during my stay. My mother was particularly tender and emotional. My father was my father; he would try to lighten the situation with funny quips as his hand rested or stroked my forehead. After their visit, I lay in bed thinking about my mother's reaction to seeing me. Through my history of illnesses, it was uncanny how my mother was able to reveal an affectionate side during crises for me, but not during the normal times. It was as if she liked me best when I was helpless and defenseless. When I was very young, without knowing why, I secretly hoped that I would get sick. From a child's perspective, if that's what it took to get her to hold, touch, and caress me, then so be it! As the saying goes, be careful what you wish for. Enduring a host of illnesses, aside from the polio, several childhood viruses, along with frequent earaches and fevers, my wish came true, and they haunt me now. In the hospital, I am that little girl again, longing for a tender touch and a voice to tell me things would be all right, but her overture didn't quite ring true anymore.

After I returned home, I was confined to bed most of the day, as I was in a very weakened state. Again, I felt abandoned. Joe would take the kids out for an event on the weekends, and I would be left with no one, and nothing to do but think about how miserable I was. When I was able to get around, Joe would often say, "Colette, you have to find your own interests." I didn't want to find my own interests; I wanted my interest to be with him. I clearly didn't like sharing his time, when I couldn't be a part of it. I was completely dependent on him.

Despite my emotional struggles, we blended our families and made the decision to marry four years after our initial meeting.

Our marriage took place in our home, with family and close friends attending. We met with a Protestant pastor who was recommended to us. He was kind and compassionate about marrying us outside of the Catholic Church, but wanted us to understand the seriousness of our vows. My sense was, just because the Catholic Church would not acknowledge our love and commitment, he recognized that Joe and I were in fact committed to our relationship after the interview.

We wanted our ceremony to take place in one of Joe's gardenscapes around the house, but Mother Nature was not cooperating. It was a warm, sultry August day, with a light steady rain, so we said our vows in front of a bay window that overlooked our pool. A singer and pianist played our favorite songs. It was a beautiful afternoon and I felt like I'd come home, for the first time in my life. After pledging our love, we danced to Barbra Streisand's song, "Evergreen."

"Soft as an easy chair, love fresh as the morning air, one love that is shared by two, I have found in you...Time won't change the meaning of one love, ageless and ever green."

We spent our honeymoon on the southern coast of Portugal and in the cities of Lisbon and Oporto. Joe's mom stayed with the kids at our home.

It was a blissful time. We had the opportunity to know each other better without distractions of daily life. We were equally eager to explore new sights and discovered how much we both appreciated the beauty of nature. Joe was sensitive and generous, and I was feeling free and secure at the same time. He enjoyed buying me gifts and taking me to the finest restaurants Portugal had to offer. I enjoyed sleeping beside him and having our late night talks about our ideals and intentions, and the excitement of spending the rest of our lives together. The time was ours now, to plan our future and to feel contentment.

I still think of Joe as my rock. No one has ever given me the stability and support I longed for, as he has through the years. He showed me a new definition to the word, love, and allowed me to grow when I was ready to spread my wings.

The Stuff Nightmares Are Made Of

I was very mindful and struggled with my emotional state during my adult years as a single and married woman. I wrestled with my thoughts, and the judgments I made, and knew they were not healthy, but they surfaced and won, over and over again.

Always feeling insecure, I developed a habitual goal to be perfect. It was most important that others not judge me adversely. I couldn't divulge the tumultuous havoc that played in my mind to others, so I strived to be everything I thought everyone wanted me to be. I was not selective; I wanted to be liked by everyone I knew. Attempting to be perfect however, came with a price—I was in a chronic state of tremendous stress. Oprah Winfrey used to refer to this specific disposition as a "disease to please." Guilty as charged.

When asked to give my opinion on anything, I often found myself in great angst. *That woman in the red top doesn't like me,* I'd think. *She doesn't agree with my remark.* It would take me days to get over my anxiety, because I could not change my perceived opinion this person must be feeling about me.

The service man arrives to repair an appliance. My house is untidy, and I am instantly anxious about his perception of me. Or a friend pops in without announcing she was coming. *Oh, my God, what will she think of me?* was always my first thought. I'd make feeble excuses, and then feel embarrassed for not living up to the expectations I thought they had of me. I'd vow to myself that I would not let it happen again. I would make things perfect next time.

At work, I had similar issues. I'd think, *That woman isn't crazy about me. Maybe I could go out of my way tomorrow and greet her with a big smile, or strike up a friendly conversation. I'll make her like me.* I became pre-occupied with how to get into the good graces of others. They may have not given me a second thought, but I was completely focused on making sure I could compensate for my comment or action in the event it was taken negatively. So many people to mend fences with, that may have never been broken in the first place, and with so much needless energy spent.

Initially, I looked for ways to help myself, because I wanted to put an end to my self-loathing and paranoia. Even though I was not reading much at the time, I did scour the inspirational /self-help section that filled the bookstore shelves. After reading this genre of book, I would often be inspired by their insights. But inspiration isn't enough; I didn't know how to change the tape that had played in my mind for so many years.

The physical and emotional residuals from an affliction like polio made me hyper-focused on my appearance as well. The most obvious difference was a noticeable limp from my shorter right leg. My right foot was two sizes smaller than my left. It's a terrible challenge to find shoes that fit, I might add. Over the years, after my numerous surgeries, I was left with scarring on my back, hip, and right leg and foot. Being seen in a bathing suit was out of the question; I couldn't handle the whispers that I thought would ensue as a result. And if the scarring wasn't enough to make me feel unattractive, my right leg had atrophied from the lack of use. I was consumed with masking my flaws. I went to great lengths, spending hours finding clothes that would conceal the things about myself I hated the most. I spent a limitless amount of time looking for shoes that didn't look like men's footwear as well. During the '80s, there wasn't a lot in the way of dainty flats that I could wear, when spiked heels were all the rage. And if I did find something more appropriate, it was invariably painful for me to wear. The shoes had an awkward feel and my ankle often turned in, putting undue stress on my muscles. Painful, raw blisters would surface with every step. The pain would eventually overtake my whole body, but I foolishly lumbered on for the sake of beauty and uniformity. Some surgeries were performed to correct my gait, but my right leg and foot just didn't have the muscle strength to walk in footwear that was designed for a normal foot stride.

Having a poor self-image was one measure of my insecurity. I longed to quiet my mind, to find inner solace and a sense of peace. I began to find it in *The Oprah Winfrey Show*, which aired every weekday afternoon. Oprah offered a candid and compelling look at the lives of people dealing with personal challenges and how they could potentially overcome them. With insights and advice from Oprah, as well as invited specialists, she used this platform to teach and inspire her viewers. Her suggestions and opinions were forthright and sincere. I admired her; no, I idolized her. I bought her biography and signed up for yearly subscriptions to her magazine. She was instrumental in my reading more consistently, and I eventually started a book club of my own that lasted twelve years. I couldn't get enough of her. My son, Dana, and stepson, Percy, were preteens by this time. They would good-heartedly tease me about my allegiance to what I considered the best show on TV. I arranged my life around four o'clock every afternoon, so as not to miss her. It was a freeing hour for me. I was a student witnessing the cathartic evolution of her guests, and felt a sense of hope that I, too, could find a way.

I began to participate in her self-improvement suggestions. I created a scrapbook. I collected uplifting quotes and assorted pictures that resonated for me. I started adding what I refer to as "feel good writings" I came across through media sources. And it grew from there: a photo of a pretty, full-length gown I loved, an article about Charles Dickens and where his inspiration came from for *A Christmas Carol,* babies, flowers, friends' photos, Joe and me on vacation, a colorful map, a souvenir from a hotel, a loving note my son wrote many years before, funny quips, and anything that could potentially open my spirit to the positive side of living.

Oprah offered a "Gratitude Journal" idea that I eagerly embraced. She urged her viewers to write five things every day that they were grateful for. Some days it was easy. I could merely look outside my window at nature itself and it would reveal its blessing to me. Other days it was harder to feel grateful, and I would turn my mind to the ones I loved and feel grateful for them.

I was thirsty for the path to my wellbeing, but how could I reach for a star if I didn't have the wings to fly and the sky continued to be filled with clouds of worry, perfectionism, and worthlessness? My health was perpetually compromised. I was in a state of what I called "Waiting For the Other Shoe to Drop" Syndrome. And it did.

One warm spring day, I decided to attack the job of window cleaning. We still lived in the L-shaped ranch that made spring-cleaning of windows reasonably easy, except for the 4½-foot Palladium window that extended across four French doors in our living room. Joe had set up the 12-foot ladder earlier, so I was ready to tackle the "beast." I knew it would take the better part of an hour to complete, since my physical limitations would slow me down. Climbing the ladder gingerly, with my left leg leading, and right leg limply following, I reached the highest part of the window and worked my way down, rung by rung. Shifting the ladder over one foot at a time to finish the nine-foot span, called for a lot of ascending and descending, but it was finally done. Catching my breath from the ladder aerobics, I was relieved that I wouldn't have to face the task again until the fall.

Looking through the kitchen window while washing the grime off my hands from my arduous task, I suddenly noticed my vision was compromised. It was as though I was looking through a glass of water. I wasn't alarmed at first. I surmised that the sunscreen I had applied must have bled down into my eyes from the sweat on my brow. A nice shower would remedy that issue. As I finished my shower, I could hear Joe's car approaching through the open window. We kissed hello and he made his way to the den. Entering the den behind him I began to talk. "I fin….fin…I wan.. was….can't…cad… talk," I stammered. *What is going on?* I went to our bookcase in the den and pulled out a dictionary, attempting to look up the word I was not able to pronounce. I stared at the page, but I was not making a connection; my mind was blocked. In a panic, I turned to Joe. "Joe, I can't...I code, I can't red," as I pointed to the page in the book.

He jumped up and went for the wall phone in the kitchen. "Should I call the doctor?" I nodded yes, standing in the middle of the room and suddenly shivering from fright. After his short conversation with my primary doctor, he turned to me and said, "He wants me to take you to the hospital now." Still filled with dread over what was happening, I headed for the garage with Joe holding my arm in his hand. My body trembled and I felt as if my brain was trapped in a vortex. I prayed I would make it on time. For what, I did not know.

My symptoms began to subside by the time I reached the hospital emergency room entryway; once again, I was on a gurney and placed in a curtained waiting area. After transferring to a room on the neurology floor, the doctor explained that I had experienced a T.I.A., otherwise known as a transient ischemic attack or a mini stroke.

Overtaken by another unexpected medical condition, I was fortunate that I had no serious residuals from the incident and was able to go home within a few days. The experience took its emotional toll, however. Having the proper medication gave me a sense of comfort, but the sudden medical crisis played on my psyche once again. I was increasingly becoming pre-occupied with the fragility of life. The habitual "what ifs" played in my head: *What if Joe got sick, passed away and left me? What if Dana had an accident, or became fatally ill? What if terrorists destroy our world? What if we destroy ourselves with toxins? What if I ate tuna and was stock piling dangerous mercury? What if the killer bees that are coming this spring? Would they sting me or even someone I know? What if the alarm reveals a nuclear war between the U.S. and Russia?*

My heart was very heavy, and I felt overwhelmed with fright, even more so when nightfall arrived. In addition to carrying the weight of my own worries, I carried the weight of others; my compassion was endless and irrational.

"Joe, I feel like I am in a funk," I tried to remark in a light tone.

"Why do you say that, hon?" he asked.

"I don't know. I can't watch the news anymore. There are so many scary things happening, everything is worrying me." Watching old sitcoms before I went to bed was the only way I could distract myself from the impending disasters that kept me on the edge of a meltdown.

I would eventually fall asleep and have terrible dreams. Once in the dead of the night, I heard an atomic bomb going off, with the capacity to destroy the entire world. The sound was similar to a droning from an electrical transformer before it blows, only so deafening and mind blowing, it felt as if it could be heard around the entire planet. I abruptly awakened. Quiet surrounded me, as I lay frozen in bed. My heart was pounding. I turned to Joe, who was sleeping peacefully. I nudged him lightly with my side. He turned and asked in a murmur, "Are you okay?" As I snuggled into his arms and cradled my head in the nook of his neck and shoulder, I whispered, "Now I am."

During the day I managed to live my life more fully, but I was plagued with a parade of ailments and chronic headaches that made sleeplessness a common occurrence. Quite usually, I managed four hours of broken sleep a night. I was alone during those long and restless times, with my many thoughts racing in my head and overwhelming me. As for Joe, uninterrupted sleep was to become a thing of the past in the days, months, and years to come. Somehow, he put up with it, and I am grateful for his love and patience.

With my nights becoming increasingly difficult, I began to experience multiple, unexplained symptoms. Each time a symptom occurred, my mind would plummet and I imagined the worse medical outcome. I was terrified the symptom would lead to a fatal diagnosis.

During numerous nightly occasions, I awakened to a physical uneasiness. I would feel like something was overcoming me. My head and body felt numb as if I were on the verge of fainting, but my heart was furiously beating. Oh no, it's happening again, I'd think in a panic. Softly squeezing Joe's arm, I would wake him. "Joe that same feeling is back. I am so scared." "It's okay, baby, you have had this feeling before. Try to think of something positive." He ran his fingertips across my forehead ever so lightly. I always loved that feeling, and he used it in an effort to calm me. I tried to do what he suggested. It didn't seem to be working. After a few minutes I would announce, "I think I might be having a heart attack. I think I need to go to the emergency room." Joe did not respond, but turned to his side of the bed to stand up. "I am so sorry honey, but I can't help it." I felt guilty for putting him through this.

Sometimes in the wee hours of the morning we would sit in the car in the hospital parking lot for a time to see if my symptoms would perhaps recede. Most times I succumbed to the prevailing symptoms and entered the emergency room. On this night, like other nights, the medical staff arrived to confirm my arrhythmia condition, but they didn't see any serious indications that my heart was compromised. I was discharged after several hours. Waiting for my release, Joe would often nod off in the chair next to my gurney. "Wake up honey, we can go home."

With each trip, I hated myself for putting Joe through it all, but still anxious about the medical distress I was in. I wanted to feel positive. After all, wasn't that the best medicine? Primarily during the night, my emergency room visits continued for a variety of symptoms— mostly heart and abdominal issues or sudden visual distortions from my severe headaches. Life continued to be volatile and unpredictable.

During the following years, I experienced additional inexplicable symptoms, some mild and some bizarre, including colds, lung and sinus infections on a frequent and regular basis, neck pain, back pain, TMJ, mouth and eye spasms that lasted for hours, underarm burning sensations, self-inflicted scratches on neck, face, arms and legs, bug crawling sensations on my legs during the night, sore throats that didn't lead to a cold or illness, sudden sharp pains in any area of the body, as well as severe and painful charley horses.

The most bizarre were my morning visual images and my chronic mind repetitions. Without fail, every morning I woke up with a stiff neck, headache, and a repeated image. During my initial moments of arousal, my eyes still closed, I would see a moving image one might call Newton's Cradle. Newton's Cradle consists of a series of identical metal balls suspended by wire in a metal frame. The balls are touching each other; with each impact from the end ball moving toward the next, creating a swinging momentum to and fro. I witnessed this repetitive image, but only if my eyelids were closed. Should I open my eyes the image would be gone, close my eyes again, and it recurred. It was so disturbing to me that I wouldn't keep my eyes closed long enough to see if it actually dissipated on its own.

Another quirky symptom I dealt with was what I called, "parrot head". Not conscious from the onset, I'd suddenly find myself repeating a phrase in my head. It would take a few seconds or perhaps a minute to realize that I was doing it, and then it was almost impossible to stop. I would make a concerted effort to "switch it off," but soon I found myself repeating a new phrase. It felt maddening. I wanted to run away from it, but it continued to haunt me at the most unexpected times.

For approximately five years, I made appointments with many specialists and underwent CAT scans and numerous tests for my multiple issues. There was no evidence of any disease and I received no diagnosis that could explain my illnesses. Joe began to say with each new ailment, "God, if it's not one thing it's another with you, Colette." He was right. I went from one condition to another. I felt like Alice in Wonderland trying to find her way back from a scary dream! Sheer madness.

We planned a trip to Florida during my illnesses to get a change of scenery and escape from the gloominess of the winter, hoping that my physical condition and mental state would be less eventful. Enjoying spring-like weather, I looked forward to our friends visiting us at our condo. I did escape from yet another and newer medical condition to deal with, however. The numerous specialists I received evaluations from had their own individual theories. They were varied but the one that perhaps made the most sense led me to consider that I was dealing with allergies. My chronic headaches seemed to be leading to an overproduction of mucous. I was going through, on average, a three-ounce can of a saltwater spray solution a day, to release the accumulation from my throbbing sinuses. The expense of these cans was costly so I researched drug web sites and bought them by the dozens to get a break on the price. I was not a doctor, but it seemed to be above the normal range of drainage necessary for allergies.

I was accustomed to dealing with my symptoms, and tried to forget about them during our friends' visit. I was looking forward to our time together and wanted to make the most of the visit. Since they were big fans of golf, we planned an early tee time for the next day. When I woke up that morning, I heard Rob, "Magpie," and Joe in the kitchen and hurried to get up. As I rose from the bed I began to cough. *That damned mucous has collected again and now I will need to clean out my sinuses before we go,* I thought. I felt something lodged in the back of my throat. Grabbing a tissue, expecting the congestion from my sinuses, I was alarmed to see a sizable bright red blood clot. During a several minute interval, the blood continued from my throat. When I finally entered the kitchen where the three were sitting sipping coffee, I announced, "I don't know what's going on, but I am coughing up blood."

Joe was the first to answer, "Well, if it continues, we'll call a doctor after our golf game."

Magpie (my nickname for her) was more alarmed then Joe, "I think you should go to the emergency room, Colette, that doesn't seem right to me." Her eyes were open wide and she looked distressed, so I agreed to her advice. Before I left I took a shower and got dressed to leave. Joe, still not realizing the severity of my situation and used to dealing with my false alarms, was not worried. "I will drop you off at the emergency room and will be back as soon as I get Magpie and Rob to the golf course."

I walked into the emergency room lobby and explained my condition to the triage nurse, who handed me a mask and indicated that I needed to put it on in case my diagnosis turned out to be tuberculosis. *Tuberculosis? What next?* I sat in the waiting room with a white mask that began to take on a red complexion from the blood I continued to cough up. I tried to stifle my coughs, but I could feel the blood gurgling up in the back of my throat. It was time to find a bathroom. One look in the mirror at the blood surrounding my mouth, after coughing up about a ¼ -cup this time, told me I could not wait any longer and headed for the triage nurse again. In an alarmed voice, speaking through my cotton barrier, I explained my worsened condition. I was finally taken seriously and brought into an examining room to face a barrage of tests and questions from numerous doctors and nurses. Hours passed with no diagnosis. Joe was now by my side, as confused as I was about what was transpiring. I was lying on the stretcher, not fully absorbing the gravity of my health until I called one of my close friends in New York.

"Hi, Ellen, I am calling you from the emergency room in Florida."

Ellen, audibly alarmed by my remark asked, "Why, what's wrong, Colette?'

"They think I have a blood clot. I think they call it a pulmonary embolism."

Ellen, her voice trembling, said urgently, "Please have Joe call me...I love you, Colette." The direness of my condition was starting to sink in.

A pulmonologist arrived, perhaps five or six hours later, and confirmed that I had a blood clot in my lung. "We are going to put you on Heparin in an attempt to dissolve it, Mrs. Aliamo." At that point, we were still unaware of how dire my situation was. Joe then asked the doctor, "Is it possible to go home tonight? Because we have out of town guests and tickets to a concert this evening."

"Mr. Aliamo, I don't think you realize the seriousness of your wife's condition; it's a matter of life and death now."

I was told with more clarity that if the medication did not successfully dissolve the clot and began to move or burst, there was a slim chance for me to survive. I was in trouble again.

I spent a week on the Heparin IV and was not allowed to do anything but lie still in my bed. I was being closely monitored for any movement on my part by an alarm that was connected to the front desk nursing station. Joe was beside himself with helplessness. I continued to spit up masses of bright red clots for another couple of hours, and then smaller amounts of brown blood surfaced as the days passed, until it was finally over. I was informed that I would have to be on a blood thinner the rest of my life, and slowly the reality of my medical state began to take me on as a prisoner in fear again. This drug was a double-edged sword—it would save my life but it would also control it.

Did terrible things happen to people when they least expected it? You bet they did, and no one knew that better than I.

A Road Less Traveled

———————◉———————

While dealing and coping with all my health issues, I strived to find ways to better myself and stay active. I enrolled in a women's group that met once a week at the church's community center. "Ruth's Table" was a forum for women of all ages, coming together for a greater understanding of our common spiritual and emotional lives. We explored many arenas. We had guest speakers, took field trips, made our own mandalas, walked labyrinths, and discussed our journeys as modern women.

Kristen, our director, announced that she had made arrangements for a speaker one Monday morning and introduced the guest therapist. The therapist began her presentation by explaining that she specialized in loss. Her patrons could be mourning the loss of anything: a loved one, a dog, a job, or any void in their lives they were trying to cope with. Her assertions were so enlightening and informative; I had to hold myself back when it came time to asking questions. I longed to grab her by the arm and say, "Maybe you and I can talk about my loss." I resigned to ask for her card when she concluded her oration. I immediately went home and told Joe that I had decided to see a therapist who specialized in an area I believed could be beneficial to me. "If you think you can get something out of it, maybe you should," was his reply.

I had gone to therapy a few years before with a Dr. Irving. I realized in retrospect that he was probably not the best therapist for me. I did find the resolve, however, to get help for myself despite my past. I hoped this time my experience would be a better one.

I did find it easy to purge myself during my initial appointments with Dr. Irving. The years of physical and emotional abuse spilled out without reservation. Layer by layer, I released all my thoughts of my family dynamics. After several months of dialogue, Dr. Irving began our session with a question, "How do you feel about inviting your mother?"

"I doubt that she will come," I replied.

"It could prove to be beneficial if she agrees to attend," he retorted. My mother, with great reluctance, came to three sessions. Reviewing the memories of my childhood and the recent years that caused me so much pain would be difficult, but I was longing for a new beginning or at the very least, for some nagging questions to be answered. I hoped seeing the therapist together would be a way to clear the toxic air that had developed between us.

We discussed our relationship during the first two sessions, but in our third—and last session—I was eager to get to the heart of the matter. I began by discussing my childhood and my father's physical abuse. In carefully selected words, I told her that she was the enabler for all the violence and abuse I sustained and fell victim to. Feeling enormous trepidation, I faced my eyes downward during my recollections. Finally, I reluctantly lifted and turned my head toward her. I saw the fire in her eyes, something I had not expected so soon into the conversation. I shifted my position, knowing it was impossible to discuss the subject with delicate dialogue, as it appeared to be ineffective and futile. I decided not to mince words at this time and asked my first direct question, "I need to know...why you didn't you stop the years of my abuse?"

She closed her eyes for a few seconds and let out a deliberate sigh. "What did you expect me to do? Leave your father?"

"Well, Mom, if I was in your shoes, one time would have been enough for me. I wouldn't have allowed my husband to beat my defenseless child."

She retaliated and spit out her defense by trying to diminish the severity of my accusation. "Look, it was only one time."

"*What*? One time?" I responded in disbelief.

Although I didn't feel like it was necessary to chronologically review the many incidents, I briefly ran through some scenarios. Looking down at her lap, with a slight sneer on her tightly pressed together lips, and moving her head slowly back and forth, she asked, "Where was I to go?"

I pressed on. I wanted to make her see she was accountable and a catalyst for my physical abuse. "How about going back to your mother or your sister in France?" I asked. I was no match for my mother; she had an uncanny way of twisting things around in her favor. In the end, you might even question the credibility of your stand when debating an issue with her.

"I couldn't go there. You wouldn't get the care you needed," she answered.

"Well, how about Grandma Penny (my father's great grandmother)? You had a good relationship with her, and I always loved my time there. She had room for us."

She hissed at me with a raised tone in her voice, "You are wrong!"

The dialogue escalated. In an effort to salvage something from our discussion, I tried a new approach. I asked her what her reasoning was behind some hurtful times in my life, and why she would threaten to send me away to a boarding school for "bad" children.

"I wasn't a bad kid. What did I do that was so terrible that you would threaten me with something like that?" I asked.

She was simmering with anger, but waved me off while looking at the wall closest to her. "I longed for you to be tender and nurturing and to see me as a good and successful person, Mom," I pressed on.

"What are you talking about?"

"You want an example?" I asked. No answer.

"I was looking forward to my 26th birthday. I felt like I had already received my best present by getting my new job, even though you didn't share in my happiness. But this was now the morning of my birthday and I was looking for a small gesture from you."

"What are you talking about?" She had a deadly expression on her face now but I continued.

"I was getting ready for work that morning, and making sure Dana was ready to catch his school bus. When I passed through the hall, I saw you loading the washing machine and I stopped to say good morning. Do you remember that?"

She did not answer again but continued to glare back at me.

"You asked me if I lowered the thermostat. I answered yes and told you I was leaving for work."

"And your point is?" she replied with an air of indignation.

"Well, since it was my birthday, I hesitated in the hallway so that you would have a chance to acknowledge it. I came back into the house after I put Dana on the bus, and called out to you that I had forgotten something. If my birthday had possibly slipped your mind, I wanted to give you the opportunity to remember. Do you remember that, Mom? I approached the open door of the laundry room again to make some small talk."

Her jaw tightened but she did not respond.

"I didn't want to have to tell you it was my birthday." I was forever trying to convince her that it was her insensitivity and not what she called my "formality" that was the problem. She wanted me to believe that we were family and didn't need those endearments.

"As I began to head for the garage, I called another, 'Bye' to you. Do you remember what your answer was?" Nothing. "I remember it well, you said, 'On your way home tonight, pick yourself up a birthday cake.'" I could have forgiven her forgetting my birthday but to not acknowledge it was crushing. I felt like a deflated balloon slowly loosing its air.

"Oh, you are too sensitive, Colette," she said dismissively.

"No, Mom, I don't see it that way. I would never dream of treating you that way, and I never have," I replied with irritation.

She knew how to manipulate words and how to defend herself, so my insistence was fruitless. The hour was not up but she was quite ready to leave. I shrugged my shoulders at the therapist.

"I will see you next week Colette, thank you for coming Mrs. Dunne." She wasn't in the mood to acknowledge Dr. Irving either. By the time I arrived at my parents' house to drop her off, she was incensed and reprimanded me for my accusations. She hissed at me like a rattlesnake. Tears ran down my face as I sat behind the wheel of the car, staring straight ahead. "You are not the daughter I knew," was the theme of her tirade that lasted a few minutes more. She was right. I used to try and please her at all costs. Now I had taken on my own defense and it left a bitter taste in her mouth.

"Mom, I was trying to find a way. I need you to understand my feelings."

"You don't need me to understand because I understand very well what you are trying to do." She opened the car door and slammed it shut. I watched her approach the garage door in the rain. I wondered what and how she would describe our meeting to my father and brothers. It was out of my hands now.

There would be no more sessions and Dr. Irving couldn't have been more wrong. He had interjected very little during our last meeting, although he had a lot to say during our session the following week. We reviewed most of the dialogue to extract my feelings from that day. One memory that stands out was his description of my mother. He simply stated, "Your mother is an insufferable narcissist." I wasn't even sure I knew exactly what that meant then, but I knew it wasn't a compliment. Before our meeting was over, however, he indicated that a few days after our appointment, he had received a threatening letter. He offered it to me since it had been sent to him anonymously. As I held the letter that consisted of only a few sentences, I read the typewritten note that accused him of poisoning his daughter with fictional mumbo jumbo. I knew whom it was from. My father was the only person I knew who still used a typewriter. Oh, how I wished I knew what was said between my parents that day. She was so good at distorting things.

My relationship with my mother, at this time, was at best, strained. I had not contacted the new therapist yet, but I had just finished a powerful, well-known self-help book. Throughout the book, I found moving passages that helped me better understand the dynamics between my mother and me. After reading the book, I asked Joe if I could read some passages to him. I knew from his own experiences, witnessing my mother's actions, he would be able to relate.

"Ready for this?" I asked.

"Sure, go ahead."

The focus of this chapter was how passive and dependent offspring can suffer because their parents fail to give them affection and attention during their childhood years.

"What do you think Joe, does this sound like my life?"

"Yeah, I see where you are going," he replied.

"Wait, there's more I want to read to you," I responded with an air of exhilaration.

"There's a chapter that fits my mother to a T. I want you to hear this."

The passage addressed how parents say they care, but on another level they don't demonstrate the care or value of their children. In turn, the children may long to believe the statements are true, but on a deeper level, it doesn't ring true for them because their acts don't equal their words. That struck my very core.

"I get it, babe," Joe commented with a pensive gaze.

"How about this description of a neurotic? It's going to blow your mind."

When I had initially read the sentence, I knew, as surprised as I may have felt, I was the neurotic the author was referring to. Should you look up the word in a dictionary, you will find a definition close to this description: *overanxious, oversensitive, nervous, tense, high-strung, strung-out, paranoid, irrational, overwrought, worked up.* The doctor's description goes a step further explaining the dynamics of neurotics versus character-disordered individuals. *A character-disordered parent treats their child/children with vicious destructiveness and is able to cast away responsibility when in conflict because they never see themselves at fault. As a result, a neurotic child/children take on the responsibility in a relationship and feels he/she is at fault. Neurotics are inclined to torment themselves whereas; the character-disordered make everyone else feel tormented.*

It was such a remarkable parallel to my life. I thought maybe if she heard it from an authority instead of me she would understand. My mind was clouded by my exuberance, but my intention to share was not.

I asked Joe if he would come with me for moral support, and he agreed. Although he was dubious about my success, he replied, "I will back you, hon."

"That's all I want you to do," I answered. I was feeling enthusiastic about my disclosure and there was no turning back. So much damage was already evident in our relationship, what did I have to lose? There was little chance that she would be open-minded. She had always had a streak of defiance, of stubbornness, and she was often unreasonable. Regardless of the outcome, I felt compelled to share my discovery with her.

We arrived at the house. My mother opened the door without a greeting. On a good day she might say, "Oh." We were used to that, and followed her to the kitchen where she took a seat at the table. We, in turn, did the same. My father was downstairs in the basement, but I was sure he knew we had arrived. I had mixed feelings about bringing him into the conversation, but at that point I thought, *Let the chips fall where they may.* After some small talk, I opened the book and spoke to her about my intention of finding a way to approach this newfound theory. I introduced the book to my mother and began to randomly read the key excerpts. I felt comfortable sharing because the theories were someone else's, not mine; I was hoping she would listen. Joe, in a most kindly way, would add a comment or two to support my point, trying to not to make her feel defensive. Her look was grim and her body rigid. In hindsight, I might just as well have pointed a finger at her, I suppose. This was a woman with tunnel vision. I stopped reading and began to give examples to support the passages I had read.

"Listen, Mom—" I began.

"You are kidding," she interrupted with sourness in her tone. Her eyes squinted as she started to give me her take on my viewpoints. "You are ungrateful and misguided," was her angered response.

I heard my father's footsteps coming from the basement stairwell. I knew this could possibly escalate, but I was unstoppable, and prepared to explain my feelings to him in hopes he would align with me. After all, he had every reason to relate to the readings since he had lived with a woman who criticized, cold-shouldered, and controlled him through the duration of their marriage. He had to acknowledge and see the truth in what he was about to hear. It could be disastrous, however, and part of me was well aware of his potential to become violent.

My father entered the kitchen through the living room and leaned back against the bottom cabinets with his feet crossed at the ankles, in a relaxed stance. After we greeted him, he listened to our dialogue, trying to get the gist of the conversation. My mother was displaying intense agitation, more so now that my father had arrived. She slowly turned her head toward him.

"What's this all about?" he questioned her.

My mother sprang into action before I could get a word in. "She is trying to say I am wrong and she thinks we don't care about her."

My father listened to a bit more of my explanation and began to stare at me intensely with his steel blue eyes slowly widening. Taking on a more threatening posture, he stood erect with his feet now firmly planted on the floor. Without a second's hesitation, he went into a fiery rage, yelling on the top of his lungs, "What do you mean we don't care about you?" He turned to the upper cabinet door that was slightly ajar and slammed it shut with the back of his fist, so hard it bounced open again. Then he grabbed a drawer handle, opened it and slammed it shut with such force you could hear the silverware jumping and clinking against each other like chimes in a fierce wind. With each step through the kitchen, he continued to bang his fist on every surface, cursing. Joe attempted to interject, but he lunged toward him and bellowed back. I began to tremble with fear. "Joe, please, don't say anything," I cried, after nudging him to sit back in his seat, positioning my body between them. The last thing I wanted was my father to engage in a fistfight. I would not let Joe become my father's victim. I was used to the victim's role, and there wouldn't be any surprises for me; I didn't want this to happen to Joe. I had traveled down this road. I could endure it, come what may. It would have killed me, though, if he hurt my husband.

Instead, my father stormed out of the room, thundering outraged expletives and slamming the basement door on his way back down to the apartment, where he now lived. My mother was relatively quiet; her face was stoic, as if she was satisfied her deed was done. She had succeeded in her plan to divide and conquer. I quickly grabbed my purse and told Joe, with alarm in my voice, that we were leaving.

Driving home, Joe turned to me and said, "You know, you have told me about your father's temper, but I did not fully understand the impact it must have had on you until today." My body began to react; I was shuddering from head to toe as if in shock. Tears pooled in my eyes. "Why did I think I would accomplish anything?"

Joe grabbed my hand and said, "I know, I know."

"I am a fool," I said through my sobs.

"Why do you say that? You were just trying to make things clearer."

"No, nothing is clearer, nothing is better."

As I gazed out the car window I remembered something else that I had read in the book. *The individuals who have been declared one with a character disorder are close to impossible to work with because they don't see themselves at fault in any situation.*

I did not have a clue growing up, why my life played out the way it did. Despite the fact that I could recall countless events when I felt an emotional void, uncertain about my mother's actions or the lack there of, somewhere in my heart I clung to the idea that there was a kernel of love for me. There had to be. Every mother loves her children, don't they?

****

Early on during my childhood, I would question her directly. "Mom, why don't you ever say you love me?"

"I don't know. That's just me. I show you love in other ways. Didn't I hem that dress for you?"

As a young girl, I accepted her rationale, even though I missed the warm and fuzzy parts. She did take care of my basic needs and daily living. She did make sure I had medical appointments and taught me how to do chores around the house so I could be a responsible person. She did make sure I went to church and had religious instruction. When I was older, she did take me to buy my first bra and taught me about the birds and the bees, despite the fact that I could have gone without that conversation.

My father, on the other hand, was capable of demonstrating loving ways. He wrote me notes that he would slip into my lunch bag or a Valentine card chosen just for me. He bought me wrist corsages for my teen birthdays when I told him, "Every girl is getting one, Dad." Once when I was in grade school, he went to my elementary school fair; I was disappointed I couldn't attend due to an illness. Coming back from the fair he surprised me. He bought scores of 45 rpms of the current music on the radio, so I could play them on my record player. He taught me how to ride a two-wheeled bike and went with me to buy my first car. After religion class, we would head across the street from the church and have egg creams at the luncheonette. On good days, he was a ray of fun in our house: tickling, teasing, and fixing things that were broken. Like his mom, he played music in the house and in the car, and took us to fun places on weekends—a Sunday drive, a stop for a hamburger or hot dog by the shore.

Despite her annoyance, he attempted to demonstrate his loving ways with my mother. I would often witness him stepping up behind my mother, wrapping his arms around her waist and giving her a kiss on the neck, maybe even a little pinch on the butt. With a knee jerk reaction, she would push him away and exclaim in an irritated tone, "Stop!" Undaunted, he would answer in a jovial tone, "What? I just want a kiss!"

One evening when I was about twelve-years-old, my long locks were tangled from swimming. I asked my mother if she could brush my hair out for me. She was seated on the sofa and I snuggled between her legs on the carpeting with my back to her so she had access to my mangled mess. Oh, how I instantly loved that feeling of having my hair brushed. I was totally spellbound. The repeated stroking of the brush through my hair was so hypnotic; I could feel myself nodding off with my eyes open.

From time to time, later on, I would ask her to brush my hair again but she was always busy, though not too busy for her own backrub. My father would offer her not the therapeutic backrubs where one might knead the muscles under the skin, but the light, hair-tickling, skin skimming back rubs that she relished. I could see how much she enjoyed it, so I would volunteer if my father wasn't around. In my young mind, it occurred to me that I was always looking for ways to make her happy, and maybe one good turn deserved another. That didn't happen.

But backrubs were not what I wanted from my mother after that pivotal, explosive afternoon in her kitchen. Truth be told, I didn't know what I wanted that day. Perhaps unconsciously I wanted her to admit to her feelings about me. I aimed to corner her. I probably would have been destroyed if she uttered the words, "I don't love you," but I was in the dance and I wanted it to end. I was allowing her to punish me over and over again for the sins of my existence. A part of me hoped it wasn't true, but a part of me needed to connect the dots. Your mind chooses how you perceive things when love is unrequited; perhaps there are times you are not prepared or emotionally equipped to face the obvious. In my case, perhaps I was ready to deal with the reality. Or perhaps if I had thought more fully about it, I would have backed down from the idea of approaching her.

That night I went to bed with the fierce afternoon scene playing over and over in my head. Before Joe was asleep, I turned on my side and thanked him for trying to help. He cupped his hand around my cheek, kissed my forehead, and replied, "It's okay. I'm sorry you are so disappointed." With my arm stretched across Joe's chest, I stared out through a window that was dimly lit from a streetlight. My body had ceased to tremble, but my mind was struggling to gain a sense of calm. I was more pre-occupied with my father's reaction now. I was always frightened of his wrath, and now I was mentally strained with irrational thoughts. I was envisioning him driving over and banging on our door, enraged and ready to retaliate. I pictured him forcing his way into our house, and perhaps getting into a physical altercation with Joe and me. I thought to myself, "You have to stay awake, Colette. If you hear the car, you need to reach for the phone and call the police immediately. Maybe you will have enough time to stave him off before they arrive." I knew his capability, and I was wired to do whatever I could to protect us. The images ran through my mind over and over with different endings, like a bad dream can often do. He didn't show up and I spent a sleepless night.

The next time I saw my parents, they were at my stepson, Percy's, wedding. I had sent invitations to my parents, both my brothers, and their wives. I had not received a reply from my parents and it was long after the due date. I called the house and my mother answered.

"I just wanted to know if you are going to come to Percy's wedding. It's past the reply date."

She replied with an arrogant tone, "I don't think we can attend, all things considered." I accepted her answer with relief, "Okay if that's how you feel," and hung up the phone.

A few weeks later, as Percy and his new wife, Monica, exited the front of the church, family members followed slowly. Suddenly, I saw my parents. *Why are they here? They had said they weren't coming.* My mind was spinning. As we headed toward the last pew, my father's piercing eyes penetrated me and I felt drained of life. His eyes possessed an all too familiar look of tremendous hostility. Even as an adult woman, he could still leave me paralyzed. I hesitated and stalled to talk to others around me, giving him enough time to leave with my mother.

****

From my perspective now, I have a clearer idea about my motive that day at my parents' house. I simply wanted to be heard. Did I really think there was a chance of salvaging our relationship? Maybe not. I knew it would be a defining moment, however, and I believed I was on the cusp of freeing myself. I believed I did not deserve their horrible treatment of me. My spirit was broken that day, but I was resolute and able to move on.

****

Within a few days after the wedding, I called the new therapist. I knew now the only way I could rid myself of pain was to sever ties with my mother. Most of my efforts to change the constant emotional discord with her only skimmed the surface. I had spent too many years trying to forge a relationship, now I made a conscious decision to break the shackles of my chronic suffering and disappointment. After all, a wound never heals unless you care for it and protect it from more injury.

I wrote a letter to both my brothers and my nephew explaining to them that I was estranging myself from our parents. I put my thoughts on paper, so as not to leave out any of my feelings. I wanted to carefully qualify the reasons for my ultimate decision. Little did I know what would ensue.

Roller Coaster

My mother once revealed to me that she didn't plan any of her children. She never said that she didn't want Benjamin, Barker, or me, but she implied that we were "accidents" and she had accepted her fate.

We called Benjamin, the older brother, Buster. He was a quiet, reserved boy and two years younger than me. Since I was a consummate tomboy, my brother and I played for hours together and rarely fought. The plastic replica of Rin Tin Tin, the painted metal Fort Apache, and Frontier Town were, by far, our favorite toys to play with. We spent hours getting lost in our make-believe stories built around the well-known TV show from the late '50s.

As he got older, his short frame became stocky and broad shouldered. Buster resembled our mother's father; his fair hair and blue eyes could be attributed to either side. He was a good student, played baseball, and loved the Yankees.

Through the years, growing up together, he seemed to be able to stay clear of my father's wrath, and I never witnessed any abuse toward him. Nor did he ever come to my rescue or lend a shoulder to cry on during the times of my abuse. Was he afraid if he aligned with me, he could be next? Or did a part of him think I deserved it? Or was there another reason that I was not privy to? When I was around twelve-years-old, my mother told me that Buster was our father's favorite. I must have looked startled by that remark because she quickly added, "But you are my favorite."

As brothers and sisters go, we had a good, healthy relationship. He was my best man for my first marriage and I was a bridesmaid in his. We spent holidays and family celebrations together, and I adored his son, Chip. When his wife died, suddenly and all too soon, we gathered together as a family to make sure Chip knew he was loved.

Buster attended college in Michigan and was successful in his business career as a marine engineer. Although I would have loved the same opportunity, getting married was the only option for me.

I cannot recall that Buster and I ever had deep discussions about the dynamics of our family. He had been untouched by the climate of our household and my personal experiences, or at least that appeared to be the case. His only contribution to the discord was a snide remark once in a while during a conversation. "Well, I am the favorite," he would say with a muffled chuckle. He was even-tempered for the most part. He could be pushed a bit too far, however, and he would become more than just hot under the collar. Generally, he demonstrated much more self control than our father or younger brother, Barker, ever possessed.

When my mother was about to deliver Barker, her third child, much later in life, her doctor indicated it would most likely be a hard pregnancy. In her last three months, I was in charge of taking care of things, like cleaning the house as best I could, while she was urged to stay in bed. After Barker was born, I was happy to be his big twelve-year-old sister, and I loved taking care of and playing with my "live baby doll." Aptly nicknamed "Shrimp", Barker was born ten years after Buster and twelve years after me, and was an altogether different type of child. He had dark hair and brown eyes, much like the coloring of my mother, but with the slender face and frame more similar to my father as a young man.

When he was fast approaching his teen years, and I left home after my marriage, he would spend time at my house, even more so when my son was born. I have beautiful photos of Shrimp cradling Dana in his arms or beaming over Dana at his first birthday party. Shrimp developed a volatile personality, however, that surfaced as he got older. School was drudgery for him. Because he didn't enjoy going, he ran into trouble—nothing serious but enough to get my parents' attention and their fair share of gray hair. There were some physical scuffles between Shrimp and my father through the years. Only now, my father was taking on a son who fought back. I once heard them above me when I lived downstairs in the basement apartment. Goosebumps raised my hair on end when I heard the furniture falling over, bodies being knocked against walls and the thundering of voices. It was all too close a memory for me. With teeth clenched and fingers clutching the back rung of my kitchen chair, I was frozen in place until it was over.

Several years after this period of time, Shrimp acquired a steady job working as an electrician's assistant, and later getting his license for the trade. We both had our own careers and separate lives now and we spoke or heard from each other less frequently. One day, however, Shrimp called and asked if I could meet him at a restaurant lounge for a drink when he finished work. I agreed, wondering about this unexpected invitation.

We kissed each other hello, sat down on the bar stools and ordered a drink. Initially, it was a cordial conversation, but I knew it was not the reason he wanted to meet. Turning his barstool toward mine, he finally broached his question. "How do you feel about our parents?" He had his share of strife living with our parents, and I knew he wanted me as a sounding board.

"Well, you know I have had lots of issues with them. Why are you asking?"

He looked down at his beer with both hands cupped around the glass and said, "I want to tell you something I know, but you can't share it with anyone."

What in the world could that be, I thought. "What is it?"

He turned to face me now. "Promise you won't say anything?"

"Anything to whom?" I questioned.

"To the family, but most especially, Mom."

"Okay," I answered, delaying some in my reply.

"Do you know that you were born out of wedlock and Mom was pregnant before Dad married her?"

"Whew, well I am relieved, Shrimp. Mom told me about that a few years ago. She said she wanted me to know because she thought I might have gotten sick as a result."

"Sick? What do you mean?"

"She actually believed because Dad contracted a venereal disease during the war, prior to their intimacy, that I contracted polio as a result." I thought her theory was unfounded but never challenged her thinking.

At this point, I was informing my brother more about our family than he was to me. Shrimp and I discovered that we shared much of the same views on the dysfunction in our family; there wasn't anything he shared that I didn't already know.

On some level, I clung to the idea that we had a bond between us, although I was beginning to see that Shrimp had issues with Joe and me. I later came to understand that he had jealousy issues.

It started when I was in my thirties and my Grandma Esther passed away. She was living in Florida for many years, but my father made arrangements for the wake and funeral to be in New York. It was a small ceremony; my immediate family members were her only living relatives, and she had long survived her friends. After her burial, next to my grandfather at a nearby cemetery, the nine of us made the joint decision to have lunch together. When our meal was done, the waitress laid the check on the table, near Shrimp. He picked it up and announced, "Joe should pay for this. He can afford it." It was a telling and jaw-dropping moment, not to mention embarrassing. We were all speechless and we agreed to split the check. Shrimp made his point and was not embarrassed in the least.

Shrimp had a crude way of expressing his sentiments. I was personally saddened by his coarseness during one of his birthday celebrations at his house. Interested in photography then, I was trying my hand at taking nature shots. Looking out from our kitchen window one morning, I noticed our front path was now graced with a row of bright, multicolored zinnias. Watching more carefully, I could see Monarch butterflies playing hopscotch from one flower to the next. On sunny mornings for a few weeks, I would snatch my camera and catch images of these winged beauties perched on the flower stamen, as they hunt for nectar. Playing around with many photos, I was delighted to find an image that was a cut above all the others. The lighting, the balance, the clarity, and the colors took my breath away. Shrimp also enjoyed photography. Since his birthday was coming up, I decided to have the photo enlarged and put into a handsome mat and frame for his special day.

After the birthday meal with Shrimp's friends and family, it was time to open his gifts. He sat several steps up on the stairs in his living room that led to the second floor bedrooms, so everyone could clearly see the opening ceremony. After opening a few gifts, he picked up mine. He opened the card, then unwrapped the gift and turned the frame around toward himself to see the subject matter. He announced to everyone, "If I wanted a photo of a butterfly on a flower, I could have taken it myself." He handed it to his older son standing on a stair above him and said, "Here, Ryan, put this in your room." It was a gut-wrenching moment for me.

That night in the car, it was all Joe and I could talk about.

"Why does he say those things, Joe?" I felt so hurt and embarrassed.

"Because he doesn't have finesse or manners," he answered. The scene echoed experiences with my mother, and I wondered, was I really too formal or sensitive with my family? No, I trusted my gut, and decided this was not how people treated those they respected and cared about.

Ten months had passed since my brother's birthday that February afternoon when I made the decision to estrange myself from my parents. Since neither of my brothers had contacted me after my decision, I sent them letters explaining my position. I wondered about their feelings. I also sent a letter to my nephew, Chip, as I was pretty confident he would understand, but the reactions could go either way with my brothers. I felt ambiguous about their understanding of my

159

situation. Since I had been completely honorable and forthcoming, I hoped they would accept and support my stand. At this point, I was learning to share my honest feelings more openly and go with my intuition about the trauma I had experienced with my parents. If I could not take this next step with my brothers, I knew it would inhibit my efforts to understand my past, and to help heal myself.

After an undue length of time, three separate letters finally arrived. They would prove to be more than what I was prepared to handle in my fragile state of mind. Had I stirred up an emotional quagmire so deep that I would never escape?

Buster's letter was typed and written in a formal manner, his name and address centered as letterhead. His first question was why had I made the decision to send a letter in lieu of communicating by phone. Questions posed followed. Why was he the first addressee, but had received only a copy instead of the original? He went on to discuss, at great length, the etiquette of letter writing. Quite unnecessary and superfluous! He excused himself in advance for any inference of sarcasm, but his letter was full of sarcastic comments. He made a mockery of my attempt to reach him. He denied any recollection of the violent encounters I'd experienced with my father. I was confused. We lived in the same bedroom when we were young, and a short hallway from each other later on. Why would he make such an incredulous statement?

He also questioned why I would suggest he was the fair-haired child of the family. He felt that our treatment was equal. Unfortunately, either his recollection was poor or he chose not to acknowledge the differences. He said he didn't believe in psychologists and felt that mine was the culprit for causing the conflict between my parents and me. He likened them to chiropractors, witch doctors, love doctors, and evangelists, all of whom he did not hold in high regard. In total, the seven-page letter made me feel we were two ships passing in the night. Instead of us being united in understanding, we were more distant than ever.

As for Shrimp, his letter was more painful than I imagined, especially in regards to his feelings for me. He claimed he had never been close to me and questioned my integrity by bluntly stating, "No one is bullshitting you, you are bullshitting yourself," and, "Enough with the shrink stuff." It was hard to digest his hurtful, coarse words. His admission, "Maybe this isn't *Father Knows Best,* but it's the card you and I were dealt. I am playing my hand as best as I can," was very telling. It was an acknowledgement of our family dynamics, and how he chose to deal with them. Lastly he wrote, "Get your shit together." Exactly what I was attempting to do but he failed to see.

Chip's note was more tender and questioning and made me feel badly for including him in the mix. At the time I believed I owed him an explanation; why I needed to separate myself from his grandparents. He too failed to understand my feelings.

In the end, I grieved for the loss of my family, but I felt I had no choice but to estrange myself from them all now. I felt no understanding and support from them, and I was devastated. I had hoped that I would not lose my entire family, but now that ray of hope was extinguished. As my brother, Buster, acerbically put it, "Let's see where you will be when you don't have family and you have all those wonderful friends of yours."

I do have friends, however. I have the kind of friends who hold me up when I fall and are genuinely interested in my welfare. I am fortunate to have them in my life.

One of my closest friends, Margot, was my salvation during those tumultuous years. We became fast friends initially, volunteering for charities together. She was a good listener and unselfish. At times, I felt guilty for burdening her with my woes, but she never made me feel our relationship was one sided. She was genuine— the kind of friend you'd want in your corner. I could tell her all my secrets and insecurities and she never judged me. Not even when I did push the envelope with our friendship.

By this time in my life, I was even more terrified of being alone, if that was possible. Joe, on occasion, planned overnight fishing trips to the continental shelf or to the islands below Florida. Those were some of the longest nights I have ever experienced. My doors and windows were checked to make sure they were secure. The house alarm would be set, my shower over, and the dog walked before dusk to avoid going out in the dark. The same efforts were made to hide behind shades and blinds of my window and lamps lit throughout the house. When I went to bed, my light and TV were on for the entire night, the dog close by, my bedroom door locked. My telephone book and phone were placed strategically on my night table for numbers to call and a flashlight in case the wires to my house were cut. As darkness fell, I would lose control of reality. After endless hours of listening for sounds of a potential intruder, I would fall asleep. Nothing had changed; the fear of being left alone when I was first married was still present in my second marriage.

One night while Joe was away, I awoke around 4am. The heart palpitations began and the fainting sensation kicked in. I felt desperate. The only friend I felt comfortable calling in the middle of the night was Margot. I stared at the phone for a few minutes, thinking how could I take a chance if this was a serious medical sign. The fragility of my life overtook the guilty feeling of waking her up from a deep sleep. I dialed her number with angst and trepidation. She answered and I explained my plight.

"Gus and I will be right there," she answered with little hesitation. I left my bedroom and sat in my den, contemplating what I had just done. I was relieved she was coming, but did my need justify such an act? My symptoms began to subside, probably just knowing she was on her way, but my guilt was increasing. How could I do this to her? Was I crazy? I timed their arrival and opened my garage door so they had access to the den, where I again planted myself on the edge of my sofa. Before long, they knocked at the garage door and entered the room. I was breathing heavily, I was clearly nervous, but it was evident that I did not need emergency care. Gus was quiet and stood in the darkness of the room by the doorway. Margot sat next to me with her arm around my back patting my shoulder and telling me everything would be all right.

"I don't know why this happens, Margot," I said as my voice began to crack. "It scares me to death and I can't help myself."

Margot leaned into me and repeated in a whisper, "It's okay, it's okay." And it was okay because she was there. Not only was she there, as a true and loyal friend, she never made me feel guilty for my unwarranted and irrational act that night.

She continues to be full of grace and kindness. When Joe and I sold our home and had nowhere to go before our new house was finished, she offered not only her home, but also her master bedroom and bath. She insisted she could sleep in a twin bed in her guest room where she remained for four months until our home was ready.

When Joe and I planned trips where we could not take our dog, she volunteered to dog sit for him.

She loves to cook and invites us for dinner often, despite the fact that she is alone now. Gus tragically passed away a number of years ago, after a horrible battle with cancer.

I only hope that I have been half the friend to her as she has been to me. It's been about twenty years now and we remain as close as we have ever been. When she can, she visits us at our winter home, and we share birthdays every year with our mutual friend, Ellen.

So much for my brother's scathing comment about the endurance of friends when you need them. I came to realize that my friendships not only endured, but also helped strengthen my resolve to heal. Friends are priceless gifts and come into our lives for a reason. I have been blessed with friends who are good listeners, patient comforters, generous of self, fun to be with, dependable, genuine gal pals. They give me pep talks when I need them and the backbone to keep myself on track, making life feel worthwhile. I have friends who have dramatically changed my life for the better. In contrast, I have even had friends who taught me our relationship was not what I wanted at all. Some friends encompass many forms of friendship; some define one aspect of being a friend more grandly. These friends have taken me through the highs and lows of my life.

My brother was wrong. I have lived without my brothers and their families for well over two decades and although it would have been wonderful to have them in my life, I chose to follow Oprah Winfrey's advice, "Surround yourself with only people that are going to lift you higher."

Reunited

"It's like getting stung by a bee. You've been there. You know how much it hurts. You try to stay away because you don't want to get stung again. But it happens even though you think you are careful." ~Colette Aliamo

A number of years had past and my estrangement from my parents remained intact. Little did I know that was about to change. Returning from a friend's birthday dinner one evening, Joe announced that my mother had called while I was out. "What? Are you serious?"

"Yes, she called and she wants you to call back."

Why now? It was hard to absorb. I sank into the sofa with great uneasiness, staring at nothing.

"What else did she say?"

"Nothing, that was it," he replied.

I didn't even consider calling her that night. I had a lot to mull over. *What does she want and what would I be prepared to say.*

The next morning, I continued to procrastinate. On one hand, I had waited for this call for a very long time. But on some deeper level, did I really want to hear or be heard now? Maybe more than anything, I did want the opportunity to tell her how disappointed I was. To be specific, why hadn't she called after the September 11th terrorist attack? She knew Dana lived in Manhattan. Wasn't that compelling enough for her to want to know of his welfare, regardless of what transpired between us? What would it have taken for her to show concern, if not for me, at least for her first-born grandson?

Finally, about mid-morning, I took a deep breath and dialed the number. My mother answered and began the conversation. "I thought you'd want to hear from me." As soon as she said that, I suspected her phone call was a result of a meeting I had a few weeks earlier with my nephew, Chip.

To my surprise and delight, Chip had contacted me and agreed to visit so we could talk in person. He had become a man in those passing years since I had last seen him, strong and sizable, on the order of a football lineman. With a few tattoos scattered on his limbs and a shaved head, he might have been mistaken for a menacing biker. I knew Chip well and he couldn't have been further from that assumption. He was a gentle soul, compassionate, sensitive, and by his own accounts, a great grade-school teacher. As we sat on my patio, catching up on the years missed, we shared our feelings about what had gone wrong within our family. I was happy to answer any questions he had that would help clarify my position.

"It bothered me very much that no one thought to call me about Dana," I said. He looked down but didn't offer an explanation.

All in all, we had a amicable dialogue with regard to our family dynamics; I felt like any misunderstandings were now behind us. We promised we would not let anything jeopardize our relationship again. Chip had a long trip home so we hugged and said goodbye. I would see him only three more times after that day; future family conflicts would demand his allegiance.

On the phone with my mother, I repeated the question I had posed to Chip. "I thought it was incredulous that you didn't think to call about your grandson." My mother pretended not to know about Dana living in New York City, even though he was living there long before our estrangement. In days to come, that would be the first of many more dubious statements she would make in order to deviate from the truth. I reluctantly accepted her answer but it was disheartening all the same.

She began to tell me about her medical condition as our call continued. She advised me that she had been dealing with emphysema the past few years, but the latest discovery was inoperable lung cancer. It was stunning news. I could only respond by asking questions about what was to come for her. My mother sounded resolute and strong, and explained the steps that her physicians would be taking. She asked if I would see her. I was reluctant, but at the same time I felt compelled to do the right thing. This could be a dying woman's request. How could I ignore it? Whether the decision was right or wrong to unite again with my parents, I did it with a pure heart.

My first visit was momentous. When my mother answered the door, I was astonished by her frailty. With the passing of numerous years, she had transformed from a relatively vital woman to a feeble, weakened self. She embraced me, saying, "Oh, my daughter. Oh, my daughter." This reunion clearly had all the makings of a good one—an ailing mother and her daughter returning home. It was unfamiliar territory though, and

I felt strangely uncomfortable. Her behavior was so uncharacteristic, I didn't know whether to believe the sincerity of her sentiments or not.

What kind of emotional reserve did I discover in myself when I heard my mother was dying? And what emotion was it really? Was it love? Compassion? Pity? Or the idea that when she was gone, there would be no reconciliation, no second chances.

I felt resigned. Whatever the future would hold, for better or worse, I would be there for her. Not wanting to live with regrets in the days to follow, I did my best to be a kind and dutiful daughter. My heart was in the right place. I hoped that I could apply what I'd learned during my therapy sessions, in order to salvage a relationship with my family.

My brothers were less than thrilled about my return. My mother didn't hesitate to share their sentiments and their chagrin. "They asked me why I would contact you, as they had been there for me, not you," she purposefully added.

"There for you, in what way? You and Dad have so far been quite self-sufficient," I answered. But I understood what she meant: my brothers still called every Sunday and visited on holidays, and I had not.

A few days after the initial meeting with my mother, I stopped by again at her request. Instead of approaching the front door, I tapped in the numbers of the garage door opener. The garage led to the apartment I had lived in years ago. My intention was to see my father, since I had missed seeing him on my first visit.

He had been assigned to the basement apartment because my mother didn't want him living with her any longer. He had settled into the apartment quite well however, and they had made a pact of sorts: a civil separation was implemented as an intercom was installed between the two levels. Now my mother could beckon him at will in the event she had a need or request, such as driving services to medical appointments, the grocery store, and mass on Sundays, in exchange for cooked meals. Cooked meals providing they didn't include anything that was off limits. There were always a handful of items in the kitchen that the rest of the family was forbidden to indulge in. Salmon in a can was hers, the rest of us ate tuna, Sara Lee croissants and coconut cream pie was banned, certain fruits were boycotted, and any cherry crepes she made were primarily for her. There was a strict embargo on the fresh croissants from the lady across town that baked them once a week. Although I'd wondered what those coveted foods taste like, I think the rest of us were satisfied with our ice cream!

My father would be responsible for taking out the garbage, changing screens to storm windows, mowing and raking leaves, and doing all that it takes to maintain and repair a home. Clearly, my mother had the best part of the deal.

After I entered the apartment, we hugged briefly. I took a seat on his sofa as he sat down on his swivel chair in front of his desk. Our meeting was an easy transition—no drama and no discussion about the interim period of our estrangement. He wasn't a man to articulate his private emotions. I knew if I brought it up, he would avoid the dialogue. I wasn't brave enough to engage in conversation about it either because I didn't want to "rock the boat." I never knew how he would interpret a discussion, and I didn't have the strength to choose my words carefully on this day.

Although I thought their arrangement was demeaning and felt angry about it, my father seemed amenable to it. He got to decorate his living space as he wished, including displaying his extensive collection of baseball caps. Hung in a row just below the ceiling line on one wall were hats from sports teams, tourist sites, and promotional advertising images. A decorator's nightmare, but it was an embodiment of his passion as a collector. Not far from his desk that accommodated his computer, business files, movies, CDs, and country and soul cassette tapes, sat a cabinet that housed binders, labeled chronologically, of the assorted coins he had acquired over the years. My mother's father gave him some of the antique coins, dating back to Napoleon's time as well. On his wall above the L-shaped desk hung memorabilia, including a musket, Civil War photos of long lost family members, an aging framed map of Long Island, and assorted favorite clippings.

He had his own kitchen oven now to bake cakes when he wished. He had a sweet tooth and would often bake a cake from a pre-mix box for himself or for someone in our family who was celebrating a birthday. No yelling in this kitchen if he didn't clean it to my mother's standards. (Though he was far from a slob!) In addition, he now had his own bathroom where he could assemble his toiletries without any hassling about keeping things sanitized and uncluttered. His tool bench on the unfinished side of the basement reflected his organized nature. He had built wooden shelves where he kept Mason and baby jars labeled for every kind of screw, nail, nut, and bolt you could imagine. Tools were kept neatly and orderly in his well-worn and shabby-looking storage cabinet. He loved woodworking and made wonderful items, including birdhouses, several of which I still own. There was a place for everything despite the fact that there was a lot of organized clutter. Vacuuming mattresses routinely as well as the inside of shoeboxes, as was my mother's routine, was not his.

In the basement apartment, he no longer had to worry about annoying her and was free to express himself.

We chatted for a while about casual events and experiences. Not for long, however. The intercom buzzed. He answered her call by pushing a button. A pause at first and then, "Okay, I'll tell her." He turned to me with a look of resignation, his shoulders now hugging his neck. "She wants you to go upstairs."

With a half smile, I answered, "Guess if that's what Mom wants, that's what Mom gets. See you later, Dad."

She was sitting in the guest bedroom that was converted into a small den years before. "I wondered what happened to you."

"I just wanted to say hello to dad."

She looked annoyed, as if a gnat was fluttering around her face, and said, "Well, I have things to go over with you that are *important*." She was getting matters in order and had a thin stack of papers on her lap. My parents had many decisions to make, especially about whether they would stay in their home or move to a facility, and it looked like I was to become the facilitator.

Trying to take everything in, I was also aware of my father in the background, heading down the hall toward the den within a few minutes of my departure. He stopped at the door and leaned against the entryway while my mother continued her litany of possible plans. When she took a breather, I turned to him.

"Do you want any tea or something to drink? I am going to make myself some," he asked.

"No, thanks, Dad."

From the couch, my mother looked up and said irritably, "Listen, I want to talk to Colette. You should go downstairs Leon."

He was miffed. Taking a deep breath with his mouth pursed, he turned and left.

I felt sorry for him. I knew what it was like to be devalued. I was very familiar with her dismissive ways. Sometimes I had the strength to ignore her. I should have said, "The hell with it, let's have that cup of tea Dad," but I didn't. She would be disgruntled if I took a stand against her wishes, especially when it involved my father, so I kept silent on this day. I can see now how easily I fell back into the "good daughter" dynamic that I had tried so hard to remove myself from.

With each passing day of being reunited with my mother, I could feel my anxiety bubbling up again. I imagined myself like a simmering pot of hot water starting to spurt over the top. I was back in the mix and feeling a lot of trepidation. She offered no apologies, but I was beyond that now because some things don't change. I had to set aside my needs because she was dying.

Days drifted into weeks and then months. Knowing her diagnosis and the decidedly limited time she had left to live, I found myself attempting to please and help her when I could. I vowed to myself that I would try to forget the past.

****

Six months after my reunion with my parents, I sat on my living room floor with my family while opening stocking stuffers for the holiday. I received a gift from my stepson, Chase, that moved me like no other. He had given me a jar of mirabelle plum jelly. Little did he know that this was my mother's favorite and the very same plums I had picked with my Papa, when I visited him as a child. I stared down at the jar in my hands on my lap, quite speechless.

"What's the matter, Colette?" Chase questioned.

"During the course of my mother's life, I remembered how much she missed and loved this fruit that grew in her homeland," I explained.

"I didn't know that."

"I know, Chase. How could you know? That's what makes it so amazing."

Falling forward to my hands and knees I reached over and gave him a kiss on his cheek and said, "Thank you, Chase, you don't know how much this means to me. I have memories of picking the fruit with my grandfather."

"Well, then, I am very happy I picked it for you," he answered sweetly.

Since my mother was losing her appetite and considerable weight during her treatments, I borrowed Chase's idea and decided I would buy her a jar of this jelly, imported from France. Maybe I could spur on her desire to eat. If this didn't work, nothing would. I scoured kitchen and gourmet stores, hunting for this delicate fruit, and came up empty. Thinking it would be a long shot, I contacted the company online to ask where I could purchase their product. Much to my surprise, within a week, I receive an email from the proprietor himself. He expressed how moved he was by my plea and my mother's plight. He explained it had not been a good season for the mirabelle orchards in their region and they were unable to supply the store chain with enough of the product. He did add, however, that if I gave him my mother's address, he would send her some jars from his private stock, free of charge! He was a man of his word and I was ecstatic to share this wonderful news with my mother. "What a kind man,

Mom. Can you believe he did this?" I asked. She was pleased with his gesture and his personal note sharing his concern and support. She in turn, savored her jars slowly to make them last. As for me, it was just all in a day's work. I knew I was a glutton for punishment, always setting myself up for disappointment and never receiving the reaction I longed for. I could see I was in an emotional ebb and flow, like the fingers of ocean waves stretching upon the sandy shore only to lose its grasp and recede again. Deep inside, I knew I was that little girl asking for an, "I love you." Oh, God, what I would have done for this woman. I would shower her with love if only she would give me a glimmer of hope. My capacity for love is boundless and it could have been hers for the taking.

I was so conflicted that I began to run the gamut of emotions. There were many times my threshold of tolerance was challenged. Countless other times, I felt committed to her as her illness progressed, with little hope of recovery. Still determined to help, I scrambled to find the best path to take. By total happenstance one morning, I caught a program on TV about a clinical trial for a new lung cancer drug. It sounded promising, and I was ready to pursue the possibility.

After some investigation with the pharmaceutical company and locating an oncologist who was authorized to administer the new drug, I urged my mother to make an appointment. Reluctantly, she did so. During her appointment, the physician explained that she was a candidate for the drug but would be placed in a lottery. This wasn't encouraging, but there was a chance that she might be chosen. The drug was on record showing a 40% success rate of isolating the cancer cells to block them from spreading to other organs. Surprisingly, she received a call from the doctor's office within a few weeks, indicating that she was chosen to begin the trial. My father and I were present when she got the news, along with Aunt Cerise, who was visiting during this time. We were ecstatic about this positive turn of events, but my mother's outlook was strangely subdued. Ironic even. Throughout her whole life, she feared everything and was always worried about death. She avoided what she thought were high-risk situations to prevent harm or her demise. She subscribed to a health magazine for years. It became her bible and she followed the medical advice religiously. She had even stopped her lifelong smoking habit about nine years before her cancer diagnosis. Now she was looking at death in the eye, but she didn't seem happy with receiving this second chance. Despite the fact that we were all thrilled for her good fortune, she began to make comments about her medical status, as if she didn't believe it could really help. She continued to complain and never displayed gratitude for the potential gift of life that had been offered to her. Hesitating and reluctant, she finally accepted the medication. I couldn't help thinking about juxtaposition: the countless others wishing they might be eligible for this drug, only to find their hopes being dashed, while my mother was dismissive and unappreciative of her fortuitous position. Her physical health remained stable, but her mental attitude became more and more difficult to handle. She was depressed and had too much time to think of other ways to be saddened. She became more demanding and her needs were endless. She began to depend on me for virtually everything.

My father on the other hand, was showing signs of his own physical illness and was unable to help as much as before. Nothing he was still able to do lived up to her expectations and the climate was becoming caustic.

As I knew all too well, he didn't have the patience of a saint, but I pondered over his resolve to abide by their marriage all those years. I even wondered if it had ever crossed his mind to leave her. I did get an answer, in a roundabout way, a few months later.

After taking my father to a specialist, his physician had him hospitalized to investigate his condition. His diagnosis was bladder cancer. He was a heavy, lifetime smoker and the doctor explained that second to lung cancer, the bladder was most susceptible to cancer from cigarette smoking. This was again a sobering moment for him as well as the family, but his prognosis seemed more favorable. Taking it very seriously, he asked while he was hospitalized, if I could find a lawyer to help straighten out their legal affairs. I researched and found an elder care attorney. After my initial meeting with her, she indicated that she could make arrangements to come to the hospital to go over any necessary documentation. Not being present at their meeting, little did I know my parents decided to make me responsible for their banking and appoint me their Power of Attorney. I did not see that coming at all.

Before long, with this new responsibility, I was visiting their bank on a regular basis. One afternoon, while meeting with one of the banking officers, I learned about a discussion she'd had earlier with my father quite by accident. A few years prior, he inquired as to whether he could financially live separately from his wife. The manager, reviewing his accounts and liquid assets, informed him it would be impossible to do so. I surmised that the basement became his only alternative for solace.

As for my mother's status, she continued her life upstairs on her terms, keeping my father in check. Meanwhile, the clinical trial drug was doing its job—the cancer was not metastasizing. What had looked like a seriously negative prognosis might now be considered a chance of hope and possible survival for her.

My father returned home from the hospital for a short interim before surgery became necessary. That day came very fast. I picked him up very early one autumn morning. The sun was shining brightly, but I couldn't appreciate the dawn, knowing what was to come that day. It was a chilly morning; I couldn't detect if I was shivering from the temperature or from the emotional strain I was feeling. A friendly nurse greeted us and my father took part in some light jovial conversation with her, as he had always done with strangers. He could be quite the charmer. She asked if he would take a seat and fill out the medical forms. During admission, he turned to me and said, "I want you to be my healthcare proxy." (My mother was originally the healthcare proxy for my father.)

"Okay, Dad, if that's what you want."

"I don't want to suffer, so don't let them keep me hanging on."

"You will be fine. You will be fine," I reassured him as well as myself. I signed the necessary paperwork and before long, they called him in to change into a hospital gown. A nurse directed me to an area just outside the operating room to wait for my father's return. About ten minutes later, he was wheeled out on a stretcher. His head was covered with what looked like a shower cap and a sheet covered him from his neck to past his toes. His false teeth were taken out. He looked old and frail, not the brawny man I was so used to seeing. I stood by his side. I couldn't help but think about the days long ago where this scene was reversed. I put my hand against his forehead stroking him lightly with my thumb. He looked resigned, and I rambled on, sharing encouraging words. It was time; I kissed him on the forehead and said in a whisper, "See you in a little bit, Dad." He passed through the doors. I waited with a heavy heart.

It was a long recovery after his surgery and he was not able to go home due to his many medical needs and complications. Initially, when I would visit, he had vivid hallucinations, despite my attempts to bring him back to reality. This was the beginning of my negotiations with the hospital staff for the next six months, on and off, for his many admissions. I was his advocate and I did my job well.

He was finally ready to be dismissed from the hospital and transferred to a rehab facility. He was acting more like himself, but continued to be in tremendous pain. I wasn't happy with the center, however. I called on my medical contacts and asked if they could help me out. Shortly thereafter, he was admitted to the same facility I had worked in for a number of years and given a private room.

Prior to my parents' health decline, I had made arrangements for them to see some alternative living facilities. Keeping the house was becoming more and more difficult. Making numerous appointments, we traveled throughout neighboring towns in search of appropriate and comfortable living quarters. With every facility we visited, my mother had a long list of requirements. So unreasonable at times, I was embarrassed that the directors had to even qualify their accommodations to her. There had to be a separate room for my father, the living quarters had to have an outside view, couldn't be far from the ancillary services, had to be on the first floor (she was terrified of elevators), not too close to the public areas, had to have enough closet space, had to have adequate lighting, adequate staffing, room to fit her own furnishings, certain types of food offered; the list went on and on.

A few months later, with many visits and tours behind us, my parents were still in their home. My father had looked forward to relinquishing his many household responsibilities. As for my mother, nothing was acceptable, even if it meant her husband would have to continue to carry the burden and hardships. She had no room for concern of his failing health, his compromised heart, and the pain in his legs or his persistent headaches. He was hard of hearing now and had a severe case of psoriasis, not to mention something was still amiss even after his bladder surgery. The writing was on the wall and it was just a matter of time.

Seesaw of Emotions

---◉---

A few months after my reunion with my parents, Joe and I left for Florida for the winter. I kept close contact with my parents via email or phone. When we returned, it was apparent to me that my mother had noticeably declined. She was becoming increasingly lethargic and continued to have a loss of appetite.

In August of that year, her physicians informed us that her cancer medication had ceased to be effective. The tests indicated the cancer cells had spread to her lymph nodes. Based on their medical expertise, they believed that she had only weeks, perhaps a few months, to live.

In just five months we would leave for the winter again—something Joe so looked forward to. I panicked at the thought of telling him the news about my mother.

"How can I go to Florida, in good conscience, knowing she might not make it before I return, Joe? She says she needs me. The hospice nurse said that even though her decline was slow, when the cancer overcomes her, it will be very quick."

"Why can't your brothers take care of her?" he asked, almost knowing the answer.

"It's not possible; you know they work," I answered, halfheartedly. "This is the very reason I wanted her to make a decision to settle into a facility, so this wouldn't happen," I said with some irritation.

"I remember that ordeal well. How many places did we see back then? It's your choice, dear. I'm not happy, but I will go along with whatever you want."

I was seeing the new therapist that was recommended to me for a few months now. My confusion about my place in the family and my growing concerns were often discussed. This time I brought up my dilemma regarding the prospects of leaving for Florida. I realized after our discussion that I had once again put my parents' needs before my own or Joe's. Had I not learned my lesson through these years of seeking help to set my boundaries? Apparently, I still had much to learn. The push and pull continued in my mind.

"Were you okay with Joe's answer?" my therapist asked.

"No, not really. I hated to disappoint him, of all people. He loves me more than anyone. Why should he have to be the one disappointed? You know I feel like my mother knew it would come to this."

"Come to what?"

"Well, there is a part of me that thinks she knew all along that I would be the easy mark out of her three children. She knew my personality, she knew my weaknesses.

"What kind of weaknesses?"

"She knew how hard it would be for me to turn my back on her, and if she didn't win me over, she would be stuck with two sons who worked and would be essentially of no help. She is that calculating, you know."

The winter was long for us all that year. My mother was weak and depressed, my father continued to have his own medical issues and Joe was miserable staying home during the long, cold months. As for me, seeing my therapist was my only shred of hope that I could get through this quandary.

Most days, my visits to my parents were pointless, outside of fulfilling her wishes. Trips to the physicians' offices, fetching stamps, buying groceries at the discount store, writing letters of complaint (she had an ongoing list), dropping off my prepared foods, finding items on the web: her videos (more *Little House on the Prairie* seasons), specific body lotions, dental floss, candy, and a horrible charcoal breath freshener that tasted and smelled like a bottle of perfume. If the right brands were not available, purchasing them on the web was the only way I could resolve her inflexibility to compromise.

"How are you getting along?"

"I feel anxious about my decision to be involved at all and I regret that I had to disappoint Joe, even thought he is trying not to complain."

"How are you feeling emotionally about your mother now?"

"I am not proud of my thoughts."

"Can you share them?"

"Well, it's becoming more and more difficult to. I am embarrassed that I have been calculating how many more months my mother might have before she passes away. I am drained and feel exhausted. I cope by numbing myself to her words or actions. I am beginning to feel used. But then, other times I catch myself thinking, *I am only as good as my word, carry on Colette.*

We survived the winter months and another year went slowly by. My mother remained the same medically, much to everyone's surprise. She was on hospice for all intents and purposes but little changed. She had recently been writing letters to her sister in Spain and was on a campaign for her to visit.

Joe and I picked Cerise up at the airport. Anxiously scanning the crowd of people coming off her flight, I was delighted to finally see her coming toward us. She was smiling from ear to ear and so was I. As soon as she passed through the gates, we embraced and almost forgot that Joe was standing nearby. Although our visits together through our lives were few, we always felt a special closeness and made the most of our time together. When I was a young girl, I secretly wished she were my mother instead of my own, even though I believed I loved my mother. She was Auntie Cerise to me, and her visits were long enough for us to savor our endless chats and participate in things mothers and daughters enjoy doing together. We went to girlie girl movies, had lunch with my friends, went shopping (she always appreciated my input on her choices), and attended any and all of the church functions I took part in. I don't know if she really liked going to the fundraisers or volunteering, but I never detected any hesitation. Life felt good when she was around; I gave her my love unconditionally and spoiled her every chance I got.

The year before my mother was diagnosed, Auntie Cerise planned a visit to the U.S. with her son. Besides seeing my mother, her main objective was for her son to make American business contacts for his growing athletic shoe business. In response to their request for help, for a week we drove them wherever he wanted, in an attempt for him to establish a network. One afternoon, I received a phone call from my mother. She had a stern tone to her voice and began the call by saying, "Where is my sister?"

"She is right here. We just got in from visiting a Nike distributor. We were just about to get something to eat. We're all starving."

"Well, I want to talk to her now," she replied, as if she hadn't heard a word I said.

"What's the matter?" I asked.

"Just put her on the phone."

My heart sank as I handed the phone to my aunt. There was a brief discussion in French between them before Cerise hung up the phone.

"She wants me to come to her house," she explained.

"But why is she so upset? She knows we were trying to help John find contacts, right?"

"Yes, but I think your mother is feeling neglected."

My aunt spent the rest of her time at my mother's. I didn't mind that Cerise felt compelled to share time with my mother, but I did mind my mother's response.

The Sunday before my aunt and cousin were leaving, my mother had planned a dinner. She invited my brothers and their respective families, but Joe and I were not invited. Was I being punished for "hogging" her sister? Coincidently, I had called my parents that afternoon to see what they were planning to do, as I knew Auntie Cerise's time was now limited. Hearing several people talking in the background, I questioned my mother, "Who is at the house?"

"Buster and Shrimp and the kids."

"Really? Why?"

"They are here for dinner."

"And you never thought to invite Joe and me?

Although I was not shocked at her display of thoughtlessness, I was surprised by her answer. "I don't know. I just didn't think about it."

"You didn't think about asking us, when my brothers were there? I really can't believe that, Mom." By this time, I could have had spit bullets I was so upset.

When I finally got to say goodbye to my aunt, she remarked about my absence that day. She said that she had asked my mother why I was not at dinner and my mother said, "Oh, she's probably busy, and I don't have enough room, anyway."

"Did you discuss it further with your mother?" my therapist asked on my next visit.

"What's the use? She has one lame excuse after another, and if I challenge her she continues to dig in her heels and justifies her stand. What disturbs me is that in all the years that Joe and I have been together, she has had him to her house to eat once! Can you believe that? She is a bead squeezer."

"A bead squeezer?"

"Yeah, that's what I call her. She says her rosary everyday without fail. But she isn't any more Christian than you are. (My therapist was Jewish.) She is so religious that she tells her own daughter, 'There's no more room at the inn.'"

A few months later, we were again facing the third winter of my mother's cancer survival, but this time I was determined to go to our winter home. I would have to make some kind of arrangements if Joe and I were to spend any time in Florida. A caretaker had to be willing to stay with her twenty-four hours a day. That was a tall order in itself, handling such a dependent woman. The choices would be slim, I suspected.

Before we planned to leave, we conducted a number of interviews and scheduled trial runs with several women who resided in a predominately Polish community. Before we left, my mother had dismissed one woman and was working on the inadequacies of the second. She would have to make do, I thought, as this woman seemed very capable.

We managed to leave for Florida, but my mind did not. Bracing for troubled waters, I called my parents regularly from my condo. I had to admit, hiring caretakers who had little command of the English language could be trying, but that appeared to be only one of many strikes against them in my mother's book. They did nothing right according to her. They didn't know how to cook the things she liked, they used the dryer too much, they never bought the right product at the store, and they were terrible drivers when she had to go for a medical appointment. I sat with the phone to my ear and my eyes closed, allowing her to voice the litany of hardships she was dealing with. If I could get a word in, I would offer some alternative measures, none of which were acceptable or even heard, I suspect.

"When are you coming home again?" she then would ask.

"I told you Mom, early April. It's not that far away. Joe would like to stay longer but I told him we couldn't."

"I know but this is just not working out. I need to find someone else," she replied.

"When I get back, I will look into it."

"I don't think I can wait. It's just not working out."

We returned home and to my surprise she had found yet another caretaker. Lena, like the others, spoke little English, but she and my mother found a way to communicate. There was an 8½-by-11-inch, lined sheet of paper hanging from the refrigerator by a magnet, with two rows of words. The left row had words written in English, the right in Polish. Apparently, there was a lot of pointing going on to communicate between them.

On my first visit, Lena was sitting at the kitchen with an American/Polish dictionary in her hands. She had a kind smile and shook my hand. Then she pointed toward my mother's bedroom. I walked in and found my mother lying in bed; I greeted her with a kiss on the cheek.

"How are you doing? I see you have a new girl."

"Yes, she is okay, but she doesn't speak enough English."

"She seems nice. Give her a chance, Mom."

After my return, my aunt visited once more during my mother's illness for a few months. At this time, my father was failing and had to be admitted to the nursing home. Lena was living downstairs in his apartment. During Auntie Cerise's stay, I confided in her about my going to therapy. I told her that I was upset. No matter how much I tried, my mother never appreciated my efforts. My aunt, putting her hands on my shoulders and looking me straight in the eye said, "Sit down Colette, I want to tell you something." As I sat at my kitchen table, she said, "I understand how you feel and do you know why?"

"Because you have seen her in action?"

"Yes, but more than that," she added. "Do you know when your mother and I were growing up, she was the favorite with my mother?"

"No," I answered.

"Well she was, and I tried very hard to make my mother see me in the same light as my sister."

Tears welled up in my eyes; I knew that feeling all too well.

She elaborated on her statement by saying when she and her sister were growing up in France, despite my mother's thoughtlessness, inflexibility, and rigid ways, she continued to be the favorite.

"But why was she like that?" I asked.

"I don't have that answer for you. Your mother could do nothing wrong in my mother's eyes, though. I do know after the war something died inside of your mother. She had no joy. I do understand how hard it is for you."

I didn't really know my grandmother, since my times with her were limited and we didn't speak enough of the same language. I could never have guessed the dynamics of their family before that day, but being told this, I now saw the strong parallel.

"So after hearing what your aunt shared with you how do you feel?"

"I feel like I have an even more significant bond with her. I have someone who understands me and that means so much."

"Did you ever consider that your mother might be mentally ill?"

"Mentally ill? No, I don't see her that way at all. I think she is manipulative and calculating and knows exactly what she is doing. She is smart, like a fox."

That therapy session made me more connected to Auntie Cerise. On the other hand, Lena didn't know what her place was, since my aunt's intention on this visit was to help my mother. Cerise worked tirelessly during her stay. If you ever want someone to do your spring or fall cleaning, my aunt is the person to call. I would often arrive at the house to find her in a sweat, her hair disheveled and her face reddened from working so hard. To add insult to injury, my parents had window air-conditioning units, but my mother's room was the only one on during the summer months. Her reasoning was to save money. I, for one, couldn't stand to see my aunt in this state, however. To give her a break, I would often ask if she wanted to come to my house for lunch, and she readily accepted.

I picked her up a few days later, after returning from my session with the therapist. She asked me how my meetings were going as we sat at my kitchen table. I shared some of my discussions. "He thinks that perhaps my mother is mentally ill, but I need time to digest that a bit longer." My aunt's response was shocking "Oh, no she is not!" she replied in a hostile tone.

"But, Auntie Cerise, you know yourself how she can be? How do you explain her actions then?" She wasn't even listening to me at this point. She took great umbrage with my remark.

"What' s wrong, Auntie Cerise?"

"What kind of doctor is this man?"

"A good one, he has helped me through so many difficulties."

She spoke not another word about it. Gathering herself, she grabbed her bag and asked me to take her back to my mother's house immediately.

"Can't we talk about this? I made lunch for us."

"No, I can't eat now, I am too upset."

"I don't understand why you are so upset!"

"My sister is not mentally ill."

"No, wait, let me explain," I retorted.

It was too late.

I kept thinking that although she spoke English quite well, she must have interpreted my remark as if I was saying my mother was crazy. Innuendos between languages are easy to misunderstand, but I was still stunned at her reaction. I had never seen this side of her and didn't know what to make of it. I tried several times to qualify the exchange my therapist and I had, but it continued to anger her. Driving the short ride back to my mother's house, I was unraveled by her ranting and cutting remarks, claiming that I didn't know what I was talking about. Turning the corner to my parents' street, I began to sob uncontrollably. This couldn't be happening! This was the aunt I loved, the one who I wrote and poured my heart out to almost every month for many years.

In my next appointment with my therapist, I rehashed the scene and my aunt's reaction.

"How does it make you feel? Do you have any idea why she would have that reaction?"

"I'm still in shock, doctor. I don't even know why your comment upset her so much. You would think she would be more upset if I said that you suggested my mother had an evil streak in her. This is the aunt that I took away with me every chance I got. Joe and I spoiled her whenever we could."

"Why did you feel compelled to spoil her?"

"Cerise lost her husband to cancer early in their marriage. Her son moved away to pursue opportunities for a better career out of the country, and she was left alone. My heart broke for her; whenever we got a chance, we would take her on trips with us. We took her to Florida twice, once I took her to Disney World without Joe. On other occasions, Joe and I set out to show her some of the beautiful and historic cities of America. She got to see the sites of Savannah, Charleston, Williamsburg, Washington D.C., and Boston, and we never let her pay for a thing. We delighted in indulging her. But now she has turned her back on me as if a switch was flipped; she left the car and never looked back. She has left me inconsolable."

"What do you plan to do, if anything?"

"I doubt that I will address anything with her. I am in no condition to challenge her. It was like I was dealing with my mother. I can't believe this is the same woman I cherished all these years." Tears began to surface. My therapist sat quietly and handed me a box of tissues.

"You know, my son asked me if everyone could be wrong and I could always be right."

"Everyone?"

"Yes, he was talking about my parents, my brothers, Keira and now my aunt."

"What did you say?"

"I don't know. Maybe it is me. I am always trying to do the right thing, but I've been told I am a perfectionist and I am too sensitive. Does that make me a bad person?"

Blowing my nose, tears streaming down my face faster than I could wipe them, I continued having trouble regaining my composure.

"I think you have been through a lot, Colette."

Before he had a chance to say more I added, "I mean if someone comes to my door and my house is messy, I freak. I guess that does make me a perfectionist, right? Or if I am working on a project, I want it to be the best it can be because I want everyone to admire it. So does that make me wrong?"

"You aren't wrong, but I think you need to narrow your choices of who you need to impress. Who is that person at your door? Is he or she significant in your life?"

"No, but I can't stand the idea of someone disapproving of me. It's funny; Joe sees the goals I set for myself so differently. He calls me his 'French cleaning lady' and I guess I am. I have a level of cleanliness I have to live by, or anxiety sets in just looking at the house. I guess I got that from my mother. I wish I was more like Joe."

"What makes you say that?"

"Well, he isn't concerned if there are snack dishes in the sink from the night before. And his closet? You would think it belonged to a kid! I am not like that at all. He doesn't even care if he wears the same outfit three times in a row. Look at me today—I have to make sure my outfit matches and my hair and makeup is tended to. I could never show up here without doing that."

"So you appreciate that he is carefree and doesn't worry about what others think?"

"I guess so. I would be a lot less stressed, that's for sure. Last night I tossed and turned the whole night from tremendous stress."

"Was there any reason you were so restless?"

"Yes, I was worried sick about my best friend's husband. He is in the hospital and no matter how hard they try, it looks like the cancer is consuming him. It's just so frustrating and upsetting that there is nothing they can do."

"Let me ask you something. After spending the whole night thinking about him and your friend, did anything change this morning?"

"Well, no, I guess not."

"I am not saying that you don't have the right to be upset, but there are times you aren't going to be able to control what is happening or what others think of your actions."

"I guess what you're saying is that I have to let things go more, like that verse, 'It is what it is,' and try to be more selective about whose opinions count."

"Yes, I am not saying that you shouldn't have any feelings, but you need to realize you can't control everything in your life.

"I get it." Perhaps.

The Beginning of the End

For a while, after his bladder surgery, my father seemed to be holding his own. Despite the fact that I believed he felt guilty about leaving my mother alone at home while he was at the nursing facility, he thrived. Because of my history working as an Admitting Director for many years, I was able to secure a private room on the first floor, not far from the lobby and elevator. It was an enviable bedroom in this sizable facility. I set him up with his own bed linens, got him a new TV that was compatible with his VCR, and adorned his room with framed photos that had meaning for him.

He didn't spend much time there during the day. His health was compromised but he made the most of his time. In the brief time he was there, he became the "mayor" of the nursing residence. He had found freedom. Freedom to do and say what he wanted, without fear of reprimand. He found things he was interested in doing. Who knew that he liked making crafty things? I was taken by his gesture to give only me his creative endeavors. He played bingo and other organized games, he went to the piano concerts in the lobby, he attended weekday mass, and most importantly, he made friends. The women were smitten with him and the men wanted to be in his company. The staff enjoyed his silly jokes that my mother so disliked. Oftentimes on my visits, armed with an ice cream treat, I would have to scour the facility to find what event he was attending. Most people would consider living in a medical facility something they would dread. I felt I gave my father a gift during the last year of his life.

Unfortunately, his health began to take a turn for the worse. A few weeks before we were returning from Florida, I spoke to a close friend of my father's. Jim was a hospital chaplain as well as a veteran of WWII; he and my Dad met at the Veterans of Foreign War's local group a number of years ago. He recently visited my father at the nursing home while I was in Florida and told me that he had some concerns. My father was failing, often in and out of the hospital, but what concerned Jim most was what he discovered in the course of their conversation one afternoon. He explained that they had a bad snowstorm and my parents' car had a flat tire. My mother called my father to say that he needed to come home to fix it, so she and Lena would have transportation. Joe said that my father was in no condition to do anything of the sort, yet he got a ride to his house and sat on the frigid, icy ground to change the tire. Jim was disturbed by this incident and wanted me to be informed. I thanked him for letting me know. Preoccupied with thoughts of my father's actions, I gave him a call the next day. I didn't bring up the incident but told him that I would be returning very soon. Suddenly, my father began to have difficulty speaking. His words were jumbled and he made no sense.

"Dad, are you okay?" I asked.

More slurring and fractured sentences. I knew what it was from my own experience.

"Oh my God, I am going to hang up and call the nurse. I'll get someone for you, hang on."

The nurses attended to him right away and contacted me to say he had been sent to the emergency room. Since Joe and I drove to Florida that year, we began to pack up our things to drive home.

I was on my way to the hospital on the day we arrived home. Walking into his room, I found him lying on his side and awake. I quietly walked up to the bed and he turned to me. He now spoke clearly but his words were chilling. Tears began to run down his face, something I had almost never witnessed—once, long ago, when his father died and once when I was a young girl kneeling before him begging that he not leave my mother that Christmas Eve. In a soft tone he said, "The doctor told me I was dying. I'm not crying for myself but for what will happen to your mother when I am gone." I didn't believe all of his explanation, but I reassured him that there were people to take care of her.

"We are just going to think about you, Dad. I am home now so I will see that you get the best care."

My brother, Buster, arrived during one of my visits to see my father. I hadn't seen him in years. We sat across from one another staring at our father, witnessing his tremendous, unforgiving physical distress. Buster turned to me after a few minutes and asked, "Are we ever going to speak again?" I got up from my chair and embraced him. Before long he was sharing his own distress about our mother.

"She is making me such a ball of nerves. Now I have a hive-like condition around my neck and chest."

"How would you like to deal with her day in and day out? Now you know why I stayed away all those years," I replied.

He didn't reply.

I wasn't sure if my father heard our conversation, but weeks later after his death, I tried to imagine that he did because of "our connection" that afternoon. His bedside rails were up as Buster and I spoke. In his utter anguish, he threaded his bruised and raw arm through the bars that were connected to IV lines and reached for my hand. I gave him my hand in return, and he squeezed it. I held on to him tightly for some time, staring at his weary face. Was he trying to tell me that he was sorry and understood how fatigued I was and how frustrating my life was? If it was what I embraced as a truth, I trusted it would ultimately sustain me after he was gone.

The anguish of my father's pain was so great that his physician told me it was time to make some decisions. I was his medical proxy and the weight of decision-making was enormous. Trying to get the best healthcare possible for my father and trying to meet my mother's emotional and physical needs were staggering, leaving me to feel unsure about which way to turn. That evening in the hospital, I turned to my brothers. From the empty waiting room, I called them individually to share the information from my father's doctor. He did not want to have any extenuating care given, but could I follow through on his wishes now? Because they had been so critical of me returning to the family, I didn't want the job of deciding my father's fate on my own. The conversations were remote and cold. Facts were discussed and neither brother would consider taking part in the process or come to the hospital to witness my father's state. I was on my own, and I left that evening feeling like I had abandoned my father.

The following morning, I returned to the hospital and was greeted by a hospice nurse. She asked if she could speak to me and led me to a private lounge area. I doubt that she asked me more than a few questions about my father when I suddenly broke down. I couldn't possibly explain all the mixed feelings and the dysfunctional state of my family at this time, but it didn't seem to matter. She was kind and gentle, and was the one who would lead me to closure. She urged me to go to my father's room and speak to him. Despite the fact that he was semi-comatose now, she suggested that I take the opportunity. "The last thing a dying person loses is their sense of hearing so say what's on your mind," she explained, while giving me a light hug.

Joe led me down the corridor toward my father's room and whispered that he would stay in the hall to wait for me.

As I approached his bed, I noticed how frail this giant of a man had become. I studied his drawn and pale face, wires and tubing attached to his limbs and nose. I only saw the father who needed me these last few years. I still wanted time to talk and share thoughts, misunderstandings, and feelings. If only he could stay a while longer, but it was too late now. He was drifting away quickly before my eyes. That morning, my heart softened, I began to share with him some poignant memories I cherished. Not necessarily the momentous times, but the small events that filled me with emotion.

I leaned toward his ear and began to share my memories that easily came flooding out. The first thing that I told him was that he was a good father. My heart did not embrace that statement, but I thought of it as an unselfish gift to him. I didn't want him to leave this world without peace. I began to hum quietly to him an old tune that Bing Crosby sang back in the '50's,

"I'll be seeing you in all the old familiar places, that this heart embraces all day through..."

"I know how much you and Johnny Carson loved that song, Dad." Knowing that my words would be the very last thing he would hear in this world, I was seeing my father in all the old familiar places, hoping he was capable of connecting to my voice.

"I've been working on the railroad, all the live long day, I've been working on the railroad just to pass the time away..." was another tune that came to mind. My father, his father and his grandfather worked for the railroad. Three generations of my family and my own connection to trains had started many years ago, and I hoped he would remember one of my fondest memories.

"It was just before Christmas, Dad, and you had to work, remember?"

My mother, Buster and I had arrived at the station loaded with boxes of holiday strands of multi colored lights and decorations, left over from the house. The train station office had a desk centered on a three-sided bay window that looked out on to the platform and the tracks. Sharing the task, little by little, we transformed the window into a niche of festivity: primary colored lights, clear icicle ornaments, tinsel, and sprays of garland framed his view. Then, like something out of a storybook, it began to snow! Not the blizzard kind of flakes, but the heavy crystal-shaped stars of a soft winter's fall.

"Look Dad, it's snowing," I cried. "Can I go outside to see?"

"Okay, put your coat on," he answered.

The window looked just as I had hoped it would. My father was sitting in the center of a picture perfect Christmas card! He spent his nights working in that office alone, and it warmed my heart to know that he would be surrounded by the soft glow of the lights, lovingly decorated for him.

I would have been remiss if I didn't also recall our trip to Rockefeller Center long ago. There are still black-and-white photos that my father took of me in front of the gaily decorated promenade. I was donned in a white, rabbit-haired bonnet. It covered my head and ears, except for my bangs, and it tied under my chin with a grosgrain ribbon. The best part of my ensemble was the matching white rabbit muff. It had a small, three-dimensional, plastic, colored head of a girl's face attached to the front. With my hands coupled inside, I proudly displayed it in my photo.

"Can we see the tree now, Dad?"

"Sure, Colette, but after we have to catch the train home. Mom will be wondering where we are."

After seeing the enormous tree standing tall in its holiday splendor, we headed back for the train station. I didn't want the day to end but I began to get sleepy.

"Do you remember that, Dad? I rested my head against your shoulder and didn't wake up till we arrived home."

The Christmas season was always my favorite time of year and he was a prominent part. My favorite story of my father was on the day I was born. I fondly remember the tale of his plight to be there for my birth, a week before Christmas.

"Do you remember the blistering winter snowstorm that night, Dad?"

His poor excuse for a car had failed to run in such inclement weather. Afraid to miss the birth of his first child, he began the four-mile pilgrimage to the hospital. The sky was darkening and snow began to accumulate quickly with each step. Finally, he reached the hospital and crossed the tiled lobby floor to the receptionist, leaving drops of melted snow behind him from his encrusted shoes. Seeing how snow-laden he was, she asked if he would like to leave his hat to dry on the radiator.

"Remember how you chuckled and said how taken you were by her request?"

In his attempt not to laugh he couldn't hide his lips that began to curl up a bit. Oh, how he loved her surprise when he bent over and brushed off the layers of snow that accumulated on top of his uncovered head.

For fear his attempt to arrive on time was in vain, he asked, "Is the baby here yet?"

"Let me check the labor room for you...no, it's not too late, Mr. Dunne."

"I savored every word of that story, Dad." It still has a place dear to my heart.

"Remember, as I got older, the corsages you always bought for me on my birthdays? You made me feel special, Dad. I especially loved the one with the sugar cubes mixed in between the flowers; I would have died if you hadn't bought me that one. That was my sweet sixteen."

He introduced me to music and we both loved to dance. He taught me how to Lindy, and from there, I danced away my life. We both loved ice cream and he made the best banana splits on earth. He could be so nurturing and gently supportive. Yet he could be so punishing with a rage that would leave me quaking. I can't forget the abuse, but I did embrace the poignant, sweet memories and the "what ifs" in those moments.

It was time to leave him now.

At home that night, I was not feeling well and went to sleep early. The phone rang and Joe woke me. The end had come.

Despite my personal loss, my duties continued, and now I was faced with meeting the funeral director. Barker was there. No greetings were exchanged as we sat down in the director's office. Decisions were made with little eye contact, as I acquiesced to Barker's demands. He was very headstrong and accepted his position with fervor.

The second day of the viewing, my illness had become more than I could ignore. I was able to get an appointment with the doctor in between the funeral parlor hours, only to find out I had walking pneumonia. I should have been in bed, but bailing was not an option now.

The morning of my father's burial, I found that my brother had made arrangements for the family to have limousines to the cemetery. I was informed no arrangement was made to accommodate Joe, my son, and me. Even in this time of sadness, I was reading my brother's sentiments loud and clear, but not really understanding why.

A small reception was planned at my mother's house after we laid my father to rest. The opportunity presented itself for me to speak with my brother, Buster, alone. "What in God's name is going on, Buster? Why have you two been carrying this torch with me? I just don't get it." He stammered a bit and before he could answer, Barker walked into the room. He was clearly angry by the scowl on his face. "I was just about to ask Buster why you two..."

"Don't give me that. We know the things you said about our father and then you act all upset now that he is gone."

"What are you talking about, Shrimp?" I asked in disbelief.

"Oh don't tell me you don't know!"

Buster said nothing.

"I really don't," I answered.

"Mom told us when you two went to therapy that you called him a monster. She was so upset after that."

"Wait, that's not true; she is twisting things around!" I said, defending myself.

It was too late; he stormed out of the room. I turned to Buster and he mumbled something and left the room—a trait inherited from my mother. I realized then she had used our therapy session to her advantage. Using lies, she had united them with her. For those five years of estrangement, she had convinced my father and brothers that she was the victim.

Lena, my mother's companion, entered the room a few minutes later as I was trying to gather my thoughts and compose myself for the guests still in the living room. I was clinging to the vision of my dad, his hand holding mine in his last days. Maybe he was trying to tell me that he didn't believe the ugly lies woven into the minds of my family by my mother. I only have that shred of hope to cling to now.

Lena was very sympathetic and held my hand as I smiled through my tears. "I don't know if I should tell you this now, Colette," she said.

"What is it?"

"Your sister-in-law and your brother, Barker, went down to your parents' apartment. They were going through your father's belongings and found what they wanted under the stairwell."

"Do you know what it was?" I asked.

"Yes, they took your father's coin collection. I am sorry."

"Thank you, Lena. I appreciate your support and kindness."

I went home that day and went straight to bed, collapsing physically and mentally from the rise and fall of my life. In the days that lay ahead, I would need to gain strength again, as new confrontations would surely arise.

Changing Tides

---•◉•---

My mother was growing more restless and delusional after my father's passing. She talked often about the love they shared, how she missed him more with each passing day. She justified their heated arguments and highly charged, near violent fights as, "Just something we did."

In addition, she began to express her feelings about not wanting to live in her home any longer. Her number one priority now was to find an alternative residence. I knew what to expect from my previous experiences with her. She was restless and decided that the arrangement with Lena and I was not enough—it didn't suit her needs. She had asked me if she could move into my home several times during this period. As much as my better judgment told me it would be a hardship, I agreed, providing Lena came with her.

"Why does Lena have to come?" she asked.

"Because I am not capable of helping you, Mom. You know I have my own physical limitations. What if you fell while I was trying to help you in the tub? Now that the kids are gone, we have two empty bedrooms so that is the best I can offer."

"No, I don't want her to come. The living quarters would be too close for me."

"If Joe and I are willing to accommodate you, you need to be willing to compromise. If you can wait a bit more in your home, we will have more room for you and Lena when we move to our new house."

"I don't know if I can wait."

"Mom, you are safe and you have chosen to live in your home in lieu of other opportunities, so please be a little patient. Our new house is almost finished."

"I don't know. I can't stand being here anymore."

That was the end of that option in her mind. The idea of an adult home became her new focus.

Visiting alternative assistance homes in pursuit of perfection was an unattainable goal with her continued standards and unrealistic requirements. In an effort to appease her however, I searched local adult homes to find a supervised environment that might be acceptable. My mother again found fault with them all. With every appointment and visit, my ongoing headaches and other health issues prevailed, and my level of frustration escalated. She finally resigned herself to a home that I personally was not all that taken with. She insisted that as long as she could have a private phone and see the lake across the street from her private room on the first floor, she would be happy. As I anticipated, I received a call from her before the end of the first day. She already had her list of grievances to share.

"Mom, you need to give the place a chance. People that live there will get to know you and then you'll make friends."

"No, they are not nice and the staff isn't very good either."

"You just got there, Mom. Give them a chance to get to know you and I am sure they will work with you."

"I can't eat that food either. The lunch was awful."

"Okay, if you want, I can bring you some food you can keep in your room. I'll bring you peanut M&Ms and some fruit."

"Look, I just can't stay here. It's not for me!"

"Please have patience, Mom."

I had to pull all the "strings" I could to expedite this move; she would have to stick it out now. Her stay was more temporary than I could have dreamed, however. Within 24 hours, Shrimp moved her out and back to her home with Lena in place. Trying to pick up the pieces of her decision, I was obliged to make an embarrassing appeal to the director for a refund of the pre paid three-month deposit, as well as diplomatically soften the blow of my mother's radical reaction.

At home again, nothing changed for her. Being chronically ill and in bed most of the time, days drifted into the following days. When I would go to check on her, more often than not she would ask, "What day is it? I am all mixed up."

"It's Sunday, Mom—the day I take you to my home for dinner." I sat aside Sundays for my parents' visit. It was a way to break up the monotony of their lives. When my father was still living in the nursing home, Joe would pick him up, along with his wheelchair, so he could spend several hours at our dinner table. They enjoyed my spaghetti sauce and meatballs or my roasts, so I never departed from those two menus.

Now that my mother was alone during her visits, I would often try to invite one of my widowed friends so she had someone to speak to other than me. Joe made himself scarce, leaving after dinner for the garden or a TV sports show.

With my father gone, she was much more elusive during our one-on-one conversations, and I felt a sense of mistrust and hesitation with her. I couldn't put my finger on it but I began to ponder on the fragility of our relationship. If she didn't depend on me for most of her needs, would she have ignored me as she did during those years of estrangement? Would she lose respect for me and treat me like she treated my father? I vacillated with my emotions. There were times I tried to have compassion for her and reminded myself how difficult it must be to be ill for so long with little hope of recovery.

"If only I could go back to my homeland, I would be happy," she once mentioned.

"Mom, you aren't well enough to go anywhere, much less France."

"Yes, but I miss it so, I miss my French friends. If only I could speak to them. I used to have French friends here, oh how I miss speaking to someone from my homeland."

"You do receive letters from them, don't you?"

"Yes, but it's not like having a conversation with them on a regular basis."

I thought about what she had expressed for a number of days. At that time, the internet offered chat rooms that I dabbled in from time to time. Sitting at my computer one evening, it suddenly dawned on me. If they had chat rooms for just about any subject, perhaps they had one for French-speaking people. I wasn't successful with the chat rooms but I did connect with a pen pal site of sorts. I scanned the list of comments when I came upon a post about French war brides. My French was rusty but I was able to make out a statement from a lady who lived in Florida, looking for someone to communicate with. Through our online conversation, I was convinced that this just might be the woman my mother would enjoy speaking to on a daily basis. By sheer coincidence, this lady's name was the same as my mother's. And even more astonishing, her husband's name was the same as my father! In any event, I thought this was a match made in heaven. I was so excited with my success; I rushed to my mother's house to give her the good news.

"Mom, you will never guess what I found! I was on the computer and there is a lady a bit older than you who is a French war bride, and she wants to become friends. Can you believe it?"

"Where is she, here in New York?"

"No, she lives in Florida, but she is anxious to chat with you on the computer."

"On the computer? Oh no, I can't do that!" she replied with alarm.

"What do you mean? I will teach you. It's not that hard. I will spend time with you until you feel comfortable to do it on your own."

"No, that's no good, I wanted to meet someone local, someone who could visit and keep me company here."

"But this is the next best thing, don't you see? She has the same past as you and she is lonely like you are. If she can use the computer, you can too."

"No, no, no."

"Wait, you won't even try?"

"No, I am too tired to learn something."

These were the times that I lost my patience. She took the wind out of my sails and squashed my efforts inside of a minute, not to mention how Julliette felt when I told her my mother wasn't interested enough to learn. I felt so bad for this lady that I began to communicate with her as a result. We have been emailing for ten years now.

My mother was vindictive toward the end of her life. It's a strong statement to make but one I believe is true.

"When they read the will, they will be surprised," she told me one day.

"Surprised by what?"

"Oh, I added a statement to my will."

"When did you do that? When you called the attorney without my knowing?"

"Yes," she said with a smirk.

I had no idea initially that this transpired. She made arrangements for the elder care attorney to come to her house to change the will that she and my father agreed upon before his death. I wouldn't have known it at all except for the fact that I received a bill from the lawyer stating that she owed $500. The distribution equation was changed. Instead of her three children equally receiving her estate, she now included her sister in Spain. It was a jolting blow to find she did it in such a manner and my gut was telling me why her sister was added. On many occasions during her illness, she would share her guilt about her sister to me. Auntie Cerise was the sibling that primarily took care of my grandparents. She was the one who often jumped on a plane to France to help them in their aging years and managed all their legal matters. When my mother was asked to visit her parents, she always made excuses why she couldn't, including not being able to fly. Even when Cerise's husband was dying of cancer and asked to see her once more, my mother refused to go. Heartbreaking for my uncle, I am sure. In the end, when my grandmother died, she did not attend the funeral, and when my grandfather needed care, my aunt took him in to live with her.

It was in fact her Last Will and Testament now. She would choose to ignore my father's wishes to satisfy her own means. Despite my mother's bold move, she could not see the forest through the trees when I pointed out a major flaw in the will's allocation. My mother had great disdain for her nephew, John. She felt that he was thoughtless with my Auntie Cerise on many levels through the years. For this, I tried to reason with her. "Mom do you realize if your sister passes away, your nephew, John, will ultimately be the recipient of the estate and not your own children?" She refused to discern that possibility. We are not talking about a great deal of inheritance, but the eschewed and inflexible way of thinking that my mother possessed was mind-boggling.

"So what is the statement they will be surprised by, Mom?"

"I added that Donna (Shrimp's wife) would receive $5.00 and not a penny more because that is what she deserves."

"Good God, Mom, that is outright vicious!"

She placed the palms of her hands on either side of her forehead and nodded east and west. "There is more to it than that," she added with a chuckle in her voice.

"What else?"

"I don't ask you about your business."

"Do I need to remind you that I do all your business?"

She didn't budge. "You might be happy when you hear about it. I know exactly what I am doing."

As I sat on the edge of my father's twin bed, listening to her, I couldn't help wonder what my father would have thought about it all. And I thought about my brothers. We had lost regard for each other, but I didn't believe in revenge and I wanted no part of her plan.

All I knew was this woman I called my mother would go to her grave leaving a message that would hurt and offend. And to add insult to injury, she justified what she was doing. *Why should she be different now?* I asked myself. For as long as I could remember, she had never found fault in her actions and had never said she was sorry. Certainly not to my father and, I can attest, never to me.

I see clearly now that she was jealous of my relationship with my father as well. She would say subtle things to sabotage feelings. Oftentimes she would ask me, "Do you know what your father said about you?"

"You know what? I don't want to know anymore."

Perhaps he actually did say something negative but I always felt it unfair to hear it out of context. Looking back now, I realize she used whatever she could to build a wall between us.

A few weeks passed and she began to conjure up another plan. On one of my visits, she asked me if she could live at the nursing home where my father spent his last year. Her desires changed like hands on a clock from one hour to the next.

"If that's what you want I will try, but you can't be going to facilities like they have a revolving door Mom. It's not going to be easy so promise me you will be open-minded."

"I can't stay here. Your father was happy there so I want to go."

"Okay, I will see what needs to be done for your placement."

My mother got her wish to be admitted to the nursing home, although it was not in the way either of us was expecting. She was sent to the emergency room for labored breathing. By the time Joe and I arrived, she was agitated, but I assured her this was the best place for her to be at this time.

"It's late, Mom. Joe and I are going to run out to get a hamburger; we will be back as soon as we are done."

She wasn't pleased lying on the gurney as we began to walk away. "What is going to happen?"

"I don't know, Mom. It takes a while to find out what is going on, and we will be right back."

When we arrived at the hospital, within an hour, a nurse greeted us. "Are you Mrs. Dunne's daughter?"

"Yes, is something wrong?" I replied.

"Well, your mother is giving us quite a time."

"What do you mean?"

"She is acting out. She just threw the bed pan from the bed."

Turning to Joe, I asked, "What am I going to do with her? Everything is a problem."

"Take it easy Colette, we'll get through this together."

My head was throbbing and my hamburger was telling me it wanted out. I went to her bedside to tell her we were back. The nurse further explained that they wanted to keep her for several days for observation, since they'd detected an abdominal aneurysm and wanted to make sure she was not in danger. With each day that past, my mom acted out like a child: crying, complaining, pleading me to get her out of the hospital.

The attending physician at the hospital was adamant about the supervision of my mother's aneurysm and recommended that she be placed in a nursing facility, since it was questionable as to whether she was well enough to undergo surgery. I once again contacted the nursing facility I had previously worked in and asked for help. The administrator had clearly remembered my father and was willing to help me with the placement of my mother. Now my mother was getting her ultimate wish; she would be transferred to the nursing home and into the very same room my father once inhabited.

This time, within two days of her admission, she began to complain. Her discontent escalated rapidly. I did everything humanly possible to make her comfortable. From bringing in her home treasures and mementos, to speaking endlessly to the staff, asking them to try and give her special attention. Nothing worked. She found fault with everything. If it wasn't about the fact that they woke her too early in the morning, it was about her not having her fresh blueberries for breakfast!

Once again, unbeknownst to me, she called my brothers and worked her magic. She begged them as if she was the victim of my cruel judgment, placing her in a godforsaken place. To my surprise, Buster called me two weeks after her admission. He went into a lengthy explanation about his elderly next-door neighbor who was requiring extra care. He asked me if I thought Lena would consider helping his neighbors out since she was not caring for my mother any longer. In truth, after acquiring Lena's number, Buster asked her to come back to my mother's house. Once that was in place, Shrimp, in his explosive manner, proceeded to pack for my mother's discharge without any notice to the staff that cared for his mother. Without the protocol of a medical discharge and social working assistance, my brother was insistent that he was taking my mother out of the facility, come hell or high water. Things became so heated between my brother and the staff, and I ultimately received a call from the administrator. He advised me that he was considering calling the police regarding my brother's assaultive behavior and disruptive actions. I hung up my cell phone and leaned against a wall nearby for support. My legs wanted to cave and my body felt like it could slide down the wall in a puddle on the floor. How much more could I endure? I vowed to myself at that moment that I would lay down the law to my mother. If she chose to follow along with my brothers' plan, then let them take care of her. This was a repeat performance and I was tired of the dance I was in. Despite the social worker and medical staff's efforts to encourage her to give it more time, despite the fact that her discharge was against the doctor's orders, she left.

She called me not long after she was back at her home and asked me to stop by. I arrived a day or two later and I read her the riot act.

"I want no part of the responsibility any longer. Let Shrimp take care of your needs. He can run errand; he can take care of your finances. I am so done Mom."

She began to cry about her life and circumstances. Through her tears she told me that all she ever wanted was a family...friends and family. I sat a few feet away from her bed and could not bring myself to embrace her or say anything to soothe her. All I could think of was that she was the reason she did not have that beloved family she longed for. She created the animosity and mistrust.

She stopped crying but her labored breathing continued.

"Take some oxygen and calm down now," I suggested as I positioned her tank closer to her.

I left her in the bedroom and met Lena in the kitchen. If there ever was someone to understand the circumstances, even without the command of language, it was Lena. We sat and had a cup of tea together and spoke about her family and her daughter's plans to marry.

I returned to my mother's room to find her awake and abundantly calmer. As I approached my father's bed, I sat down and faced my mother. In a quiet and calm voice, I said, "I have a question for you I want you to answer."

She turned to face me and pulled her covers over her shoulders.

"Why didn't you ever express your love for me?"

She answered, "I don't know. It's just the way I am."

"But, if you knew you couldn't stand to lose someone you loved, why wouldn't you find it in heart to show your feelings and claim the relationship?"

Her answer was always the same. "It's who I am and I can't change. You don't understand me."

She was right; I did not understand her. She had at times even gone so far as to say it was the fault of her ethnic background. "French people think differently than Americans." I knew that it was not so; I believe she knew that in her heart too.

She had no friends because it was always one-sided. She expected much but made excuses for her lack of reciprocation to others. She was disappointed and always questioned why people didn't do more for her. As much as I thought I wanted to hear those three words, I didn't know if I could embrace them now. She had made that statement once at the urging of her sister but it didn't ring true for me. Furthermore, I felt uncomfortable when I heard it coming from her mouth. How can something I naturally longed for make me feel so squeamish?

****

We had all reached our levels of frustration and exasperation. Buster complained of his jumbled nerves and shingle-like condition. Barker had difficulty keeping his temper in check. And with a five-year estrangement under my belt, I found that nothing had changed in my relationship with her. It was all about Mom, despite her attempts to act like she had an interest in me.

****

During this period of time, I had the added responsibility of packing up twenty years of essential and nonessential "stuff" that would be transferred to our new home after the finishing stages of construction. In one of my guest room closets, I came across my mother's personal affects, tucked away on one of the upper shelves. She gave me the weary, corner-frayed box years ago when she was first diagnosed with lung cancer. The box had a yellow sticky note attached to it in my mother's handwriting, "My Baby Clothes." She explained that she gathered some of her faded, tissue-thin baby garments along with cards and letters I had sent her many years before. She implied that my correspondence was something I should reread, but I chose not to look at them at the time. I was having enough trouble trying to figure out how I felt about seeing her again; I didn't need another element to bungle my mind. Now I needed to decide whether I would include this box with many the others being prepared for the move. I sat myself down on the bedroom floor with the box on my lap, and proceeded to scan through the stack of cards and letters. Most of the letters were written when I was single and traveled to Spain to visit my aunt and uncle, and some, around the time of my first marriage. Some were thank you cards for various occasions with brief notes inscribed— one in particular was written just before I was being admitted to the hospital for back surgery. The rest were personal holiday cards that I faithfully sent with each occasion. I scanned through them one by one. I was unsettled by the nature of my words. Extolling many terms of endearment, I must have believed my mother was verging on sainthood. With each letter I gleaned over, I was taken by the love and devotion I expressed for her. Digesting the inscriptions, I felt I needed to hesitate for a few moments. I positioned myself against the nearest wall and gazed out of a nearby window. Who was I back then? Why did my mother want me to have them now?

As years passed, I slowly began to establish an independence from her. Fearing that she would loose control of me, she never failed to engage in her common ploy, "You are not the daughter I once knew." Was this collection to remind me of the daughter I once was? Guilt often worked for me in the past. How could I not be the best daughter possible?

Then again, was it to affirm her position as a "good" mother? The longer I dwelled on the motive, the more it began to repulse me. One of the letters I reviewed even emphasized the fact that I was away for an entire summer and hadn't heard a word from her. Making the decision not to dwell any longer on her intention, one by one, I methodically tore the cards and letters up. As I ripped them into small pieces, I had a fleeting thought: would I ever be sorry I did? Looking down on the scraps before me, I reminded myself that these were letters I wrote to her. None of them were from her to me. I possessed no box with mementos, cards or letters from my mother to cherish. Her baby things would be addressed at another time. Placing her garments in their original box, I added it to the many boxes ready for temporary storage and transit.

Family (Un) Ties

---○---

I had just attended a meeting at my mother's attorney. I was drained and disheartened. My headache rendered me in a non-functional state, so I took to my bed. It did not prove to be a restful hour, however. Recollections of the day and enumerating past memories dominated my consciousness.

During a number of my sessions with my therapist, I was trying to make sense of my mother's lack of concern and attention toward my son, Dana. I coped as best I could with her absence of affection for me, but thinking that she had reservations about Dana was so much more than I could bear. As his mother, there would always be the undeniable truth. My loyalty to him would be boundless and my motherly instincts would compel me to be protective. This mother hen would not let her chick be treated unfairly.

Wandering through the myriad of flashbacks, I drifted to a memory long ago that jarred my senses.

During a visit Dana made to my parents one Sunday, he noticed a two-inch plastic figurine sitting on my mother's windowsill. She had bought this diminutive statue of a donkey at a well-known souvenir shop located on the border of North and South Carolina. Dana, at that time, was into a musical group called Gov't Mule. He had acquired a few similar images over time that reminded him of his favorite rock group. Approaching my mother, he asked, "Grammy, can I have this for my collection?"

"Oh no, I have had that a while now and I like it where it is."

In light of what had just transpired at the attorney's, I was dismayed that his minor request was denied.

There was no denying her disposition with regards to Dana. She once made a confession to me of an incident that had transpired between them twenty years earlier.

"We were at Buster's house and Dana was sitting outside by the pool studying for his school final exams. He was arguing with me and I had just about had enough." She paused with a fevered intensity in her eyes and continued, "I told him if you don't stop right now, I am going to take your books and throw them in the pool. He never made a remark to me again, I'll tell you that much." I couldn't miss the satisfaction and pride in her tone as she recalled the event.

"Maybe he shouldn't have argued with you that day, but what about your demeanor when he was just a little boy and he needed a grandmother? You had the opportunity to bond with him but you chose not to." She was equipped with an alibi.

"I was taking care of Chip back then. Dana was just jealous."

"No mom, Dana was not jealous. He was hurt. What did you expect from him? He saw the difference in attention you gave."

She shrugged her shoulders and replied, "I've done things in the past but I can't change them now."

Oh yes, you could have, Mom, but after today I don't think it would have ever been your intention.

In her mind, her statement was enough to exonerate her. Amazing how my conscience ruled me and yet she could mentally brush an action away like dandruff on the shoulder.

Another memory reemerged. Lena needed to leave for a few days and my mother more than dreaded the thought of being left alone for any length of time. Outside of my staying there, I realized I had no other options. I had been on the phone with Dana, telling him about my mother's concerns and not having any solutions. "What about one of my uncles?" he asked.

"No, they aren't going to do it. Besides they see it as my responsibility, not theirs."

"Listen Mom, I am in between contracts. If you want, I will come out and stay with Grammy."

"Would you Dana? That would be great!"

While defending my son and needing to vent my pent up feelings I held inside, I reminded her of another memory. "Who was there for you when Lena left for a few days?"

"What are you talking about?"

"Did you forget when you couldn't be alone for one second of the day or night, who came to stay with you? Dana came out by train, remember?"

"How much did he do?"

"There's just no reasoning with you, Mom," I answered angrily.

Dana stayed during that week in the basement apartment my father was formerly relegated to. He was able to work from his computer and yet be there for my mother when she beckoned through the same intercom my father had installed a number of years ago. All went well and Lena returned as promised.

Before heading back to his own apartment, Dana noticed a framed map my father had hanging in the bedroom. While working for the railroad, he acquired the map by happenstance. He was present when a demolition crew was taking down the interior walls of a train station in dire need of renovation. He noticed the map of commuter train paths on the waiting room wall and asked the construction foreman what he was going to do with it. The foreman replied that it was going in the trash. It was in very poor condition—the frame was damaged and the corner-mitered joints were skewed and separated. The map itself was unprotected by exposure and revealed numerous water stains. The glass pane had slipped below the image by an inch. Despite it's deteriorated status, I assured Dana I would ask if he could have it someday. Dana had a longtime interest in maps and I knew that it represented remembrances of several family members that worked for the railroad, including his father.

Not long after, I mentioned Dana's request to my mother. "I don't know," she replied. I dropped it then, not wanting to make an issue of it. I had to pick my battles since my stamina was waning.

One day, not long before the meeting, I asked my mother a question that had been nagging me. "What were you thinking about when Dana came to visit you?"

"What do you mean?"

"Okay, you were lying in bed and I was the first to walk in and greet you. Dana was close behind me. You didn't acknowledge that he was there to visit you. Why?"

"Oh, I don't know, I couldn't turn to see him."

We both knew she was more than capable of doing that. "Is that your reasoning?" I asked. The words hung in the air.

I could see Dana sitting alongside of me on the edge of the second twin bed, listening to our conversation. During our stay, all her questions and dialogue were directed toward me. Even if Dana made a remark during our chat, they fell on deaf ears, despite my efforts to include him. I didn't want to make Dana uncomfortable but later I felt compelled to question her.

"Why didn't you asked Dana how he was, or what was he doing? He did make an effort to come out to see you."

"I had a lot of things to go over with you," was her only response.

****

When I discovered that my mother, brother, and nephew were to meet with my mother's attorney without me, I knew we were at our lowest point as a family. During a phone conversation, my mother mentioned the meeting briefly and quite off the cuff. When I asked her the reason, she indicated that my brother requested the appointment to review her finances. Since Buster and his son were going to be there, I became suspicious of their intent. I had to be. I had already experienced Shrimp's efforts to swindle my mother out of a Medicare check that was due her.

When my mother declined to offer any more of an explanation, I contacted her attorney. The secretary indicated, "Mrs. Aliamo, I believe your mother's attorney assumed you were coming since you are the power of attorney and handler of your mother's finances."

"No, I was not informed but I will be there, thank you."

Before we hung up, I was reminded that the appointment began at ten o'clock. I called my mother the following day to let her know I would see her at the law office at ten. She replied, "Oh no, there was a mix up, the appointment is at eleven, I confirmed that with the attorney."

The morning of the meeting, I was on my way to have blood work done beforehand, only to receive a call on my cell phone from my mother's attorney at 10:14 am.

"Mrs. Aliamo, are you still attending the meeting or did you change your mind? Your mother, brother, and nephew are already here."

I felt it in my gut. The appointment was always at ten o'clock and my family wanted to have it without me.

"No, I didn't change my mind. I am five minutes away."

After receiving the surprising phone call, I became very anxious and was anticipating that this meeting would perhaps prove to be the showdown of all showdowns. To keep myself together, I called Joe and attempted to take deep breaths to calm myself as I headed toward the law office.

Joe met me in the waiting room with a big hug. "If you need me, I am here." How did I get so lucky to have a man like this? His selfless acts balanced my life and I was so willing to do the same for him. This was the way love was supposed to be. He was my human life vest. If I thought I was drowning, he made sure I stayed afloat.

I was as ready as I would ever be and took the plunge. Walking into the conference room, I found Buster, Chip, and my mother seated at the large wooden conference table in ample, leather, upholstered seats. There were no greetings on anyone's part. I passed my mother's seat and asked, "Why didn't you let me know the right time?" She waved her hand and said something unintelligible. I had become accustomed to her murky, fragmented remarks over the years when she wanted to avoid giving an answer. I dropped the inquiry. As I took my place, my brother started to question me about why I was not speaking to him. This time there was an altogether different posture in his question, unlike before, when we were seated at my father's bedside. When I didn't answer him, he persistently badgered on. I knew that he wanted to incite me emotionally. Feeling under attack, I got up from my seat and left the room. My mother did not shield or defend me as I exited toward the waiting room. I broke down in Joe's arms, hoping my family did not witness my act. I felt bruised, intimidated, unnerved by my brother and not appreciated by my mother. This is not my family. These are combative people I understand nothing about. Joe kept his arm around my shoulder as thoughts flooded my mind...

You can't just cast me away. I am here because I am a responsible person doing the right thing. I may not always have a clear head, but I always conduct myself with integrity, without regret, and without underhanded ways. I may feel beaten down and I shake some today, but I am a fighter. Like a boxer in the ring, they go back to their corner when the going gets tough, but with some encouragement from their trainer, they are back in for the fight. I am driven by my principles. I took on my job with a sense of honor. I would venture to say that most parents strive to treat their children equally. I, in turn, have strived to be worthy of my mother's love, but on this day I only ache for fairness and equality. And perhaps in the end, I hope beyond hope, that I will earn her respect. I won't let the injustices, the dishonesty, and the betrayal win this battle. Someday I will look back and feel good about myself, despite this quagmire they have initiated.

Within a few minutes, the attorney arrived and invited me into the room. I returned to my seat and tried my best to act composed and unnerved.

The attorney turned her attention to my mother and asked what was the purpose of the meeting.

"I have decided to make legal arrangements to have an apartment built adjacent to my nephew, Chip's house," she announced.

The room became still for a few seconds. My mother had been on hospice going on a year now and she was growing increasingly weaker by the day. Finally, I spoke. "Mom what are you talking about?" She turned and broke the news to me directly. "I have made the decision to give Chip $125,000 to build an extension."

I couldn't begin to comprehend her rationale, considering the fact that in all probability she might not live to see the extension finished. Or maybe she didn't even care.

"Mom, this just doesn't make any sense at all." She was willing to pay for an extension for her nephew while reducing the inheritance for Barker, our respective children, and myself, not to mention my aunt. Buster, the opportunist, didn't pass the fortuitous moment to mock my disbelief. With his well-known smirk, he remarked, "Oh, that's right, Chip is her favorite." I ignored his remark and continued, as there was even more at stake. "Does Chip understand how often someone tends to your needs? Do you think he or his wife, raising a toddler, will have the time to care for you? I know all too well how much it takes to be there for you. Will you feel comfortable with all new doctors? You often voiced your opinion on how important it was to have the same doctors following you these past years."

No answer. She stared at the wall of law books beyond where her attorney was seated.

It was clear that they hadn't wanted me to attend this meeting because they knew I would be the voice of reason and would object to the plan. I briefly wondered if Shrimp even knew about this meeting, but I wasn't going to dwell on his part of it now.

As if I had not spoken a word, I sat facing my mother, brother, and nephew, while they began to go over the details of construction. During their conversation, there was no discussion with regard to the time element required to complete the apartment until Chip succinctly questioned my mother, "If you die in a month Grammy, I will be paid in full for the extension, right?" She agreed, without a blink of an eye.

I wanted to leave; I felt foolish and discounted on yet another level. The attorney excused herself from the room to take a call and my brother took the opportunity to harass me once again.

"What's the matter? You can't speak unless an attorney is around? Don't you think of us as family anymore? I guess you like it formal." My mother did not utter a word in my defense.

The attorney returned, and I decided to make a last ditch effort to appeal to my mother's better senses. "Mom, if you think my idea is a reasonable one, perhaps you might want to consider this. Since Chip will be gaining the funds to pay for the extension on his house, would you consider deducting it from Buster's share of the inheritance?"

She looked at me sternly and said, "No, I don't see it that way."

"Why, Mom? This way, whatever is left of your inheritance, it will be divided equally between your other grandchildren."

"Oh no, I am not leaving anything for Dana or Shrimp's children." She wasn't at all subtle, and I was dumbstruck, to say the least.

"Why are you concerned? You don't need the money."

Despite the fact that she was right, she continued to ignore my suggestion to leave my share to my son. "It's always about the money," she added.

I answered, "No, it's about being fair." Regardless of how her remaining assets would be divided, I was left with a crushing blow to my heart. In the end, I would make it happen for Dana, even if by default.

Maybe somewhere along the line, when I entertained the idea that her feelings for my son or myself were questionable, I should have thrown in the towel—the money is not good money when given without love. While the truth was still incomprehensible for me, I was driven to not let her ignore or abandon Dana even if it meant beyond her grave. After so many years of not having control of my life, I felt I needed to control this.

Months later, when I thought the storm had past, I was faced with one more gale. My mother's attorney contacted me: all the loose ends of the will were finalized. She suggested I stop by and pick up a copy. One of the staff members handed me the document and offered me a seat. "Would you like to read it over in case you have any questions?"

"Sure."

As I skimmed over the pages, I noticed a clause that heightened my attention. The checking account I had used to pay my parents' bills and everyday expenses was left to me.

"Excuse me, what does this mean? I am entitled to the amount that remains in the account?"

"Yes, it looks that way since you and your mom cosigned when she opened the account."

227

I opened my handbag and pulled out the book I had been writing checks with and turned to the back. On the bottom, in very small print, the staff member pointed out the part where it stated, the remaining funds would be given to the surviving member.

"Oh my gosh, it didn't dawn on me," I replied.

"Yes, but I understand from your mother's attorney, other members of the family can contest it."

"Contest it? Really? Even if it clearly states that I am the survivor?"

"They could."

As I drove home that day, a comment my mother shared with me had come to mind. The day she discussed the surprising changes she had made on her own, she did say, "You might be happy when you hear about it." Could this be what she was referring to? But why did she say might? I wasn't sure if this was what she meant, but it sure seemed the only possibility since there was little to be happy about in her will.

As predicted at the law office, the account would be contested. Not only by my brothers but also by my Aunt Cerise. If someone said my brother would be willing to fight over the distribution before hand, it wouldn't have surprised me, but seeing my Auntie Cerise on the lawsuit document was jolting and distressful. I was being summoned to court by my own family—what a sad and hurtful time it was for me.

At the advice of Joe and a few close friends, I contacted an attorney. After several harrowing meetings of reliving much that had transpired and the statements being made by my family, my attorney offered her advice.

"Mrs. Aliamo, you have been through a tremendously tumultuous time these last few years. I know your family's attorney and his reputation precedes him. It will be a most grueling event if you were willing to appear in court. I will do whatever you wish, but having known you for several months, I can readily see you are in a very fragile state. I know on principle you are entitled to this account, but do you think you want to put yourself through the ordeal?"

I was actually relieved when she offered her opinion. I was tired and assailable; I had nothing left to draw on.

****

When faced with this kind of culmination, it takes a lot to extricate yourself from it because the vortex you're in whirls faster and tighter, keeping you in its tunnel. I felt responsible to care for my mother and to find solutions to make her life easier. I was obviously incapable of setting boundaries for myself. Still, at this moment in the attorney's office, I glimpsed at an important truth and opened my eyes: no mater how much I thought I deserved respect and acknowledgement, I couldn't assume that I would receive any. And if I didn't get my needs met, then I needed to move on. I had to conger up enough respect for myself to understand that concept, so I could ultimately save myself from further grief and pain. Life is too short to waste it on the wrong people. Now, I can forgive myself for the blindness I had in my journey's path about those who betrayed me.

The Legacy

———————◉———————

My mother's end came suddenly and grotesquely. She had called me early one morning, complaining of stomach pains, and I urged her to have Lena take her to the emergency room. Unlike all the other times, I did not run at once, but instead took care of a few personal appointments. I felt torn, but with Joe's urging, I did so. Should I drop everything and run again to her aid? He was right. I needed to think about me.

Joe was still home when my sister-in-law, Karen, stopped by for a cup of coffee. I turned to her to explain the phone conversation I had just had with my mother. Joe was not at all sympathetic and felt that Lena could handle it. Turning to his sister, he began to share some of the trials and tribulations I had been through with my mother.

I turned to my sister-in-law and replied, "I am having a hard time dealing with anything these days and my threshold is so low, I often don't know where my responsibilities lie."

This was a sobering point in my relationship with my mother. I was being forced to face some difficult truths. The mother I longed for, with loving connections and fair, unwavering values was not to be. I could no longer live with false hopes that I had in the past. Through my adult life, I thought that just because our relationship was poor at best didn't mean that it would never happen. I compared the sad reality of my connection with my mother as a chemotherapy treatment. You took the dose because you had hope. You suffered through the after affects because you had hope. You went on again and again, surviving the assault because you had hope. I was ready to let it go because I realized there was no hope and it was time to turn in another direction.

"You can't keep doing this to yourself, Colette," Joe added. "You run yourself ragged and then your health is compromised."

Joe was right again. Throughout these past years, the local hospital was beginning to feel like my second home and my headaches of thirty years governed me.

Still, in the recesses of my mind, thoughts of my obligation nagged at me. I was anxious to be on my way so I bid them goodbye. Karen called out as I walked toward the front door, "Take care, Colette, let me know if I can do anything." Joe walked me to the door and kissed me goodbye. I smiled and said, "Thanks honey, I needed that."

My cell phone rang about two hours later while I was at the hair salon. It was the emergency room physician. "Hello, is this Mrs. Aliamo?"

"Yes."

"I am the attending physician at hospital emergency room taking care of your mother Julliette Dunne. Do you know your mother's diagnosis?"

"Yes, she has had lung cancer for more than five years now."

"No, Mrs. Aliamo, I am talking about the abdominal aneurysm."

"Yes, I am aware of it. My mother was advised a year ago that she should be monitored with 24-hour nursing supervision for her condition. She had been placed in a nursing facility but she wasn't pleased with it and was taken home after about two weeks."

"Had anyone suggested surgery?"

"Surgery? It was my understanding that my mother was not a good candidate; her pulmonologist felt her lungs might be too compromised to risk the surgery although there was some talk about it at your hospital during another hospitalization."

Long before this day, I recalled my mother telling me that her internist had described the severity of her condition. "If your aneurysm bursts, Mrs. Dunne, you will have fifteen minutes to make peace with your God." My mother seemed to take it in stride while explaining her condition, but it was a very disconcerting to me.

"Well, your mother's aneurysm is leaking, Mrs. Aliamo."

"Really...as soon as I am finished here I will come straight away," I replied.

"Cancel whatever you're doing."

"Oh! I will be there as soon as I can then." I knew this day would eventually come but I was startled by the urgency in his voice. After I hung up with the physician, I contacted Joe to ask him to meet me at the hospital. With a semi-damp head of hair, I apologized to my hairdresser and rushed to my car.

I was starting to panic some as I drove to the hospital. My mind was jumbled with all kinds of thoughts. I vacillated during those moments—it did and it didn't occur to me that this could be her demise. If it were, how would I handle the inevitable? I knew I would do whatever was possible to help her and push aside my angst and frustration. Questions still popped into my head. *Was a leaking aneurysm the same as a bursting one? Would I make it there in time? Why hadn't I jumped the minute she called me this morning like the thousand times before? No Colette, you have done your best.*

As I entered the emergency room, a nurse directed me to the stretcher behind one of the many curtained units. I found my mother lying on her back with one end of the gurney tilted upward where her feet were positioned. Her thin, sallow face was the only part of her body that could be seen above the blanket she was covered in. Her eyes were closed so I approached her cautiously and bent down near her ear. "Can you hear me, Mom?" She nodded yes. Sitting down on the only chair available alongside her bed, I took her hand in mine. At one point, she opened her eyes and stared away at the curtained wall on the opposite side of her stretcher. She was the master of the averted stare with me. "Do you want or need something?" I asked.

"I'm cold." She was still coherent. Above her head were two stacks of folded, snowy white sheets. I grabbed a handful and began to layer them on top of her blanket. After she was bundled up, I sat again and threaded my hand through the sidebars to hers. Here I was again at the end of my parent's life. As I stared at her bony, blue-veined hand in mine, I thought of my father. I remembered holding hands with him too. Only this time it was different. Despite the fact that he had been in the most unmerciful pain, he had reached out and squeezed my hand. Perhaps she was too weak to squeeze my hand, but the fact that she chose not to look at me spoke volumes. As the minutes past, my thoughts surfaced. *How many times did I need to share*

but you always had something more important to do?
Those rugs needed to be vacuumed, those windows
needed to be washed. I remembered how much I
wanted you to see me in my original homemade plays,
singing Grandma Esther's songs but you "didn't have
time." How many times did I want you to be pleased
about my artwork and you couldn't bring yourself to
admire it no matter how bad or good it was? There was
such avoidance between us.

She stirred some. "Mom, do you want me to call
your sons?" She nodded yes.

"What about Auntie Cerise? Do you want me to
try to get through to Spain?" She nodded yes again.
Staring straight ahead, she asked, "Can I go home?"

"The doctor wants to admit you. You wouldn't want
to go home the way you feel now, would you?" She
shook her head no. When I returned after making
the phone calls from the waiting room, I sat there
pondering how long she would last. I couldn't stop from
wondering again how wonderful it would be if she said
something kind to me. An, "I love you" would be too
much to ask, but perhaps a, "Thank you." After all, I
was her daughter, and this was goodbye. I suddenly felt
like a child again, yearning for her love and praise. Our
history was repeating itself and nothing was making any
sense at the moment. I felt empty, desolate, bereft,
and broken. As I stared into the face of this old woman
with her sparse hair disheveled like a haystack and her
eyes now closed, I saw my whole life with her. A life of
waiting, a life of yearning.

I was trying to be perfect for you, Mom. I tried so
hard but you never gave me a break. Nothing I did to
please you was good enough. You always turned away.
Did you even want me at all? My baby book was the
only thing that gave me hope that you did. But that was

a crumb, Mom. That wasn't enough to sustain me for my whole life. What I am yearning for now is another crumb.

I didn't ask to be born. I didn't want to live my life with the struggles of a disability. You didn't have a perfect baby. And I spent so much of my life loathing my imperfect body. I wanted so desperately to be like everyone else. I wanted to be loved for who I was. My self-loathing became an obsession. Like a drug addict who needs a fix, I tried to hide my imperfections. I couldn't bear to think of anyone not loving me if my own mother didn't see me as lovable. I was sure that if they could see my imperfections, they wouldn't love me either.

I needed to have a safe place in your heart. A mom who would shelter me from the harshness of the world. But I was on my own. Didn't you see, Mom?, If you chose not make me feel special, then I would spend my life putting up the best front I knew how to the rest of the world. Always hiding my fears of failure and criticism, I struggled to live up to an unachievable standard that ultimately led to my health issues, exhaustion and emptiness. I was a runaway train with no control in my life.

Look Mom, I bought you the perfect handbag. Look Mom, I married even though you thought no one else would love me. Look Mom, your grass is green. Look Mom, I chaired those fundraisers. Please be proud, Mom, and be a part of it. Look, Mom, I did get the job! Look Mom, it's me sitting beside you now.

There was nothing to do but wait now.

During the second hour, my mother began to mumble incoherently. I left her side for a moment and indicated to the nurse that she was becoming more and more distressed, and it seemed like the end was near. "Do you have an idea how long she has?" She smiled weakly at me and with a compassionate tone she answered, "Not too long."

"Can you please get my mother a priest for last rites? It's very important to her."

"I will see if there is a chaplain in the house," she replied earnestly. Forty-five minutes later, I was losing hope about the prospect when, to my relief, a priest finally arrived along with Joe and Lena.

By this time my mother was very agitated with the oxygen tube attached to her nose. Attempting on her own to pull the tube off her face and shifting her head back and forth, I removed it with the nurse's consent. As the priest began reciting The Lord's Prayer, he asked us to join him and anointed my mother with the oil of absolution. *Please, Mom, give me a sign. Tell me I am more to you then just another person who took care of your needs. Give me something to hold on to, something to embrace in my heart, something that will make me believe that you were happy and proud to have me as your daughter.*

When the blessing was done, I thanked the priest. He nodded and stepped out with Joe and Lena.

I was alone now with my mother. I was about to witness death for the first time in my life. I didn't know what to expect. Within a few minutes, my mother's face suddenly became violently contorted, demonic looking, and she was looking at me. Her jaw shifted to the left, leaving her mouth pinched and twisted in the opposite direction. The pull was so hard to the left that the right side of her face was deeply hollowed out. Her eyes opened wider and were terribly fixed and staring straight at me. They were so piercing at that moment, it felt as if she had lifted her head to glare at me. I was horrified to see someone appear so unnatural and to possess the kind of look only movies fabricate. Her unyielding trance slacked after a few seconds as she let out her last breath. Her face looked normal again. Her time had come. No sign for me except for the look that haunted me for a number of years to come. She died as she had lived—harsh, rigid, and without softness.

Years later, wanting to believe there was a medical explanation for her contorted face, I asked a friend in the medical field about it and he suggested that she could have experienced a stroke just before passing.

I returned to my mother's home to gather the outfit she had chosen to wear for the wake viewing. I knew exactly what she wanted. She once asked me to go through her closet as she lay in her bed a few feet away. "Look on the left side and go through the blouses. When you find the white one with the bead work on the front, pull it out." I remembered this top. It was one that she wore on special occasions such as Christmas. "Now go toward the right where you see the slacks, there is a black pair." There were several black slacks but as soon as I pulled out a few she spotted the one she wanted. I had a fleeting image of her wearing the very same outfit in a photo. She was standing next to a staircase and her hair looked as if she had just come from the hair salon. She was smiling. She must have thought that she looked well because she rarely smiled or allowed anyone to take a photo of her. I allowed myself a moment to think about her. She never had much in the way of good jewelry or upscale clothes. What little she had she took very good care of so they would last. This outfit was the personification of her perfectionist ways.

She said she didn't want anyone else but my nephew or me to take care of this job because "they" might get it wrong. (I assumed she was referring to my brothers or sisters-in-law but it didn't really matter to me.) After finding the clothes she chose, I decided that I would gather some of the items I knew she had listed on a piece of paper and in her will. They were items that had little monetary value, but my mother valued them, and I wanted to make sure that this time they would be delegated properly. After what had transpired following my father's burial, it was important that the items went to the rightful recipients that she'd previously chosen. As I collected the mementos in and around my mother's bedroom, I found another note in her bedroom. Only this one was ripped into several pieces: some were lying on her nightstand and more on the floor and waste paper basket nearby. As I picked up the fallen pieces something caught my eye. She had underlined a sentence several times. "Maybe some of you will get mad at my wishes, but it is my own, mine alone, wishes as I have seen fit." That was a powerful statement and I shivered to think what the rest of the note said. I pieced them together pretty easily as she'd left the shreds in sizable sections. I began to read and slowly started to sicken. At the top of the draft, a sentence seized my heart. It started, "My sister has always been the <u>most devoted person </u>to me."

She did feel the need to satisfy her guilt about my father as well. "Should there be any questions, your father and I always had shared everything. He always would want it this way. Your father would agree with what I ask and stand by me."

Yes, Mom he would, did he have a choice? It was your way or no way. Did you add that you loved him dearly?

Months before her demise, she spoke about the draft she had made up for her will of personal affects. She hadn't asked if I wanted anything but I decided I would offer my thoughts. "There are only two items that I would like to have, Mom. I always admired your crucifix and your communion prayer book." On idle days of my adolescence, I would sit on her bed cross-legged and skimmed through the leather-bound and gold-leafed pages of her book. Inside the book was a photograph of my mother wearing her communion dress and veil and holding the very same book. I would gaze at her, admiring her holiness. When asked, she once told me that both the sizable, frosted glass crucifix with a tiny glass font attached for holy water and prayer book were given to her for her communion. I saw them now as well-preserved treasures during the times of her innocence.

Before me now, in black and white, were the words that will always linger in my mind. "I want my sister, Cerise, to have my prayer book and my crucifix."

When my mother was making her final bequeaths and decisions, I too decided it was the time to ask for the map again that Dana had expressed an interest in. Much to my surprise, she stated that Barker wanted it as she had promised it to him. How bizarre. Weeks before, while she sat in my back yard one Sunday after dinner, she had stated how angry she was with my brother. "I want to take him out of the will."

"Mom, that's a drastic measure. Dad wouldn't have wanted it that way. It was his wish that the will be divided between his three children evenly."

"No, he can't be trusted." I thought she'd come to her senses at this point since he had committed some underhanded acts in the last year. After she questioned his deception, Barker made little contact with his mother. He was angry and cut himself off from her, except for phone calls.

Once again there before me, it clearly stated, "Barker Dunne will inherit the framed map."

There were written admissions on her part about her delinquency and about my aunt's untiring efforts to take care of everyone, including their parents, that led her to make yet another condition. She indicated that her sister would be the only one who would have access to the house and any and all of her belongings that were not specifically assigned. As it turned out, my aunt had no interest in my mother's belongings. Chip was next in line.

****

At my mother's funeral mass, the priest who had visited her from time to time described her as a loving mother, an angel. The words made me shrivel as I sat in the pew in front of him. Seated on the left side of the church in the front row with my husband and son, my brothers and their families chose to sit on the right. I knelt through most of the ceremony and robotically followed the rituals of the service. While kneeling and with my hands cupped around my face, tears began to stream down my cheeks. Many of my friends attending the service grasped my hand momentarily as they passed from communion. I am sure they mistook my glistening tear-stained cheeks as tears of mourning and loss. Only I knew the raw truth of my emotion that day. I knew they weren't tears for my mother. They were tears for me.

In the days that passed, following the funeral, my mother's attorney asked me to sort through a file of paperwork so the will could be finalized. Most of the folders were filled with Medicare and insurance statements. Quite by accident, I came across a legal document. It was a will that my parents had drawn up many years before. As I scanned through the pages, I noticed a penciled in area in my father's hand. Initially the document indicated that their inheritance would be divided equally between their children. But those words were crossed out and above the statement were the words: Barker Dunne, 45 %, Benjamin Dunne, 45%, Dana Olivieri 10% and Colette Aliamo, $9.00. I have no idea what that meager amount signified. My best guess was that perhaps the attorney said if an amount were indicated, there would be no question about the possibility of having overlooked me. This was the original will, changed when I estranged myself from my family ten years ago. That would explain a lot. Since my parents changed their will once again, during the time of my father's initial illness, my brothers could have taken umbrage with my inclusion. I was now an equal partner in the inheritance. Not knowing for sure, it could have been the reason they reminded my mother often that they were there for her when I wasn't. Adding insult to injury, I was made Durable Power of Attorney to boot! Perhaps there would never be any amount of care I could give to my parents that would subdue their begrudged feelings.

A few weeks had passed since my mother's passing. Joe and I were driving around town one Sunday morning. I turned to him and said, "You know, my mother did me a favor."

"Why do you say that?" he asked.

"Well, I was thinking in my mother's last hours of life she gave me nothing to be remorseful about," I replied.

"That's a hard reality for you to embrace, hon. I am sorry."

To make my point, I continued, "There wasn't anything to dwell on that might have redeemed her in my eyes. The memory is so black and white that it leaves me with nothing but emptiness about her. You can't miss someone if you never really had her. I can't speak for the rest of my family, but looking back today I think, what a sad legacy you have left your family, Mom."

To put closure on my responsibilities, the last job I had was to sell my parents' house. Walking through the nearly empty house where my parents had lived for thirty years was a jarring experience. I wandered through each hollow room and downstairs to the garage, where the remains of their lives were thrown carelessly in piles. Chip, my brothers, and their respective families had taken what they wanted or could sell for small profits through an indoor/outdoor house sale, leaving behind remnants discarded and strewn on the dirty, oil-soaked floor. I began to sort through the mounds of bits and pieces.

My first discovery was an elaborately wood-carved photo frame, engraved on the bottom with the date, 1946. It accommodated three separate photos and I could see the black-and-white images in my mind that had its place there for many years. Insignificant mementos but things that vividly brought back my childhood and pangs of melancholy. Tiny round cut glass salt and pepper shakers with bright yellow plastic tops, a deep green drinking glass stamped, with a mustached man gaily driving his "buggy," that the local gas stations handed out each time you filled your tank. Connections of my parents were there too. I knew the starred embossed brass button I found was once a part of my father's military cap.

In a corner there was an old enlarged framed photo of my family, approximately 24 X 36 inches in size. Although I can't recall the source or the reason, it was a result of a prize we'd won as a family. We dressed in our Sunday best, went to the studio, and had our family photo taken. All donning a happy face and sitting close together like a loving family. They say a picture is worth a thousand words. The only problem was the message in this picture was totally wrong. And now I noticed something added to this forty-year-old photo. Someone had scratched a mustache on my upper lip. It was a bold reminder of the mentality I had dealt with in those last years. I packed up a small box of mementos and closed the garage door for the last time.

Through the years I have learned that only you keep yourself locked up with pain. I knew I had so much more in my life to feel grateful for and I was not going to let it pass me by. Just like that day at the World's Fair with my boyfriend, I was resolute that I would try to get past the moments that I had no control over.

What made you Tick?

---⊙---

"Life becomes easier when you learn to accept an apology you never got."
~Robert Brault

I stared at the two-inch, white-footed tub, filled with pale blue bubbles, a rubber ducky, and a sweet faced bear that had sat for years on my bathroom shelf. It was a diminutive ceramic figurine that my mother had given me close to thirty years ago when she and my father visited us in Florida. It was a spontaneous gift. I had admired it as we passed a gift shop one afternoon and without asking, she bought it for me. A rare occurrence in our relationship. She has been gone for more than six years now, but the figurine still sits on a shelf as a bittersweet reminder of her unusual gesture. I have learned how to forgive her.

As I looked at the symbol of my mother's kindness, the old questions that I had about her came to mind. Who was she? What made her so insensitive, fearful, and inflexible? If my therapist's analysis of her was correct and she was mentally ill, then I would definitely have to consider that her background had some bearing on her actions toward her family. If I contemplated on her own history, I could see where she felt things went wrong in her life. During one of the most horrific of wars, World War II, she found herself single and pregnant, marrying a solider she barely knew, and having to leave all she loved for a foreign country. All of that surely contributed to her discontent. Regardless of my father's tireless efforts to give her a home and family, she held him responsible for what she perceived as her misfortune. Knowing that she had the added unwelcoming of a sickly babe must have made her even unhappier. Restless with a man who didn't live up to her expectations, she expressed her unhappiness through constant criticism. Despite the fact that my father worked three jobs just to support his new family, she was inconsolable. In turn, he lashed back out of his own frustrations, often losing his temper and better judgment.

There were nights when I was young that I would be awakened by the exchange of violent arguments and the sound of my mother's cries from their bedroom. I could hear my father slapping or violently pushing my mother. After the assault and hurtful words between them, my father would often storm out of the bedroom and sleep on the sofa.

I remembered her once telling me when I was about twenty-one that even if she didn't want to have sex with my father, she did because that was expected of a woman.

I asked, "So he didn't know you weren't interested?"

She obliged my question with advice. "Even if you don't want sex, you fake it. It's the only way to keep peace."

Shoot, that sounded like a terrible way to live!

On those nights that I was abruptly awakened, however, I would wait in silence a few minutes till I was sure the violence had ended, quietly ease myself out of bed and enter their bedroom in the dark. Standing alongside my mother in her bed, I could hear her muffled sobs and my heart ached for her. Wanting to console her, I would slide in beside her under the bed covers and stroke her arms and face in an effort to comfort her, the best I knew how. I knew what it was like to be the object of his abuse. I was scared he would find me there and feared I would be the next to experience his mighty blows, but I stayed. I wanted her to know she was not alone, something that I never experienced in return.

The morning after, nothing was discussed, and we went our way as if we had all enjoyed a peaceful night. One morning, however, as I lay by her side, I remembered she didn't get out of bed right away and she began to tell me a story that I heard of a few times thereafter, growing up. Lying face-to-face, she began to share her story of a soldier she met during the war whom she fell in love with before meeting my father. Although they only got to see each other periodically, he wrote her often. One letter she received was, in part, about a comrade he fought with. He said that his friend had lost his arm during a battle in the fields of France.

Julliette, do you think any woman would still be able to find themselves attracted to a broken man? He had written.

She admitted to me that at the time, in her return letter, she didn't know quite how to respond and said she didn't have an answer for him. She never heard from this soldier again, even after her repeated letters to him. Years passed and she often thought of this

246

man. She suspected later on that he was in fact the soldier who had lost his arm. Perhaps my mother's lost love haunted her. In her mind, the life she had was not the life she was supposed to live.

The timing was poor though; I was too battle worn in my own survival to even acknowledge her state of mind through the years. And perhaps I didn't have any emotional room to sort out the reasons back then.

So the sentimental connection that continues to sit on my shelf has become a fleeting remembrance of my mother attempting to make me happy. When it catches my eye as I pass, I have a twinge of regret for that moment in time. I now wished that she could have found the means to wash away all the fears and bitterness that festered in her over the years.

Two Hands

---●---

*"If I had my life to live over again, I'd find you
sooner so that I could love you longer."*

~ author unknown

I sat at the foot of the hospital gurney, staring at my
best friend and my rock. This time, my Joe was the
one in need. My heart was breaking to think he was the
one in peril and his life could virtually be balancing on
a string. Perhaps he didn't know it, but I took my job
as his caretaker seriously and I would do everything in
my power to assure him he would not be alone in what
he was about to face.

His face was stoic, but his eyes darted back and
forth at the preparation going on around him. Knowing
the familiar scene more than I would like to remember,
I explained the procedures and reassured him it was all
routine work. I could feel my inner strength surfacing. I
would be his comforter, his protector, and his guardian.
I needed no one. I knew that I was meant to do this
job for him. This was my time to show him that I would

not let him down. I would be his rock simply because I loved him that deeply.

A few days prior to his admission, the surgeon reviewed his cat scan and was clear about what we suspected was true.

"Mr. Aliamo, you have a tumor in your kidney approximately three inches in diameter. It must come out."

Joe responded without much hesitation, "Let's do it. I have no choice."

Joe and I sat in the doctor's office pondering the next step when the doctor picked up his phone and spoke to his medical scheduler and asked, "Do I have any time free on Thursday? Put Mr. Joseph Aliamo in for me."

I knew time was of the essence; the surgeon had indicated that his other organs didn't have any defining signs of metastasizing as far as he could tell. But we were made aware that a mass this size could in all likelihood be malignant. Malignant. What a heinous word. How could the love of my life be facing this? He was a good man. He didn't deserve it.

Joe, to my astonishment, remained strong and resigned to his possible fate. I would have fallen apart at the thought of the unknown. Since his first sign two weeks before, when he had urinated a sizable amount of bright red blood and a clot, he had seemingly remained calm.

He was Italian and had his fair share of doom and gloom in his personality. And he was a "scaredy cat" when it came to any medical scenarios. If someone described a surgery or injury in any detail, he would often grimace. With the palms of his hands in the air, as if he was being arrested, he would cry out, "No, don't tell me anymore. I hate that stuff." He would even get "sort of" upset with me if I suggested a movie that had a lot of suffering and physical pain. Exiting the theatre, he would comment, "I didn't like it very much. You know I only like funny movies and happy endings." And he has his moments of depression, mostly over money matters. I always said to others, if he has money in his pocket, he is a happy camper, but if money gets low, he is a different person. He has learned to value other parts of life, which has been a wonderful transformation for him, especially as he grows older. But as they say, you can't change the spots on a leopard.

He was most definitely scared now and had his share of anxiety but no sign of depression or "cashing in his chips." He still kept active and his sense of humor continued to keep me level. Perhaps he was afraid that if he showed how truly frightened he was, he knew he would definitely find me crumbled on the floor somewhere. The more I thought about it, the more I believed his upbeat attitude was most likely for me, because that's how good he is to me.

His surgery was three hours as expected, and the post op report from the surgeon was hopeful. He removed the right kidney and mass in totality as well as an adrenal gland and lymph nodes in the surrounding area. The words I clung to that day from the surgeon were, "I saw nothing suspicious." Of course, we still needed the pathology report to know if in fact he was out of the woods.

I was so very grateful to see the face of a very caring friend and cardiologist who came to see Joe after his surgery. He surveyed the chart and questioned Joe's low blood pressure while he was in ICU recovery. Despite the RN assigned to him, and dozens of staff coming and going, I felt much more reassured that Raphael was there asking questions. The RN told him, "We think the narcotics he is on are affecting the pressure," as she lowered the head of the bed some. Raphael again pressed with his concerns, asking a number of other questions while going over Joe's chart. After his evaluation, he approached me to say goodbye. I thanked him for taking time to check on Joe. We embraced and he left, or so I thought. Not long after Raphael's departure the RN turned to me and announced, "The doctor that was just here is calling your husband's surgeon."

"Really?"

I wondered why Raphael hadn't mentioned it to me. Perhaps he was just double- checking on the surgeon's directives. During Joe's on and off moments of awareness, he kept urging me to go home. "Go get something to eat, Babe, go walk Sneakers." It was close to 9pm and I had been there since early morning. Turning to the nurse, I asked, "How much longer do you think it will take before he can leave recovery and transfer to a regular room?" That would be a gauge on when I would feel comfortable leaving and a sign that things were going along well. Her eyes widened and to my surprise she answered, "A few more hours." I knew nothing about the recovery time for the kind of surgery that Joe had undergone. Besides, Raphael didn't appear to be alarmed, so I caved to Joe's insistence, and relinquished the idea to stay until his move.

It was good to get home after such an eternally long and intense day. I took Sneakers out for his last walk, put my pajamas on, and crashed on the sofa. With a cup of warm chocolate milk and a bowl of cereal, I stared at the TV screen, while listening to the many messages left by caring friends. I was too sapped of energy to think of returning the calls. Little did I know the night was far from over for me as I turned out the light on my nightstand.

At 1am, the phone rang. I was startled into alertness—no call in the middle of the night was ever good unless someone had a baby. A doctor was calling about Joe.

"What's going on?" I said with alarm in my voice.

"We had to take your husband back to the operating room."

I felt like I had been just dunked in a vat of ice-cold water! I sat in the darkness, scrambling to understand. But no words passed my lips. "They are going to reopen the thirteen-inch incision to find out the source of the excessive bleeding and the extremely low blood pressure. We will call you when it's over."

"Oh God, please do!"

I fell back onto my pillow after hanging up the phone. Staring at the ceiling, I prayed for a long time. *Please, don't take him from me. He is everything to me; he is more than that. He is my Joe. He has all the qualities someone finds in the love of their life, but you already know he is all that and more. He has always embraced my passions and been part of my roller coaster journey to fulfillment and freedom. He has always supported my endeavors and picked me up every time I fell or felt they were unachievable. He sees specialness in me. How many times has he been flexible and always willing to "aid and assist" me when I called out to him? He believes in me, respects me, appreciates me, honors me, and even tolerates me! Please, don't take him away from me now. I promise to be a more patient wife if you keep my Joe safe.*

I was so frightened and needed to talk to someone. I called Raphael. He and his wife were both in the medical field. They could help me understand or at best, make me feel more grounded. *Ring...ring...ring.* Oh geez, I hated to do this to them but I thought I would just go mad alone with my thoughts in my bed.

"Hello," it was Raphael.

"I am so sorry to call you at this hour Raphael, but something has gone very wrong with Joe's surgery."

"I know Colette, but he is in good hands," he answered. I was now at the point of gasping for air as I struggled to speak, my entire body in tremors. To say Raphael and Angela were a comfort to me is an understatement. Their calm and confident demeanor gave me something to hold on to, and I slowly pulled myself together. In the past, Joe always thought when it came to health issues that I saw the glass half-empty instead of half-full, and this was a time when I needed to be convinced of otherwise, pronto!

After their reassurance, I hung up and lay on my side of the bed, still shivering but taking deep breaths and holding on to every word of support they had given me. A band of thunderstorms were passing through that night; the lightning illuminated the whole room and thunder shook the bed. The rain pelted the window with a vengeance, as if to say that nothing was right in my world.

At 4am, the phone finally rang again. This time I bolted across the bed, knowing all too well who was calling. With my heart heaving and hammering in my chest, I heard the surgeon explaining that one of the vessels had ceased during the surgery, and later managed to relax and open. They not only had to seal the vessel but remove a clot that had developed after the surgery. He assured me that the issue was resolved.

I so wished I was with Joe, but I would have to wait for an hour or two before I could push my way through the hospital to his bedside due to their policy.

When I arrived early that morning, he was in still in ICU. His pain was intense, but his color had visibly deepened; I knew he was feeling better. As I walked down the hallway toward his room, I overheard a joke from Joe's repertoire that was being shared among the nurses. I knew then that part of my Joe was back again.

It was a long recovery. Each day I would arrive early and leave after dinner, but I didn't mind a bit. When he slept, I read or did crossword puzzles or just gazed out the panoramic view of the body of water several miles from the hospital. When the pain would awaken him, I would tend to his needs or get assistance. Being an advocate for him was easy, but helping him through his state of pain was quite a different task. Feeling helpless about what I could do to ease his suffering, I began to softy stroke his forehead and run my finger through the wisps of his hair. I asked him to breathe deeply. In time I felt a slight release within him.

"Oh, please don't stop," he replied.

Now I had direction and was resolute about helping him through the agony. I began to massage his feet and legs, then his hands, and back to his head. I showered my love on him. I did my best to comfort him and let him know he was not alone in his most painful and scariest hours. The kind of feeling I had longed for during my most frightening times—a touch, a tender word, a hand held. Joe was able to do little after his surgeries except take my hand. And I gently held it. It was a hold of love and caring, providing and protecting. The feeling of two hands clasped when someone is in need has a language of its own. The hand cupping over the other with fingers entwined says I will keep you from harm, trust in me. It was the best hand holding I had ever experienced.

Raphael stopped in Joe's hospital room with the lab reports one afternoon, a few days after the surgery, and uttered the sweetest words I ever heard, "Looks like you dodged the bullet, Joe."

Joe was still in tremendous pain and very uncomfortable, but I understood and savored Raphael's remarks: Joe's margins were clear and he was in very good shape. I don't have strong religious beliefs but I do believe Raphael is our angel. I will forever be grateful to him because I believe he saved my husband's life that night. I also believe the adage that people do come into your life for a reason, and my longing spirit was answered.

A Long and Winding Road

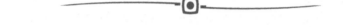

"Be the change you want to see in this world."

~Mahatma Gandhi

Secret places are often part of growing up. At the age of nine or ten, I would often ride my bike to my secret place. My home was a fifteen-minute walk, but just a two-minute bike ride to the town's vast ballpark. It largely consisted of an open area that offered baseball fields, racquetball and tennis courts, and a site for the best firework displays I had ever witnessed. Things remembered as a child often offer a more grand scale in memory.

Riding along the west side of the park was a wooded area that had no real access, except for one small, dirt path. As a young girl, it was my belief that I had to be the only one who knew about this entry, aside from the people who lived in a small house halfway down the dead-end trail. I never saw anyone at the home or witnessed a car coming or going during my many visits, hence, it was "my" secret place. It was also my safe haven where I could be free from the constraining, overbearing eye of my mother and the trepidation of my father's ultimate reprisal and abuse. It was a place where I could breathe, feel freedom from criticism, and connect to my own private thoughts. I was not sophisticated enough in my earlier span of life to understand the draw of my haven, but now I discern that gravitational pull for solace and safety.

What a perfect hideaway it was. Turning off the pavement onto the dirt path that was scarcely wide enough to accommodate one car passing at a time, I pedaled slowly so as not to hit a stone or rock on the way. I had my share of skinned knees so I was ever so cautious. The craggy road was perhaps a quarter of a mile long, with thick woods lining both sides. At the end, in a small clearing, a splendid large maple tree stood before me. Wearing short shorts and a midriff top that was all the rage then, I would leave my bike on its side and weave my way through the drooping, untrimmed branches. Some days I would lay down with my hands cupped under my head. During long hot summer months without school, I would daydream under the cool of the tree, observing the light filtering and flickering through the leaves above me from the lazy summer breeze. The same kind of musing I had experienced on my magic carpet, outside my bedroom window, a number of years before.

The majority of the time, however, I carried along my diary, secured under cables on my bike's back fender. I often wrote, leaning against the strong, mature tree for support. Alone with an occasional carpenter ant making its way up and down the tree roots, that bulged from the damp earth, I felt content in my isolated world. Writing was freeing. I could erase my worries and fears from my mind and resolve events that were stressful or that preoccupied me. By attempting to give some incidents closure, and describing them in the spiral bound notebook, I could tuck them away mentally... until the next time.

Spending my afternoons in this verdant oasis seemed to be the perfect spot for cloudy dreams to float on— dreams of a time when someone would understand, hear my pleas and my fears, and help me feel safe.

Today I find myself inclined to do the same, writing my thoughts in quiet retreat. Writing has always been a release for me. In my present home, I have created reflections of peaceful sanctuaries and scattered reminders of deeply moving and joyous images. In my library, my writing desk is against three spacious windows that look out onto one of the several lush gardens Joe has painstakingly developed: with looming evergreens, a stone bird bath surrounded by crescents of assorted rose bushes, and perennial hedges that compliment the border of brightly colored annuals. Facing south, I have a bright and cheery spot in which to reflect and write. My sense of peace comes from my home primarily. It allows me to focus on positive, visual reminders within my surroundings.

In addition to this alluring space, my Happy Wall is in a nearby workroom. I have collected photos and images of moments that have profoundly touched my heart. I can't help but soar when I gaze upon them. Some are simply the images we all seem to derive a smile from, photos of children's faces, puppies and kittens, wonderful representations of the simplicity and purity of the young and innocent; some are photos of far away images that conjure up a spiritual peacefulness or the wonder and beauty of nature at its best; a few reflect a love between two people against all odds that reaches deep in my core. My favorite example is a photo of a homeless man sitting against a building in shredded, soiled clothing, cradling and embracing a German Shepherd dog that is, in turn, nuzzling against the man's neck and shoulder. I can identify with this raw and transparent love. Its sadness haunts and captivates me in its emotional message.

I take the time to read my other messages scattered through my house as well. Little wooden signs propped here and there, remind me why it's so good to be alive and emulate those feelings.

My biggest achievement, however, was designing our center hall by stenciling uplifting messages expressed by my heroes or heroines. I am exhilarated each time I see the names of Eleanor Roosevelt, Oprah, or the Dalai Llama and their words of wisdom. One quote, which I have cherished for many years from a far less celebrated individual, was by Bette Reese, "If you think you are too small to be effective, you have never been in bed with a mosquito." It signifies human resilience for me; something I knew and believed could be true even for myself. Something in my core that makes me rise to every occasion, because I believe there is goodness and joy to be had. I often embrace the words of a Zen Buddhist monk, teacher, author, and peacemaker; a man I greatly admire, "If there is no mud, there is no lotus."

My center hall quotes welcome all who enter. I am connected to and honor the words of those I so admire for their wisdom. Some are witty, and some are clear, basic ideas on how to live your life. My quote humbly stands next to the others: "I love words, they talk back to me."

Lastly, I would be remiss if I didn't share a quote by Thoreau that was posted for ten years in my office, "Happiness is like a butterfly: the more you chase it, the more it will elude you, but if you turn your attention to other things, it will come and sit softly on your shoulder." My story is a good example of this message after writing for more than thirty years. My initial intent was to simply journal my experiences so I could put them to rest, but then I longed to share my story with others. I was going nowhere with it and I was in the wrong place mentally. The more I could taste the idea of writing, the less I knew what to do with it or how to express myself. When I found my editor, it was totally unexpected, like the touch on my shoulder. I could see my story more clearly and I was more grounded and ready. Lucky for me, turning my attention away, allowed me to receive my wish at the right time.

Early on, while writing my life story, I was making conscientious decisions to turn away from negativity that plagued me. I didn't allow myself to watch the news before I went to sleep. Instead, a sitcom rerun would take me away from all the negativity of the world and allowed me to fall into a peaceful sleep. More recently despite the chagrin of others, Facebook continued to help me when I needed an "injection" of hope and positive strength. Like flash cards, spiritual quotes popped up onto my screen, reminding me how to replace my old ways of thinking with new possibilities. Always seeking reinforcement of the positive and the possible during my need to heal.

Volunteering helped me become more of who I truly wanted to be. The more I became involved in charities and gave back to my community, the more useful and joyful I felt. Am I a Pollyanna? I don't think so. I still get in slumps and don't always think in a favorable manner—that's what being human is all about. Still I sought out ways to create joy in my life to reinforce the individual I yearned to be.

While discovering the delight and contentment of charity work, I also discovered I had untapped leadership skills. I was so enthusiastic that I sought out more and more activities to help others. With my confidence growing in baby steps, I took on jobs I would have never dreamed of doing in the past. After spearheading a drive called Operation Christmas Child in our parish with unprecedented results, I became a runaway train, so to speak. I realized I now had a platform to work with, and I looked for other ways and opportunities to give back.

My next not-so baby step, was to convince the parish leaders that we should start another charity drive for Heifer International—an organization which provides livestock animals and training to people so they can become self reliant for their food and income. With some persuasion on my part, the founder of the charity, who lived a few states away, visited our parish to explain his lifelong mission.

Once I had the approval from clergy, I urged them to allow me to include an article in the Sunday bulletin explaining the fundraising goals. After every mass, I made pulpit speeches while my lips quivered and my hands feeling like damp dish rags. I went on to make presentations with my Heifer VCR tape to every organization within our parish, religious education, choir, and the ministries. This endeavor finally reached our goal, as a whole, over the better part of two months. To this day, a plaque from the Heifer Organization hangs on the community parish hall congratulating the efforts of our parish members and children. Who knew I had it in me? Looking back now, I believe my passion drove me beyond my own expectations. Perhaps there are times when passion has no boundaries. Or perhaps in my struggle to find myself, those sparks of light kept me hanging on.

I wish I could say to you that the insights and revelations I have shared so far meant I was capable of figuring it out all on my own, but was is not the case. To say I was mentally ill at one time would be fairly accurate. Years of fear, poor self-image and self-loathing, with no outlet to see myself otherwise, made me feel crippled in more ways than one. Time after time, I would wonder why all the self-help aids I attempted to incorporate in my psyche didn't solidly change my views or actions. How could I make that leap to find a real sense of well-being and confidence in myself? I couldn't give up though; I was a mosquito in the bed, indeed.

There were times during the years when yoga would be the closest thing to feeling some level of nirvana for me. A time I devoted to my inner self. I took classes for years and practiced the spiritual discipline to guide me to a place of serenity to still turbulent thoughts.

When I first began practicing yoga, I was very grateful to have found my instructor, Lori. She was a gift. With her understanding, sensitivity, and the gentle modifications made for me, I was able to overcome my physical limitations, and learned modified positioning and the ultimate benefits of yoga. I attended Lori's classes religiously for years but one day in particular will always come to mind. Lori had just finished the stretching part of our yoga and was easing us into the relaxation period. The room was darkened and I was waiting for her approach as I lay on my mat. Ordinarily, while quietly guiding us into a deep breathing mode and suggesting peaceful images to focus on, she would tip toe between the students' yoga mats. Softening into tranquil state, I didn't expect what was about to happen. To my surprise, Lori knelt down beside me and subtly placed a drop of lavender oil across my forehead with her finger. Her gentle touch aroused my senses in an unexpected way. My eyes filled and a tear trickled down my face. A flush of heat infused my face. What was this? I tried to connect. Perhaps it was just the kindness of her touch and her essence of good will that I felt. Perhaps it brought me back to the connections I so longed for in my past.

Oftentimes I would conduct my yoga postures in my own bedroom when I felt especially stressed. Sitting on my bedroom floor, ribbons of air would drift through my open window. The scent would take me back to my days as a child, alone with lots of time to pipedream under a tree. The memory connected me to the sweetness of Lori's touch of lavender, as I lay prone in class.

I used to say, "nothing stays the same," but was I right? The points of starlight I gazed at from my bedroom window after yoga, was the same ones I had wished upon while gazing out of my second floor bedroom in earlier years. The same comforting breaths I had taken so many years ago were the same familiar fresh, scented breezes that were now filling my lungs.

Although still plagued by my illnesses, I held on to my yoga and counseling sessions for years. They were moments of release for me. Whether I was sharing my inner most private feelings to a willing ear or taking time to find a momentary sense of repose, it was all I had to keep me from perhaps the point of no return. Escaping from the reality of life, if even for an hour, was how I managed to muster up the courage to face my personal challenges.

To the outside world, I presented a polished, cheerful image, a woman who was stable, fun to be with, and carefree. Only Joe saw the true depth of my depression and despair and how difficult it was for me to be mentally and physically healthy. I still tortured myself by trying to live up to demands I placed on myself. I continued to second-guess every comment I made, every act I took. Again and again, I put myself to the test. I wanted to make myself appear flawless in everything I did. I was good at covering up the real motivation in me, so as not to show my desperate neediness. A large price to pay in the end.

I considered yet another measure to find relief for my tormented state. A friend recommended that I read a book, written by a well-respected orthopedic surgeon. The premise of his book, by and large, were his theories of the mind and body connections and the end results that caused relentless, chronic pain. As I read the book, I was astonished. It was as if he was writing about me. I had high hopes going to his office to be evaluated by him. If I did in fact have the syndrome that this physician described in such detail, perhaps he would give me the solution to rid myself of my pathological ailments. I called for an appointment and was ready to pay his extraordinary fee, out of pocket, because he carried no insurance. If there was a cure to all of my madness, then Joe and I agreed it would be worth it. After an hour of questioning and a physical examination, he confirmed that I did in fact have the mind/body disorder. When I asked essentially, "What can I do to break this process?" He suggested I try his mantras, in addition to seeing a therapist. But I was seeing a therapist and a few months of his mantras led to no change or cure!

I was at my wit's end. My mind felt like a spinning plate, balanced on the end of a juggler's pole, not knowing when and if it would eventually fall.

Help is on the Way

---◉---

I was approaching my 60th birthday, and all was not well. I didn't have the stress of taking care of my parents anymore and life was more peaceful, but I couldn't shrug off my constant fear of illness and doom. I continued to go from one malady to another. And when I thought I could not go through another day worrying about it all, I would often burst into uncontrolled weeping for long periods. What if I have some strange disease? What if I have the big C? It was a vicious cycle—worrying led to more symptoms. How much longer could I go on being the person I only wished I could be? Tethered between suffocating thoughts and reality, I walked a fine line.

My greatest fear during those years was flying. As much as I attempted feel excited to plan a vacation, I would end up canceling it. I couldn't dismiss what I thought might be my impending fate. Thoughts about how many ways a plane could crash would run through my head for days and more nights than I would like to confess to. The more I thought about it, the more I crippled myself. My greatest embarrassment and failure was when Joe and I planned a trip to France. We were going to take a transatlantic liner to England to avoid a flight and then take the Chunnel from England to France. Again, the paralyzing fear set in. My anxiety about being in an underwater railroad tube for hours forced me to call the travel agent and cancel the whole trip. I cried not only because I wanted so much to go, but also because I disappointed Joe as well as myself.

Despite all these feelings, I persevered; looking for a way out and this time it would be my dear friend, Angela. About ten or twelve years prior to this time, we met Raphael and his wife, Angela, at a local golf club Joe decided to join. Joe was now retired and it seemed like the opportune time to play the game more often and develop a social circle as well. Upon meeting Raphael and Angela, we became fast friends. We enjoyed each other's company and looked forward to our dinners and golf games and began to take trips together. I was taken by how much they had achieved in their lives and, even more importantly, how grounded and humble they were at the same time. Angela is a psychiatric nurse practitioner and received her Doctorate of Psychiatric Nursing a few years ago. Raphael is a well-respected cardiologist who also specializes in cardiac electrophysiology and has received a number of prestigious accolades for his work.

My admiration for them was boundless and I was proud to call them our friends. But now in my desperation, could I call Angela and ask for her help? Always trying to live up to everyone's expectations, could I risk the chance of losing our friendship? What risk would I take if I told her the craziness I had been hiding from mostly everyone? In my own thoughts of unworthiness, I was delighted that despite my lackluster background of accomplishments, she saw something valuable in me. Could I be brave enough to expose my hidden side to her? Yes, I knew had to take that chance. Taking a deep breath, I picked up the phone and called her late one morning.

"Hello."

Oh good, she is home. I was afraid she had left for work. "Hi, Angie, it's Colette."

"Hi, what's going on?"

"Do you think I could see you today? I really need to talk to someone." I was sure my voice had a tone of despair, even though I tried to mask it.

"Sure, why don't you come for lunch and we can talk then?"

Oh, what a relief. I was worried she wouldn't have time for me, and I didn't think I could stand to wait another day. Not being able to unburden my anxiety, my loss of mental control, and the wounds I so closely coveted, I thought I would literally burst or collapse from the pressure. I was living my own hell. In medical terms, I suspect you would call it being on the verge of a nervous breakdown. But something told me I could trust her; she was a person of integrity and I felt safe about being vulnerable, so I went with my gut.

I brought my letter where I had written to the orthopedic physician, as well as all the courage I could muster to let my guard down.

Lunch was already laid out on a table on her screened-in porch. We hugged and sat across from each other in the lovely garden setting. As we had lunch, I pondered how I could break the ice. How would I start my story? I felt like I was going crazy living two sides of myself. I wondered if I could come right out with, "Do you know the person who sits in front of you today has a multiplicity of physical and mental issues?" I was a jumble of nerves, afraid to open up and afraid of what would happen if I did not take this leap. All the while I continued showing my well-worn facade, smiling and conversing about everyday life and events with her.

Angela knew previously that I had made the appointment with the physician I had been evaluated by, but never offered any opinions about prospect. This letter would serve to open up a window now as to why I was sitting here before her. Her husband had saved my husband's life that night in the hospital. Perhaps she could save mine. Could two angels live under the same roof?

Angela listened to me earnestly and read the letter in which I literally begged for an appointment, justifying my need. (At the time, he was so busy that he wasn't seeing anyone outside of the metropolitan area he worked in.) After reading the letter, she placed it in her lap.

Tucking a soft brown curl of hair behind her ear, she said, "Colette, I think you have been through too much trauma in your life and no matter what you have attempted to do to help yourself, it's just not enough."

"What do you mean by that?" I asked in a shaky voice, on the verge of tears.

"You can't do this by yourself, Colette. I feel you would benefit from an anti-depressant."

I hadn't expected that response, but after discussing my history for the better part of an hour, I was open to considering the possibility.

But I am not depressed, am I? I am surely not the actor on TV promoting the medication, staring out the window looking forlorn and not having the desire or energy to do anything productive. I have a number of friends I cherish, and I keep myself busy when my physical health allows me to. But she is right, I'm trapped in a darkened room and no matter how much

I try, I am still blind to how I could escape from my life, as I know it.

With tears streaming down my cheeks at this point, I told her that I would talk over her recommendation with Joe.

"It should be your decision, Colette, because it's your health and your welfare," she reminded me.

I knew on some level that she made a valid point, but I was not prepared to go at this alone. My husband and my partner was at home and I wanted the opportunity to share my feelings and possible intentions with him.

As I left, we embraced and she told me that I was a remarkable woman. That meant so much coming from her.

As I had suspected, Joe was alarmed at the idea of my taking an anti-depressant and couldn't understand why I had to take such an extreme step.

I HAVE extreme issues, I thought to myself. I knew that Joe had a lack of understanding about mental health issues. He still had the antiquated view that people on psychotropic medications are the ones in mental institutions and he clearly didn't see me in that realm. After much discussion, I suggested Joe call Angela. They spoke for a while. She listened to his view, advised him of her point of view and was firm about what she believed I needed. He was reluctant, but now it was ultimately my decision.

With the guidance of Angela and my primary doctor and the physician's assistant, I began to take an anti-depressant. I am truly not big on pills and am not recommending this kind of drug to anyone, but for me, it was the beginning of a new and better life.

Initially, it was rough. For a number of days, I was bedridden with unrelenting headaches. Strangely, I likened it to an exorcism! I would call the medical office daily to advise the physician's assistant of my reaction, and she would tell me, "Hang on, Colette." And I did. I was running out of choices and this was what I felt was my last hope.

My physical symptoms and pain, including my relentless headaches, began to vanish. More subtly over time, I noticed that I began to have better coping mechanisms and felt more at ease with any decisions I needed to make. I was the same Colette, only with a new lease on life—the rough edges were smoothed. I was beginning to see the life I always wanted to have.

Nowadays, although I am still not a good flyer, I do allow myself to plan trips that require a plane flight. My trepidation has greatly lessened and I focus more on the wonderful things we will do when we arrive. My mother's fear was instilled in me many years ago, and although she couldn't find the strength to fight her demons, I possessed the determination to break through my fears and seek relief from the shackles I towed for decades. Now I have a sense of pride that comes with finding a better way to live. I understand fully just what President Franklin D. Roosevelt meant when at his first inaugural address he stated, "The only thing we have to fear is fear itself."

With a steady pace before me in healing, I was able to say goodbye to the aches and pains, goodbye to those morbid thoughts that nested and made their home in my psyche. *Hello sweet freedom, I am ready to live.*

What Doesn't Kill You Makes you Stronger

———————●———————

Being a sensitive person can be both a positive and negative trait. While things people say or do can easily upset us we are also compassionate and sympathetic with others.

I've been on both sides of this "coin." My mother was good at reminding and admonishing me for how sensitive I was. And she was right. It didn't take much to hurt my feelings. I could barely stand criticism and would often cry with little provocation.

I know that I have the "good" sensitivity, too however. Although I am not sure why others don't feel the way I do, for as long as I can remember, I have always bled for those who were dealing with difficult moments in their lives.

When I was in grade school, I used to faithfully watch the *Little Rascals*, one of the most popular shows for children on television during the '50s. Watching a show one afternoon, I was terribly shocked and saddened by a bullying scene the show demonstrated.

The story was about the lead character, a boy named Spanky. Spanky's mom urged him to enter a show in school. During his performance, his mother is annoyed when a prank is pulled on him. She decides she cannot stay still any longer and attempts to rescue him. During her attempt to save him from embarrassment, the stage curtain she was near began to rise. A hook on the bottom of the curtain in motion snagged her dress. Spanky's mother frantically tried to get the hook out of her dress hem as the audience began to howl with laughter at the predicament. The curtain continued to rise quickly, hiking the dress and eventually ripping the dress off of her. Spanky looked up to see his mother's dress attached to the curtain rising to the ceiling and looked in disbelief. The audience was in near hysterics. He rushed to his mother's aid. She was humiliated, stunned, and immobilized to see her garment dangling above her. In his haste to hide his mother's compromised attire from the audience, he dragged a stage prop and placed it in front of her to shield her from the audience's view. Unfortunately, his earnest efforts backfired. Adding insult to injury, the prop he held in front of his barely clad mother was a caricature of a headless body of a dog. His mom's head coincidentally sat atop of it and the audience was shown roaring with laughter.

I never spoke about that show to anyone, but it stayed with me through my life. How could they laugh at her? Didn't they know how awful it would be if it happened to them? I was incensed at the audience that day and my heart went out to that woman as if the event was real or it had happened to me. Perhaps the experience hit too close to home, as I had experienced my share of being made fun of. The humiliation and pain was all too familiar.

Through the years I continued to abhor shows or incidents that ridiculed others, even though most people seem to find them funny. There were real life events I was equally disturbed by, but turning off the TV was not an option.

Joe and I were invited to my sister-in-law's home for a small party some twenty years ago. At one point the guests decided to play a game. I loosely recall the idea was similar to the children's game Telephone. Only instead of whispering a message from one ear to the next, the eight couples would mimic each other by touching the next person on the face. I remember feeling suddenly very distressed when I realized that one wife was secretly selected: she would be the laughing stock of the group. Her husband was happily in on the practical joke. When it was his turn to draw a pattern on his wife's face with his finger, that she was to duplicate it to the next. Little did she know that he had black ink on his finger. The other party guests thought it was quite amusing while this woman had no idea. I became enraged with each turn her husband took, allowing her to be and promoting her as the butt of their joke. The giggles and snorts from the others and the puzzled looks from this woman rattled me. I stood up abruptly and excused myself. As I leaned against the kitchen sink with my hands shaking from the scene, I was in disbelief. Why did these people find this funny? What was wrong with me and why couldn't I see the game the same as they did? I didn't even know this woman, but I ached for her embarrassment. By the time Joe and my sister-in-law entered the kitchen, my emotions had turned to heightened anger. I looked at them both and declared that I could not be privy to such a game. I had the greatest urge to go back to the living room and reprimand the husband for allowing his wife to be the subject of mockery. But I was not interested in ruining the party for my sister and brother-in-law, so I didn't.

"Why are you so upset, Colette?" they asked.

"I don't know if I can explain it but it's not at all funny to me."

"No, Colette, it's just a game," was their universal response.

"You think it's a game to her when she finds out what they did?"

"I think you are taking it too seriously, relax."

But I didn't relax nor did I when I experienced similar instances through my life.

Many years ago, I walked out during the movie *Clockwork Orange* by Stanley Kubrick. I felt the violence and vile acts were so deplorable, I could not sit in the darkened theater one minute longer. Joe and I were with a group of five couples I worked with that night. We planned to go to the movie together and dinner afterwards. When I left for the lobby before the movie was over and never returned, Joe soon followed and found me weeping in a corner of the theater lobby. He tried to comfort me after I explained my distress. "I can't stand to see them torture that couple, Joe!"

"I know it's hard to watch."

"Hard to watch? I thought my system was revolting on me! How can any of them find this redeeming?"

"There must be some kind of symbolism that they are seeing," he replied.

"Well, maybe there is somewhere, but I can't get past the brutal, bizarre, and savage acts!"

"Let's go honey, you need to get some air."

Joe and I decided to head out to the restaurant where we had previously planned to have dinner with the other couples. When we arrived, I excused myself to Joe, telling him that I wanted to use the bathroom to collect myself and make sure my eye makeup didn't transform me into a raccoon. When the rest caught up, no one questioned our absence. I was still in a bathroom stall when two of the women I worked with entered. They began extolling compliments on what they considered amazing symbolism and creativity. I am all for that, mind you, but this was truly beyond my level of tolerance. I pondered while standing in that stall, now not wanting them to know I was there, my disbelief at their reaction. *God, what was wrong with me? Didn't anyone see this film the way I did?*

These kinds of memories have never left me, but today I have compartmentalized them. I still feel emotional about experiences but they are more balanced now. And I feel differently about my personal views. I am proud that I have compassion for others and I am not afraid to expose my inner self. It doesn't matter anymore if I am alone in my views, because they are uniquely mine and I am content with that.

A Song of Celebration

---⊙---

*"Everyone has the power of greatness,
not for fame but greatness,
because greatness is determined by service."*

~Martin Luther King

My only regret to date is that I have reached the "golden years" of my life. It's not a bad thing, but I am hoping I still have lots of time to pursue my purpose in life and to enjoy every day I have.

Sally Field won an Oscar in 1985 for her performance in *Places in the Heart*. In her acceptance speech, which is often quoted and perhaps even mocked, she shared her thoughts, "You like me, right now you like me." It was a moment of heartfelt validation for her work. There is a part of me that continues to look for that, whether it is in my writing, my jewelry making endeavors, my volunteer work or any other aspirations I may attempt. I believe everyone needs a degree of validation. Perhaps I can never completely be content with myself since there is always a drive within me to do better. But now I think it's a healthy one and I am more balanced in my approach to improving my mind, my skill, and my heart.

In the past, I had an insatiable desire to accomplish my goals and stand out whatever the cost. If I wasn't going to be the best daughter, I needed to be the best wife and mother to a fault. I wanted to be the best girlfriend, employee, neighbor, and volunteer—the list goes on. The more I strived, the less positive I felt about myself. Being the best was an unattainable goal.

I have reached a point now where it is finally sinking in, allowing my true inside to come out. I don't have to pretend to be someone else. I am not afraid to show what lives in my core now, and I am feeling more whole with every day. I have a full life. I still have bumps and humps along the road, but it gets smoother on my journey, day by day.

I am learning to accept myself now both mentally and physically in my later years. If you ask my husband, he thinks I am plenty attractive, and that's a good thing since there's nothing like a guy who is in love and wears rose-colored glasses when he looks into your eyes!

Accepting myself goes beyond my physical image, however. I have been pursuing interests that reflect my essence. Now I look for other ways to find purpose and fulfillment.

Most recently I decided I would like to start knitting and took some classes at a lovely yarn shop not more than five minutes from my home. During the time I went for instruction, I met a woman who imparted such a profound gesture, I knew I wanted to mirror it in my life. She was making an exquisite little girl's dress. The detail and the care that she put into it were remarkable. Not knowing the woman outside of being introduced, I questioned my instructor, "She appears too young to be a grandmother but perhaps too old to be a mom. Who is she making that dress for?"

Surprisingly the instructor replied, "Nobody."

Of course, I couldn't let that lie and questioned the instructor again on her remark. She then explained, "This lady was a high-powered businesswoman who lived in Miami for a while. On her lunch hour she was walking with a friend through the streets to a restaurant. Alongside one of the streets were long banquet tables with several women standing behind them. On the table were piles of fabric scraps of assorted sizes, patterns, and colors. This woman's curiosity got the best of her and asked what these women were doing. One woman answered that they were collecting first or second hand fabrics to make dresses for young girls."

Still spurred with interest she asked, "And where are these young girls?"

"They live in Haiti, Poland, Russia, and any other country that witness severe poverty, often times with the only dress they have on their back."

The instructor's explanation captivated me. I looked over to the dress this woman was working on and thought, *This dress would be delivered into the hands of a girl who has never seen such a delicate and sweetly made dress, and it would be hers!* As I struggled with my stitches, I began to wonder what I could possibly do with my newfound ability. If you have ever knitted, you know that the first and easiest thing you learn is how to make a scarf. So here I was, knitting my first scarf and wondering, *Who is going to get this soon-to-be masterpiece*? Shazammm!

It occurred to me that I could follow this admirable woman's lead! I would knit scarves for the homeless. Of course, receiving a scarf was not going to keep them warm enough, but maybe it would warm their hearts, on some level, and provide a little extra comfort. I was excited about the prospects of the endeavor, especially if I could gather my friends to help. I decided my venture would be called, "Handmade Hugs for the Holidays."

In summary, ten women worked tirelessly for six months, cellophane wrapped the scarves, tied hand stamped messages of love with gay colored ribbon, and delivered 140 knitted scarves to the shelters with the greatest need.

I felt euphoric with outcome. I didn't even have to earn an income, as I once felt was an essential part of being successful. There are so many paths to take and this was my start. I have learned that getting beyond my own perception of who I am, and embracing with the needs of others is the key to finding my true self. Now my own mantra is about being the best I can be, but knowing I will fail because I am human. I will try because I can and because my attempts are for the right reasons.

There are times that I feel more connected with my maker than ever before. I am in a better place; I feel grounded and follow my passions. My life is full, my love becomes more and more boundless, and I am so much less critical of others. I thank the creator of all during my moments of silence and solitude because of the transformations and opportunities in my life.

Several years ago when Joe turned seventy and I turned sixty, I had the greatest desire to host a large birthday bash for us. Since our birthdates are only three weeks apart, I was passionate about having an affair that would not only be a celebratory night for all but one that would invoke lasting memories for years to come. I envisioned all the components that would be required to accomplish my goal. I hired an old friend who was in the entertainment business. He was very obliging. I intended and planned to pick every single song that was to be played that night. I burned CDs with countless songs that had meaning for me. I chose songs that I loved to dance to, songs that had emotional meaning for Joe and for my son, Dana. I wanted to dance with both of them to a specific song that transmitted my emotions about each of them. Celine Dion's song, "Because You Loved Me," was chosen for Joe and I.

"........*You were my strength when I was weak*
You were my voice when I couldn't speak
You were my eyes when I couldn't see
You saw the best there was in me..."

I must admit the atmosphere was bordering on a wedding event but I couldn't help myself—I envisioned a love fest, and a love fest it was going to be. Early on before our night, I spent a good deal of time preparing a speech for our guests that consisted of close friends and family. I wanted to live in the moment with them and acknowledge from the depth of my soul how much they meant to me.

I chose everything from the food to the decorations to the table settings, the cake and invitations. As a favor, I handmade holiday ornaments with a tag attached that revealed a spiritual message I wanted to share. I was a control freak in every aspect, but Joe knew it was important to me, and he would tell you that I am good at it! Maybe I missed my calling!

I couldn't wait to dance with my Dana that night as well. I chose the Five Stairsteps song, "Ooh, Child." Perhaps not the best title I have ever heard but the lyrics fit us perfectly. Through our toughest years together, I sang this song to him with the hopes that we would pull through and triumph.

Ooh-oo child
Things are gonna get easier
Ooh-oo child
Things'll get brighter

The last song I wanted was to orchestrate in particular was Andrew Gold's song, "Thank you for Being a Friend." I printed out the lyrics and as previously discussed, the DJ invited all to the dance floor. During those moments, in a large circle, everyone who attended stood side by side and sang.

"And if you threw a party
Invited everyone you knew
You would see, the biggest gift would be from me
and the card attached would say,
Thank you for being a friend..."

It was glorious!

It felt like a dream coming true. I could feel emotions emanating from my core and I couldn't be happier. While embracing those memorable hours with loved ones, friends, and life, I kicked off my shoes and danced all night. I haven't danced like that since, but it was by far the best birthday I have ever had! Unlike my mother, I love parties and celebrations of life and my house is an open door, sometimes revolving more than I can handle, but always welcoming.

These are the steps that I have found along the way that made a difference for me. They have given me a sense of clarity to see my true north. Despite the callous and hostile ways mankind often treats others, perhaps this will make you a believer that you are the person that can change circumstances.

My brothers and I had no choice but to be siblings. Who knows what the future holds. Families can be made up of many different dynamics. I survived the family I was born into but I thrive with the family I have now.

Do I miss my parents? I feel a kind of numbness but the anger and disappointment are gone now. Memories will always be there, but the hurt doesn't have to live on. I am at peace with not having that part of my life now. I have turned the page. May my mother rest in peace.

I think of my father from time to time. He was very misguided and had his own challenges to deal with. Deep in my heart, I have loving feelings toward him and have forgiven him.

This past Mother's Day was one for the record books for me. Being with two of the most significant men in my life, my husband and my son. No more pity parties for me, only elated, loving feelings. Dana has become a sensitive and altruistic man and I hope he knows that my pride and acknowledgement for him will always be steadfast. Joe, always giving of himself and knowing my needs, is a special and personal gift each day.

Was it the dinner we shared together on Mother's Day, the help and patience Dana had teaching this old brain how to work the computer? Was it seeing the both of them in the garden center sharing ideas and their mutual enjoyment of gardening? Or the proud moment I felt, listening to my son speak to a colleague and realizing how accomplished a man he has become? I think it's everything and maybe it's me. My perspective on life has changed dramatically. When George Bernard Shaw said, "Youth is wasted on the young," he expressed what I am feeling right now. I will savor every morsel I have as long as I can. And as the poem is entitled, "When I am an Old Woman I Shall Wear Purple," by Jenny Joseph Elizabeth, maybe I can't make up for all the years behind me, but I sure can try and "wear purple" every chance I get!

Beans Beans Beans

———————●———————

"I am not what happened to me, I am what I choose to become."

~Carl Jung

When I awake in the mornings, I often turn to face the man I married. Sleeping beside him for so many years now, I can tell when he is deeply sleeping or is beginning to stir to face the new day. About a year ago, I wanted to connect to him first thing, but didn't want to rudely force him out of his dreamy transition. I considered how I could subtly awaken him. Lying on my side, wondering what to do, I came up with something I thought was relatively clever. His bare arm was in reach and I began to act out a nursery rhyme from long ago, while whispering the words in his ear.

"Incy Wincy spider went up the water spout, down came the rain and washed the spider out, out came the sun and dried up all the rain, so the Incy Wincy spider went up the spout again." Joe enjoyed the soft tickling movement of the spider's journey up and down his arm.

With a tender smile he asked, "So you are the Incy Wincy spider?" Like a child at play, I answered with a resounding yes and giggled lightly, grabbing his face with the palms of my hands to kiss him good morning. After a recent "spider massage," I thought of his question to me and decided that no matter how many times the rain came down, like that spider, I did find the strength to try again. Call me Incy Wincy!

My mornings continue in the kitchen while breakfasting with Joe. The TV is always on a morning talk show. Unlike me, he has no need for peace and quiet this time of day. As we sit side-by-side with a bowl of homemade granola, assorted berries, yogurt, an ample dose of almond milk, and fresh brewed coffee, we leisurely chat about what we plan to do that day or comment on the morning news and features. On this day, the host and guest are discussing the value of healthy eating. My ears perk up because I know the importance of a healthy diet and try to make that a habit with Joe as often as I can. The Blue Zones, as they refer to it, are the areas in the world where the population appears to live the longest. After observing these groups, researchers concluded their longevity in large part is due to the emphasis on their diet, with beans in particular as the important staple of their meals. I personally could live on beans, cut out meats for good and not look back. Joe, on the other hand, is much more resistant to that idea. He likes his traditional meals— chops, steaks, a starch, a few veggies and, if he can get away with it, a dessert.

After the feature story on the Blue Zones ended, I began to tease him on his preferred diet and vowed I would get him to eat beans regularly.

"Yeah? We will see," he responded, with a twinkle in his eye. He left the room but was apparently still within earshot of my voice. I was busy feeding our dog Sneakers, and mindlessly began to sing a tune. "Beans, beans, beans" were the only lyrics, but I continued to sing these words with a lilt in my voice. "Beans, beans, beans....beans, beans, beans," I went on, as I finished making our pet's morning bowl of food.

With my second cup of coffee in hand, I was off to my computer to open it for the day when Joe returned.

"You know what? I enjoy being married to you," he announced.

Surprised by his statement, I asked, "What do you mean?"

"I was listening to you sing your beans song and thought, it's so nice to be married to someone who has an up personality."

"Really? Gee, well that's nice to hear," I replied, smiling back at him.

On a more serious note he said, "No, it's a gift to have you."

"Thanks, honey," I answered with my own big smile and appreciation in my voice.

I thought about his statement for a few seconds...I *am* happy. I have everything to be happy for. Lucky for me, he has forgotten I wasn't always this way!

Dwelling on his statements after he left for the post office, I was reminded how far I have come. I was a master at suppressing the insecurity, fear, neediness, and depression that consumed me. Having said that, however, I am aware that even during some of the darkest parts of my invented self, I always had an unyielding spirit. Throughout my life, it eked out. Singing happy tunes with Grandma Esther in her car was clearly an early sign of my spiritual zest. Little did I know back then that I would someday be that woman thinking, *Look out world, here I come.*

As much as life can be unpredictable, I think there was always a glimmer of hope for my future.

Even at the early age of six, I experienced an event that transformed my soul. It became an indelible part of my being, and because of it, I believe that my spirit always wanted me to survive and revel in what was my nature.

It was my birthday, and I had the good fortune to be sitting on the floor that night, under the arched opening that separated our dining room from our living room. I stated my good fortune because I could have missed the black and white movie that was just about to begin on our television. My mother was cleaning up the dining table of dishes from my birthday cake. My father and Grandma Esther was also there, as she was for all our birthday and holiday celebrations during my adolescence. I doubt that the movie was on by design. While they continued their conversation I was slowly being lured into the age-old tale, *A Christmas Carol.*

At the time, I had no idea that Charles Dickens was such a warrior for the people of England, using his gift of writing to reveal how the economic and political powers of his country oppressed the poor and disadvantaged. All I knew as a young girl was the impact it had on me that night and how it has lasted a lifetime. Even at such a tender age, I could feel the intolerance, indifference, redemption, compassion, and good will of the story; it filled my heart and mind and left a permanent mark on my being. Although Scrooge learned his lessons well, Mr. Fezziwig, the jolly old soul in Dickens's novel, would also have my lifelong admiration. I mean to say, he really got it! His success as a businessman was not enough for him. His life was only complete if he shared his success with kindness, generosity, and affection for

287

his family and employees. With that seed of awareness, I have always strived to really "get it" too.

Now I embrace the realization that life isn't just about existing, it's about thriving and experiencing the pleasures surrounding us every day. I know the difference in me now—it's not to hope for pleasure as a result of my actions, but to receive pleasure from the deed itself with no expectations. With every passing day, I focus on glorifying who I am and not condemning who I was yesterday. I am a work in progress.

Ebb and Flow

---•⊙•---

Just when you think you have a relatively good handle on life, new challenges and disappointments surface. I recently learned first hand the strength of their impact and the unsteadiness my outlook and ideology became.

A few months earlier, I faced an emotional challenge that totally took me by surprise, despite my new found beliefs. I had been experiencing considerable pain in my weakened foot. Until now I have had negligible walking difficulty, outside of a duration before my hip surgery several years ago. The discomfort became persistent over several months. After a short sprint to the store one afternoon, it became impossible for me to bear weight on that ankle. Within minutes, the pain escalated and I was immobile. With the help of the store cart, I hobbled to my car. Something was definitely amiss. During that same period, my opposite knee suddenly collapsed one evening, leaving me on the bathroom floor with two stress fractures in my foot.

Much to my chagrin, I knew I needed to see a specialist. I made an appointment with an ankle and foot physician and the affected areas were scanned and evaluated. Dr. Matthews explained that my ankle had become too weak and lacked the muscle strength to finish my stride. Since the affected foot was always predisposed to weakness and my age was now against me, I wasn't surprised at the news. My knee, on the other hand, was a surprise. I was told the nerve damage that caused my knee to give way was generating from my spine. Perhaps back surgery is again in my future.

While sitting on the examining table and Joe nearby on a chair, the physician dismissed himself momentarily and explained that he would have a therapy technician come in to see me. It didn't occur to me what this meant until I turned toward the open door and noticed a young woman walking down the hall toward my room. With two hands, she carried a sizable black brace with multiple appendages: numerous Velcro straps dangling, metal hinges, patches of netting, and two oversized range-of-motion controls on either side of the knee area. As she entered the examining room, I was in shock. I looked over at Joe with such intensity that he returned a look of confusion to me. A flush overwhelmed me as if I was being drained of all body fluids. The only fluid left was a mantle of wet lashes from the tears that began to puddle in my eyes. The therapist, now squatting on her knees before me, began explaining the function and proper fit of the brace as she adjusted the straps of the high thigh-to-ankle apparatus. I could barely nod my head at her in return. As I looked up across to Joe, I knew I couldn't hold in my emotions any longer.

With teardrops now spilling over the rim of my eyes, I shared my thoughts with him, "I am coming full circle Joe. I always said I didn't want to end my life as I had begun but it looks like it's going to happen." The therapist stopped linking the straps around my leg and excused herself. Crying with little restraint left in me, Joe came to my side.

"Try to be strong honey. I know it's hard to understand, but the doctor is trying to help you."

"I know Joe, I know. I have always run from anything that would single me out, now I am going to look like a cripple again, it's so hard to swallow that thought."

The doctor returned and sat on the stool before me and reviewed his plan, "Okay, you have the brace for your knee, now we have to get you an appointment for the brace for your other ankle. The orthotic specialist will also make an appointment to fit you for some supportive shoes."

"Do you mean orthopedic shoes?" I meekly questioned. I was thinking about how much I despised my orthopedics so many years ago. Esthetically, they are a fashion designer's nightmare. Far more crucial for me however was the harsh perception I had of myself. My reflection felt stripped of my feminineness and sensuality.

Dr. Matthews held up my slip on canvas shoes and responded with a coy smile, "These shoes may be attractive but they are doing nothing for your gait or to support your feet."

My voice crackled, "I am sorry Dr. Matthews, it's so hard for me to accept the idea of having to wear braces and Frankenstein shoes again."

Now, in a more softened and thoughtful tone, he slowly replied, "Mrs. Aliamo, you have obviously been a strong person throughout your life and I understand your disappointment. But you have nothing to prove to anyone. You have a loving husband, family, and friends who care about you. That's all that matters."

He was right. Every single word he said was right. Despite my moment of despondency, I knew I could not let this define me. I thought about his words for days even though I remained sullen. My appointment with the orthotic specialist essentially echoed Dr. Matthews's words. While a cast was made of my foot and I was fit for shoes that afternoon, I decided it was time to walk the walk, if you will. I chose to embrace my own truth.

After the initial inquires regarding my visible medical appliances, I decided that it was just one more hurdle I could rise above. I even felt indulgent and self-absorbed when I began to think of all the strife and hardships others endure on so much greater a magnitude than mine.

Joe tells me how brave he thinks I am. For me, I think courage comes from confidence and the trust in others around you. Yes, I have come full circle. Not just by enduring the adversity of my limitations in a more decisive vein, but also by realizing that I am not alone in my battle, as I had once felt.

This Much, I Know and Believe

---●---

I don't pretend to be an authority on how to live life in the most fulfilling way. I can only share my experiences. I know for sure most of my greatest moments were when I gave back in some way. It's a super high I can't even put into words. I believe everyone embodies this calling if they are willing to seek it out, no matter how clouded their life might be. A paradigm shift of your mind that only you can call upon.

I have no more cloaks to hide behind. I put aside the focus on my limp and all that it represented in my life. I used to hate when people stared at me. Likened to a knee-jerk reaction, passersby would look down at my legs very deliberately. Sometimes it was so obvious and rude, I would bark at them, "What are you looking at?" As I got older and wiser, I decided that I would try to ignore the ogling and imagined they were unconscious of their actions. Now I use a cane and a brace because age has weakened my afflicted side, I don't even have to offer an explanation. Besides there is an abundance of people my age walking around with canes in hand!

The experience was a good lesson learned. I never stare at anyone who has a disability or some kind of affliction when I pass by, for the very reason I used to feel. For me, it's an act of kindness not to stare. You allow them to blend in and be seen as an equal. Of course, if they need help, that would be all together different matter, but I don't have to tell you that!

As for my spiritual beliefs, as of late I have been called a tree hugger. I think that is entirely accurate, but I feel like I am so much more. As Neale Donald Walsch remarks in his book, *Conversations with God,* our Creator offers you signs of happiness, but oftentimes we are not paying attention. If that is true, I have become more observant of my surroundings, not letting signs or opportunities pass me by. It's therapeutic; allow me to give you examples.

One morning I recently caught a feature on TV about a man named Robert Thorton and an experience that turned his life around. His mom was driving a school bus for children with special needs. One of the little girls drew pictures everyday and would hand them to Robert's mom. She, in turn, would post them on her refrigerator. Robert decided after looking at this girl's drawings, he could segue her creations into something beneficial. During his interview, he explained that he began to print the disabled children's artwork on to t-shirts. He went on to further explain. He hired workers with special needs to pack the t-shirts up for delivery and indicated he couldn't be happier with their performance. Teaming up with foundations, his company, *Paper Clouds*, has raised $87,000 toward research, due to his philanthropic efforts. This profound story and outcome led me to think what a shame it was that the media doesn't devote enough time to the events we need to fortify us.

Later the same day, I was driving down my street when I noticed a woman emerging between two cars to cross. I slowed down and noticed that coming up behind her on a leash was a large greyhound dog. I stopped momentarily and lowered my passenger window, "Was that a race dog?"

She nodded yes. "He was rescued." We both smiled as if we could read each other's mind.

Driving on, I began to think about the notion that goodness in this world exists but how we often easily overlook or don't notice it. It's my resolution and goal however, to do just that: look and savor the goodness of others. Since then, I see signs of goodness and generosity everywhere because I choose to see them. Countless people are trying to make a difference and it has been a sure way to lift my spirit.

It's the 66th year of my life, and I am at my condo, sitting at the top of a staircase that leads to the ocean. The tides are receding but the waves are breaking, reaching the shore with percolating enthusiasm. On my perch, I gaze at this natural beauty of waterscape as far as my eye can see. The profusion of the waters appears multi-colored against the pure white sea foam and the sun reflects on the water's surface like diamonds before me. This is when I feel closest to my creator.

For more than thirty years, I have sat before this very same vista outside my condo, but not until now have I appreciated its majestic glory. I believe I am in the right place in my life. I choose to distance myself from the Yin and gravitate toward the forces of Yang. I choose to see people the way Filomena taught me by example so many years ago. I am drawn in more each day, witnessing the purity and beauty of people in the same way I see the surroundings of nature.

When I examine my life now, I find the courage to believe that I am a worthy person and no longer depend on the approval of others. I enjoy making people happy,

I enjoy being thoughtful, and I enjoy helping others in need. The difference now is my motive. I am much the same person now inside and out! No longer do I try to second-guess what people want me to be. I stopped hating myself for everything I wasn't and began to love myself for everything that I am. The good part of not attempting to be a perfectionist is that, aside from being emotionally sapping, the more I allow myself to be me, the more my confidence grows.

I don't have to continue to be a best friend to everyone I meet either. I didn't need an abundance of friends, just a number of friends I could be certain of. What a surprise to know that your friends don't turn away and still like you even with faults. And speaking about my faults, I still have flaws I haven't gotten over; I think it's part of being human. I yell at the guy with a few choice expletives when he cuts me off on the highway, I get *totally* disappointed when my hair isn't cut just right, and I lose my patience when I have to wait in line. I also can't erase my cautiousness. The difference now is that instead of being a negative sponge and becoming immobilized, I have the tenacity to push through my fears, or at least lessen the intensity of my concerns. "No guts, no glory," right?

You may be saying to yourself about now, but Colette, it wasn't just your mental attitude and change of your perspective that allowed you to become who you are. You depend on a drug. You are right, and I will be the first one to tell you that it was and continues to be an important part of my healing and how I balance my life. Would I promote or suggest you go on a drug yourself to help you along? Absolutely not. I am not a big proponent of medications, but in my case, it was mandatory that I have the assistance. I had used every tool I could think of to better myself to no avail. It was a last ditch effort on my part. Although there still is, to date, mixed feelings about hypertrophic medications, I can only share with you my own experience. The medication allows me to feel like I always wanted to feel but didn't know it. It makes me feel even and more logical and realistic about my choices. It gives me peace in my choices. I believe there are instances when you can't accomplish your goal by yourself. If you had a broken leg, you wouldn't deny yourself crutches to get around more easily and with less pain, so there are times when you need to heal your mind in the same way as your body.

Do I wish I had the opportunity early on in my life to improve my mind and body, to be happy to the core, calm as a whisper, and content as a sleeping babe? You bet. But there is still so much to do, so much to connect to, and it's never too late to become who you always wanted to be. I am learning how to find harmony in myself; the acceptance of my age when I see young beautiful women in their prime, the flexibility to bend in the wind when things aren't going the way I planned, and the mindfulness to let things go when I have no control, opening up my heart and forgiving when it's the hardest thing to do, knowing in turn, it will make me happy and free. Hurdles to jump, one at a time.

****

Life can change so fast and so unexpectedly. It's my goal to love when and as much as I can, for as long as I can. My wish is that by sharing my story and the peace I came to feel, I might allow you some insights on your own journey. I don't mean to suggest that I am completely centered and whole or that I have all the answers, but it would be my greatest pleasure if, in some way, my journey helps you with yours.

Do I wish my life were different? I can't lie. Yes, it might have been wonderful. But maybe, just maybe, I wouldn't be the person I am today. There were many mistakes I made along the way as well as many lessons presented to me, and I believe I am a better woman because of them. It's not a cross to bear, as my mother used to say, but a badge of honor. And the badge reads, *She didn't just live, she became. She is proud to say she is her authentic self and loves deeply.*

Life can so damn hard and for many, so much harder. I consider myself lucky and blessed. I experienced hardships that have made me even stronger, more resilient and irrepressible. We all have a choice. Your life can become bitter because of your hardships or better for having overcome them. I have found that it is easier to detect the altruism when you have tasted the bane. I take nothing for granted, and am grateful for all that is wonderful in my life.

Resist defining yourself by how long a relationship lasted. Define yourself by how much you have loved someone and are willing to love again. Don't recall the many times you have felt knocked down but by how many times you have raised yourself back on your feet. Never define yourself by your past or your pain, but that which you have emerged from. Find your best self and live your best life. As far as I know, we don't get second chances.

My heart and soul are in this book and it's my gift to you. It is my hope that you too will find your path to wholeness, peace and joyfulness.

Namaste

Bibliography

"Infectious Diseases and Pandemics." Harvard University, T.H. CHAN School of Public Health, Fall 2013 Centennial Issue. Web. 29 June 2015.

"Poliomyelitis." New World Encyclopedia, 4 July 2013. Web. 29 June 2015.

"Poliomyelitis." World Health Organization, Media Centre, Oct 2014. Web. 29 June 2015.

Soriano, William J. St. Charles Hospital: the First 75 Years. Port Jefferson, NY: St. Charles Hospital and Rehabilitation Center. 1984. Print.

Dedication

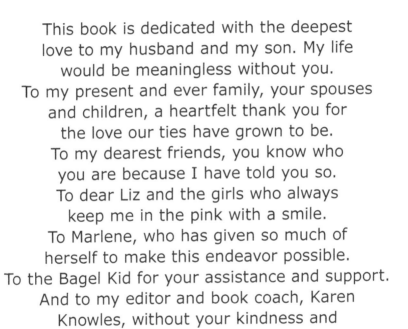

This book is dedicated with the deepest
love to my husband and my son. My life
would be meaningless without you.
To my present and ever family, your spouses
and children, a heartfelt thank you for
the love our ties have grown to be.
To my dearest friends, you know who
you are because I have told you so.
To dear Liz and the girls who always
keep me in the pink with a smile.
To Marlene, who has given so much of
herself to make this endeavor possible.
To the Bagel Kid for your assistance and support.
And to my editor and book coach, Karen
Knowles, without your kindness and
expertise this page would not exist.

About the Author

Cece Gardenia was born and raised in New York. She is married and lives with her husband on Long Island, where they raised four children.

Bringing the Inside Out is her first publication.